HIGHER EDUCATION

Social, Political and Economic Challenges

HIGHER EDUCATION

Social, Political and Economic Challenges

Divya Sharma

MD PUBLICATIONS PVT LTD
NEW DELHI
www.mdppl.com

Published by :

MD Publications Pvt Ltd
"MD House", 11, Darya Ganj,
New Delhi - 110 002
Phone : +91-11-45355555
E-mail : contact@mdppl.com
Website: www.mdppl.com

ISBN : 978-81-7533-363-5

Published and Printed by Mr. Pranav Gupta on behalf of **MD Publications Pvt Ltd** at Mohit Enterprises, Delhi.

PREFACE

Higher Education is an educational level that follows the completion of a school providing a secondary education, such as a high school, secondary school, or gymnasium. Tertiary education is normally taken to include undergraduate and postgraduate education, as well as vocational education and training. Colleges, Universities, and Institutes of Technology are the main institutions that provide tertiary education. Examples of institutions that provide post-secondary education are vocational schools, community colleges, independent colleges. They are sometimes known collectively as tertiary institutions. Completion of tertiary education generally results in the awarding of certificates, diplomas, or academic degrees, but the students who do not receive these outnumber those who do. High performance is expected of students in Higher Education, and those who cannot meet the standards must leave.

Higher education includes teaching, research, exacting applied work (e.g. in medical schools and dental schools), and social services activities of universities. Within the realm of teaching, it includes both the undergraduate level (sometimes referred to as tertiary education), and beyond that, graduate-level (or postgraduate level) for very highly-qualified students who wish to go further in their education and skills. This level of education is often referred to as graduate school.

"Higher Education" in India generally involves work towards a college-degree-level or foundation degree education. The general higher education and training that takes place in a university, college, or Institute of Technology usually includes significant theoretical and abstract elements, as well as applied aspects. In contrast, the vocational higher education and training that takes place at vocational universities and schools usually concentrates on practical applications, with very little theory.

In addition, professional-level education is always included within Higher Education, and usually in Graduate Schools, since many postgraduate academic disciplines are both vocationally, professionally, and theoretically/research oriented, such as in medicine, the law, dentistry, and veterinary medicine.

The demand for quality higher education is continuing to outpace the supply due to growing population of young people, gains in school education, growing middle class and their rising aspirations. The country has a unique opportunity to convert this demographic surplus to its economic strength by providing its young people the right kind of skills. Thus, higher education now occupies a central position in the country's strategy for global competitiveness and inclusive growth. Steps have been initiated to augment supply, improve quality and fix problems. The National Knowledge Commission has made several useful and important recommendations and the government has significantly increased funding during the Eleventh Five Year Plan.

The editor spells out the needs, identifies the gaps, and based on the lessons learnt from the experiences of other countries provides perspectives to shape its future.

I am very grateful to Mr. Pranav Gupta, Director of MD Publications Pvt. Ltd., New Delhi, for his kind cooperation and support for this book.

Divya Sharma

Contents

1

Policies in Higher Education

Introduction

The programs and policies of higher educational institutions and systems are increasingly subject to review by agencies external to the campus; and a growing sphere of educational activity is dependent upon some form of public support or affected by governmental regulation. The long cherished myth of the separation of education from politics has lost its claim to reality.

Despite this growing interaction between higher education and public policy structures, most of the serious scholarship on the politics of higher education has been relatively recent, with much of it appearing within the past decade. As a result, the politics of higher education as a field of study is in a formative stage of development. An extensive review of the literature, published earlier, suggests several major patterns within this broad area of concern and the status of this area as a field of study. Many of the impressions summarized here are consistent with both previous and subsequent literature reviews.

The study of higher education politics and policy is by its very nature an interdisciplinary field of inquiry, exhibiting tremendous diversity in theoretical perspectives and topical coverage, with a generally underdeveloped methodological base and a lack of consensus on the meaning of basic concepts. According to Paul Dressel and Lewis Mayhew, the defining characteristics of a discipline include "a general body of knowledge a specialized vocabulary and a generally accepted basic literature some generally accepted body of theory and some generally understood techniques for theory testing and revision a generally agreed upon methodology and recognized techniques for replication and revalidation of research and scholarship." According to several observers, the study of higher education politics and policy is lacking in all of these respects. While it may not be necessary for this field to advance to the status of a discipline, according to Cameron Fincher the field will not mature until it begins to develop at least some of these characteristics of a discipline.

Patricia Crosson and Charles Adams assessed the status of the literature on higher education politics at the state level, and since the literature on the state level appears to be the most extensive and advanced, their findings may apply even more forcefully to the field as a whole. There is little explanatory, disciplinary research, and researchers do not attempt to develop or test theory in their studies. Much of the research is descriptive, relying on very broad ill-defined concepts as a means of organizing data rather than using theoretical frameworks. Where such frameworks are used, they are borrowed from a number of social science disciplines including sociology, economics, and political science. While much of the research at the state level qualifies as policy research, there is little explicit discussion of theories and methods for policy analysis. In terms of methodology, case studies predominate, although there are a growing number of studies concerned with more generalizable or comparative data; and finally there is limited but growing use of quantitative research methods. These problems are not unique to higher education research. Frederick Wirt and Douglas Mitchell have similarly characterized the more generic field of educational politics as having a weak theoretical foundation which leads to contradictory findings.

The politics of education as a field of study also lacks consensus on the boundaries of the field. According to Paul Peterson, "The range of topics that is quite properly considered part of the educational politics field cuts across virtually the entire political science discipline." Peterson further suggests that the politics of education lacks a conceptual or theoretical focus and that its only defining characteristic is the common interest in the substantive policy area of education: "Even viewed as a field of policy analysis the politics of education is no more a separate field of study than, say, the politics of agriculture, the politics of housing, or the study of political activity in any other substantive policy area."

Research on the politics of higher education exhibits this same limitation of sharing at best only a common substantive focus on higher education, but not a cohesive theory or conceptual orientation, or a consensus on basic concepts and terms. This is partly a function of the difficulty in defining politics, and distinguishing it from policy. Moreover, it may also be a function of the topical diversity evident in educational research in general.

Many of these concerns can be summarized in terms of the characteristics of the field. First, the field exhibits a broad diversity of theoretical perspectives and topical foci. On the one hand, this merely parallels the rich, multifaceted character of higher education and its numerous points of contact with the political process. On the other hand, this diverse menu of subject areas presents a panoply of possibilities. Such disparate concerns as higher education finance, institutional governance, statewide coordination, faculty unionism, institutional planning, student financial aid policy, and state budgeting, can all be properly considered within the purview of the politics of higher education.

Second, as Crosson and Adams's analysis of the literature aptly demonstrates, there is wide variation in the extent to which theory is used in higher education politics research, the character of that theory, and its uses as explanation, as a principle of data selection, as description, or as prescription. Crosson and Adams also identify one major category of literature that cannot be classified as research or related to any but the broadest conception of theory, but which provides commentary on important issues by individuals with extensive research and personal experience in higher education policy. While not research in the traditional meaning of that term, this largely prescriptive literature contributes in important ways to the research agenda in this area.

In summary, there are varying purposes or agendas within higher education policy research. That research can be oriented to description, explanation, criticism or evaluation, or some combination. Second, it may emphasize educational policy or politics. Third, policy research exhibits the basic tension between the purposes of the scholar for basic research or advancing understanding and the needs of the policy participant for applied research directed to immediate action.

A taxonomy of higher education politics and policy is offered as a heuristic device for mapping the field, suggesting both the range of topical diversity and its boundaries and outlining some of the relationships between higher education systems and public policy structures. Second, this framework is applied in a discussion of the concerns surrounding accountability of higher education to public policy structures. Third, the various research agendas noted earlier are examined by use of an analytical paradigm for political and policy research. The divergent perspectives of the researcher and policymaker are discussed in terms of three levels of analysis: descriptive, explanation, and evaluation. The implications of this paradigm for research on higher educational politics and policy are suggested, as are some of the potential relationships between the discipline of political science and the more applied policy research.

Mapping the Field

Politics is a protean term, and its meaning varies with the context in which it is used. More formal definitions of politics are familiar, such as Harold Lasswell's "Who Gets What, When, How", politics as "the authoritative allocation of values," or the acquisition and uses of power and influence. As Heinz Eulau notes, a universal definition of politics may be an illusive goal: "Political seems to be a residual rather than a generic term. This makes it futile to search for characteristic features of political behavior apart from an institutional or situational environment that shapes and patterns certain types of interpersonal relations."

Even when politics is limited to the realm of higher education, the term can be used in numerous ways to refer to a variety of activities. The enactment of federal legislation for higher education and the dynamics of the faculty meeting bear little resemblance to one another, but they both can be viewed as forms of politics. However, to what extent should we be concerned with the latter at the expense of the former? By adopting a broad definition, we risk trivializing politics. One of the strengths of David Easton's definition of politics as the authoritative allocation of values is that it underscores the idea that for a set of behaviors to be political, they must involve some authoritative action. Further, lest we become engrossed in the politics of the PTA, this authoritative action should involve something of a public purpose or, in the case of higher education, it should be concerned with educational policy in some form. Thus, educational policy and politics are related in important respects.

At the same time, it is equally important to distinguish between them. Public policy is set within a context of societal expectations, demands, and constraints, and it involves purposive collective action directed toward the solution of a societal problem or the resolution of a common issue. Policy does not just happen; policy is "made" through a complex, more or less deliberative process, which can be characterized as having various stages. Politics in contrast, can be described as the interaction of competing interests, individuals, or groups over the preferred formulation or outcome of a given policy issue. Political activity may occur at each stage of the policymaking process. Put simply, policy is the "what" of the process; politics deals with the "how" and "whom."

Politics can affect any aspect of the policy process; indeed it is a driving force behind the process. Further, to the extent that policymaking involves the exercise of power, then all policy can be seen to be political in character. However, the converse does not hold. The policy process does not subsume all of politics. There are many forms of political activity (e.g., machine politics, party politics, group conflict) that may be only tangentially related to formal public policy. Consequently, we also need to be wary of definitions that confine politics to the realm of public policy. This is particularly true for higher education where educational policy has become increasingly a matter of public concern, thereby blurring the traditional distinctions between public policy and educational policy.

The implications of all of this are that we need a conception of politics that is sufficiently discriminating to differentiate politics from random conflict, and yet flexible enough to accommodate the varied contexts in which higher education interacts with the political system. For present purposes, we suggest a working definition of politics that is predicated on the assumption that politics occurs at various levels within higher education or between the academy and the broader political system. In this sense, politics is concerned with patterns of interaction and conflict over values, interests, and goals relating to the perceived needs of higher education and public authority.

A Taxonomy of Higher Education Policy

Politics and policy both relate to a process. Policy is viewed in terms of the content or substantive purpose of decision making, while politics is viewed in terms of the process itself, including the antecedents and results of a policy decision, relationships among the various actors in the process, and their underlying interests and purposes. In this respect the institutional context of policy becomes important. For example, political conflict within an academic department is quite different from the politics of federal financing of post-secondary education. Each can have far-reaching but radically different effects upon the outcome of a given policy process.

Politics has two dimensions: (1) it occurs at various institutional levels or *loci*, and (2) it is focused on a variety of substantive areas or *policy domains*. These two constructs, the locus of politics and the policy domain, can be viewed as two dimensions of a matrix, which can be extrapolated to produce a logical taxonomy of the politics of higher education.

Three loci of politics are identified: institutional, extramural, and governmental. The *institutional* column indicates political activity within a single institution or issues largely oriented to institutions. Institutional governance would be one example. By *extramural* we mean activity beyond a single institution. This includes both inter institutional relationships (e.g., the development of institutional consortia) and the relationships between institutions and quasi-governmental educational agencies, such as statewide coordinating agencies and multicampus governing boards.

Table 1.1. A Taxonomy of Higher Education Policy

Policy Domain	**Locus of Politics**		
	Institutional	**Extramural**	**Governmental**
PURPOSE	Missions	Master planning	State policy on scope and
	Broad academic policy	Accreditation	quality of H.E.;
			Public/Private balance;
			Land grant tradition;
			Federal higher ed. amendments
VALUES & NORMS	Academic freedom	Professional	Policies on access and choice
	Institutional	Standards and norms	Philosophies on who benefits
	Autonomy		and who pays
PROGRAMS	Academic standards	Professional licensing	Program budgeting
	Program planning	Program review	Categorical aid
MANAGEMENT	Personnel policy	Collective bargaining	Administration regulation
	Campus management	Multicampus Coordination	Court rulings
			Audits
RESOURCES	Budgeting	Resource allocation	Educational finance
	Resource acquisition	Competition	

The *governmental* column indicates the numerous points of contact with as well as the mutual influence of higher educational institutions and their intermediaries on the broader political system.

The policy domain is conceptualized in terms of five levels in a hierarchy from the most broad and abstract to the specific and concrete.

Purposes: The first level deals with the fundamental purposes and goals of higher education. Political conflict over issues of purpose and mission occurs within and among the institutional, extramural, and governmental levels.

Within an institutional locus this is manifested in general academic policy, institutional charters or mission statements, and the basic identity, purpose, and constituency from which the institution draws its legitimacy.

At the extramural level, comparable issues of purpose are articulated through such activities as master planning, statewide coordination, and reviews by accrediting agencies. Examples of interface between institutional and extramural concerns are the tensions between institutional aspirations and the constraints of a statewide master plan; or inter-institutional competition for status, clientele, resources, or political influence within a state.

Government influences the institutional missions and purposes for higher education in at least three respects: (1) in the design and legitimation of the structure of higher education through constitutional or statutory provisions such as the establishment of institutions, their governing boards and statutory powers, establishing state boards, coordinating agencies, or 1202 commissions; (2) in reacting, reviewing, and responding to policy initiatives for higher education such as approving state master plans; and (3) in more proactive policy initiatives directed toward higher education through study commissions, task forces, and legislative investigations.

Values and Norms: Higher education is by its very nature value-oriented, for several reasons. Colleges and universities are custodians and purveyors of society's values, traditions, and norms. At the same time, higher education is dedicated to the criticism of society and the rearticulation of society's values, consistent with its mission to discover new knowledge. Second, colleges and universities themselves require adherence to certain values of academic freedom, peer review, and institutional autonomy which differentiate them from most other kinds of institutions. Third, higher education attempts to serve multiple values, many of which are in conflict. The tension between the loyalty of faculty to the professional discipline beyond a single institution and the demands of that institution is one case in point. The inherent tension between meritocratic and egalitarian values reflected in the policies of colleges and universities is another source of intra-institutional dynamics and conflict.

At the extramural level one can identify tensions between academic and societal values toward research, and the relative ambivalence of some institutions toward public service, perhaps due to fears of becoming a captive of the constituencies or interests they attempt to serve. There is also an inherent tension between the role of colleges and universities as active participants with responsibilities for involvement and leadership in the community and the responsibility of higher education to serve as disinterested social critic.

In the governmental locus basic values are manifested in major policies, which are indications of the level of public confidence in higher education or the public commitment to such goals as quality, access, and choice. This nation's long-standing leadership in science and technology, the nearly universal access it provides its citizens to post-secondary education, and the significant public and private investment in higher education testify to the value this nation has historically placed on education. There is also another sense in which higher education is used as an instrument of social policy. Federal and state policies directed to affirmative action, accessibility for the disabled, health and safety regulations, federally aided training programs, etc., all exhibit this tendency by government to enlist the participation of higher education in activities deemed to advance public, governmentally sanctioned social policy goals.

Programs: Academic program planning and administration are among the most significant policy functions at the institutional level. Analogous functions at the extramural level include program review, regulation, and professional licensing. Program budgeting and categorical grants by state and federal government are parallel functions of the governmental locus.

Management: The management area is concerned with the development and administration of personnel policy as well as other administrative activities necessary for the effective functioning of an institution. As illustrated in Table 1.1, these are reflected in activities like multicampus coordination and collective bargaining at the extramural level, and administrative regulation, judicial review, and financial auditing at the governmental level.

Resources: Institutions require the careful budgeting and management of several types of resources, including human, financial, and physical. They must also seek financial support from government, private philanthropy, or through student recruitment. Inter institutional activities include multicampus resource allocation and intercampus competition for resources. Educational finance, including institutional support at the state level, and student financial aid programs from state and federal governments are also illustrative.

Implications

The taxonomy discussed above outlines some areas of interaction between education policy and politics as well as the forms that interaction can take. As such, its use is primarily analytical. In the real world many of the activities cut across categories. To cite one illustration, faculty governance within an institution could be concerned with all five of the policy domains. Other activities, such as strategic planning, not only transcend many of these categories on a vertical dimension (e.g., purposes, programs, resources), but also deal with several loci of the horizontal dimension (i.e., the relationship of an institution with its external environment). Despite these limitations, the taxonomy serves a heuristic function by identifying the range and diversity of phenomena that can be considered within higher education politics. To that extent it could be a useful device for mapping the boundaries of the field and for beginning to describe the inter-relationships among various facets of this diverse area of inquiry. The taxonomy may also serve a heuristic function by identifying areas where further research is needed. For example, research is needed in the area of the interface between state and federal policy for higher education, or such phenomena as inter-institutional competition for enrollment and resources, and the relationships of educational institutions to the local community, to name a few. One conclusion to be drawn from the taxonomy is that there are numerous points of interface among higher educational institutions, the political system, and their intervening structures. Second, within each policy domain there are parallels between institutional policy and public policy. This underscores the point that the traditional belief in the separation of education from politics no longer describes this complex system of relationships. Rather, as the taxonomy illustrates :

- There are several levels at which political and policymaking activities occur in higher education.
- Various forms of political relationships occur within and across institutional and governmental levels.
- Relationships between higher education and public authority are characterized by interdependence, with numerous points of interpenetration.

The Accountability Problem

One of the classic issues in the higher education literature involves the tension between independence or autonomy of higher education and the countervailing pressures for greater public accountability. This accountability issue has often been viewed in absolute terms. One of the implications of the present analysis is that government and higher education interact on a variety of dimensions, and the effects of this tension on higher education will vary with the form and context of the interaction.

A great deal of popular and scholarly literature has dealt with the growing role of government in the governance of public higher education. State governments and state coordinating boards are exercising more control and introducing more levels of review over universities and colleges. Governors and executive budget agencies are having a growing impact on the financial independence of public universities. The accumulation of additional layers of review and coordination in higher education, the imposition of new forms of control over individual campuses, and the rise of multicampus systems and statewide coordinating boards are related concerns. The Carnegie Commission and others have recommended institutional arrangements that will enhance university autonomy, particularly in the areas of intellectual conduct, academic affairs, and administrative arrangements. This could be accomplished by encouraging the states to use broad instruments of coordination, by preserving independent boards of trustees and by continuing to vest the faculty with power over academic matters.

A number of factors have contributed to the perceived erosion of institutional autonomy. Chief among these has been the growth in the scope and magnitude of public higher education, which has not only heightened political attention but also extended bureaucratic control. These in turn have increased the demands for more specific and detailed information. In addition to the increasing size and complexity of higher education, several other developments have also affected higher education's situation: increased competition for public funds; problems with inflation, productivity, and enrollment; a perceived decline in the value of the college degree; and the recurrent imbalances in the supply of and demand for trained manpower.

The issue of accountability is generally posed in zero-sum terms: Increases in external demands for information and additional measures of coordination and control result in a direct loss of institutional autonomy. To cite the Carnegie Commission on Higher Education, "External authorities are exercising more and more authority over higher education, and institutional independence has been declining. The greatest shift of power in recent years has taken place not inside the campus, but in the transfer of authority from the campus to outside agencies."

Ironically, the persistence of this view may have hindered research on the relationship between higher education and government because of the failure to recognize this problem as simply one special case of a much broader trend. Higher education may not be unique in the extent to which it has become subject to governmental regulation. In fact, this over-regulation may be symptomatic of the decline in power and legitimacy of institutions throughout society. Moreover, a fixation on the intrusiveness of government can lead to a "victim perspective," which fails to recognize the extent to which the subjects of governmental regulation can influence that regulation. According to Richard Halverson, "By overemphasis on the regulatory powers of governmental agencies, it is easy to slip into a perspective on the politics of higher education in which colleges and universities are seen as the victims of politics, as disadvantaged contenders in the endless struggle for money and autonomy." Finally, we need to be more discriminating in our discussion of governmental involvement in higher education. Robert Berdahl suggests a useful distinction between substantive autonomy, which deals with issues of policy and programs, and procedural autonomy, which is essentially a concern for administrative flexibility. According to Berdahl, although procedural controls may have some nuisance value, they do not affect the more fundamental concerns of substantive autonomy.

We would argue that the accountability issue needs to be viewed in political rather than moral terms. The meaningful question for analysis is not which sector has what authority, but rather what decisions are made, by whose authority, at what level of detail, and with what effect on the perquisites of either the university or the state.

Forms of Accountability

Drawing upon our taxonomy, several forms of accountability can be identified. Each may be viewed in terms of its effects on higher education. We suggest five distinct forms of accountability, each corresponding to one of the five policy domains of the taxonomy.

Systemic Accountability : The fundamental purposes of higher education are inextricably linked with and dependent upon societal goals as reflected in public policy. While public policy should never dictate or impose a mission upon higher education, government does influence higher education in at least three respects: (1) in designing the structure of higher education within a state or by determining its role in the pursuit of national objectives; (2) in responding to policy initiatives by higher education (e.g., approving master plans, establishing new programs, appointing members of governing boards); and (3) through policy initiatives directed to higher education (e.g., study commissions, legislative hearings, landmark legislation). This order of activity is concerned with establishing and maintaining the basic system of higher education.

Table 1.2. The Accountability Paradigm

Policy Domain	Form of Accountability
Purposes	Systemic
Values/Norms	Substantive
Programs	Programmatic
Management	Procedural
Resources	Fiduciary

Substantive Accountability : Higher education, like other institutions, is subject to a growing volume of incentives, mandates, and regulations intended to serve some broader social policy objective. They range from civil rights to civil defense. As an educational enterprise, higher education can be seen as carrying a special responsibility to set an example in the community. To the extent that our institutions live up to that standard, external inducements may not be necessary. In other words, higher education responds to substantive accountability through its involvement in specific substantive public policy goals.

Programmatic Accountability : This represents a type of contractual obligation to achieve certain stated objectives in exchange for financial support. One example on the state level is the politics of the budgetary process, particularly where appropriations are based on some form of program budgeting or funding explicitly concerned with the achievement of programmatic objectives. These objectives may vary in sophistication or comprehensiveness, including statewide planning systems, performance budgeting, or enrollment planning. This can also refer to the proverbial strings attached to federal categorical grants. The important point is that the educational system can be held accountable for the achievement of stated program objectives.

Procedural Accountability : Educational institutions are subject to a myriad of administrative requirements and controls such as laws, judicial rulings, administrative regulations, contractual obligations, collective bargaining agreements, etc. While compliance with these requirements can be costly and divert energy from the primary missions of teaching and research, the thrust of this form of accountability is largely procedural in nature.

Fiduciary Accountability : This refers to the extensive system of financial control, pre-audit, and related safeguards that have developed over the past several decades of public sector accounting. Beyond the purely technical ramifications it can have, fiduciary accountability is often used as a vehicle for affecting substantive policy. For example, the budgetary process can open major policy disputes under the guise of efficiency or budgetary propriety. Fiduciary accountability also frequently leads to extensive reporting requirements which may also have far-reaching ramifications.

To summarize, higher education politics and policy are complex and multifaceted, operating in a variety of institutional contexts and substantive domains. A major implication is that any analysis of these relationships should attempt to discern among these various forms of accountability, and should treat separately the impact of each upon higher educational institutions and systems.

Political Analysis and Policy Research

Earlier it was noted that the field of higher education politics and policy tends to be dominated by descriptive research lacking in theoretical rigor. Even among the examples of research that do display a fairly high level of rigor, a plethora of theoretical frameworks and approaches is apparent. One possible explanation for this is the number of agendas or purposes that higher education research is being called upon to serve.

In their insightful analysis of the literature Crosson and Adams employ James S. Coleman's distinction between disciplinary research and policy research: "According to Coleman, disciplinary research is intended primarily for the accumulation of knowledge and theory about a certain group of phenomena and thus for further development of the discipline. In contrast, policy research is intended to provide guidance for action and for policy development." Since the policy sciences are relatively new and undeveloped, some overlap or blurring between policy research and the host disciplines of sociology, economics, political science, and others is probably unavoidable. When dealing in the realm of policy, there are additional research agendas that need to be considered. Wirt and Mitchell suggest four types of research relevant to policy: descriptive, explanatory, critical, and forecasting. Descriptive research deals with the collection of basic information on the policy area and some comparisons among different cases. Explanatory research deals with the antecedents of a given policy, and it also deals with its effects. In this respect it is similar to disciplinary research. Critical research is concerned with an assessment of the results or effectiveness of a given policy, or the effectiveness of a policy process in producing a satisfactory outcome. Forecasting involves the analysis of policy variables and their inter-relationships for the purpose of projecting or extrapolating potential policies and their future consequences.

Of these, forecasting could be viewed as a special case of explanatory research in that the understanding of a past event is epistemologically related to projecting that understanding forward in time to forecast potential future outcomes of known relationships among variables. For this reason we will be concerned only with the three activities of description, explanation, and evaluation.

Since this field is concerned with the politics of higher education, it may suffer from some of the same difficulties facing political science in general. Specifically, there is some ambiguity in separating politics from policy. Second, there is a historic tension between the study of politics as a discipline concerned with basic knowledge and as a more applied policy science.

Robert Spadaro identifies two long-standing dimensions of this issue: normative prescription versus a positivistic commitment to value-free description. More recently, this has been manifested in the tension between social scientists committed to applied research on societal problems and advocates of a more analytical, predictive, and theory-dependent social science. Within political science some eschew the current trend to reorient the discipline toward public policy, while others argue that failure to embrace public policy analysis will leave the field moribund. One advocate of the public policy position has even argued that "policy research is political science."

Policy research means different things to different analysts. Those who are primarily concerned with policy tend to view policy research as an applied activity directed to the analysis and solution of specific public policy problems. The more disciplinary-oriented social scientists are concerned with research on the nature of the policy process. This latter form of policy research begins to overlap, if not supersede, traditional political science which similarly has been more concerned with the policy process than the content or impact of policy.

This debate between the policy sciences and the social sciences produces competing conceptions of politics. There is a clear risk in defining politics solely in policy terms. While policy is important as an area of research concentration, it is only one concern in the field of politics. What is needed are conceptualizations of policy and political analysis which allow for different forms of policy research. At the same time, this should be sufficiently differentiated from politics so as not to limit political science to a sole and potentially mundane concern with policy issues.

An Analytical Paradigm

Given these competing agendas for research and practice, it is understandable that the term "policy research" can refer to a number of analytically distinct activities. For the sake of analysis, it may be helpful to differentiate these various activities in terms of two dimensions: the primary focus of the research and the level of analysis, as shown in Table 1.3.

Let us first look briefly at the focus research. Policy research may exhibit a substantive focus on policy as such; or it may focus more on the policy process, including but not limited to its political dimension. Several scholars have cautioned that research on the politics of education must move beyond a focus on inputs to the policy process and deal more directly with the substance of policy, policy implementation, and its impact upon the policy environment. According to Grant Harmon, the field of higher education research needs to deal with both process and product: "Unless policy studies link formulation and output processes with implementation and impacts, their practical value, as well as their contribution to theory, will be severely limited."

Next, we need to look at the levels of analysis. Policy research and political analysis both operate on at least three levels: a primary level, that of the policy practitioner involved in applied research; a secondary level where academic scholarship is concerned with disciplinary research; and a third level, dealing with meta-analysis or evaluation.

Primary research is conducted by applied researchers who are close to the policy process through their formal role, experience, or recognized expertise (e.g., professional staff, advisors, consultants, etc.). Such research is largely descriptive and is concerned with identifying policy issues and recommending alternatives. In contrast to more scholarly research it is problem focused, and its goal is to participate in or influence the decision-making process.

Disciplinary research, by comparison, operates at a level once removed from this primary activity. Rather than engaging in policy, the intent of disciplinary research is to explain and ultimately to predict policy processes and outcomes. It has a more nomothetic orientation, seeking

Table 1.3. Research in Politics and Policy: An Analytical Paradigm

	Level of Analysis	**Focus of Research**	
	. Mode of Analysis		
	. . Objective	Substantive Policy or Impact	Policy Context or Process
	. . . Actors		
(I)	Applied		
	. Descriptive, problem focused, idiosyncratic		
	. . Participation or influence	Policy Analysis	Political Feasibility
	. . . Practitioner, professional staff,		Analysis
	consultants		
(II)	Disciplinary		
	. Objective, explanatory, nomothetic		
	. . Understanding, hypothesis	Policy Research	Process Research
	testing, theory building		
	. . . Scholar		
(III)	Evaluative		
	. Critical, Meta-analytic		
	. . Improvement	Evaluation Research	Meta-Policy Analysis
	. . . Evaluator		

general patterns of behavior rather than an idiosyncratic focus on a specific policy problem within a given setting. The object of this research is developing and testing theory, rather than participating in the policy process or influencing policy formation.

The third level corresponds in logical structure to the relationship of the philosopher of science to the scientist. It represents the activity of explicating and reflecting on the conduct of policy and policy research. In this sense it also has a strong evaluative orientation. It deals either with an evaluation of policy and its impact upon the policy environment, or an evaluation of the policy process itself.

Applied Analysis : Applied social science research directed to a particular policy problem or issue is what we generally refer to as policy analysis. This is what Carol Weiss and others are concerned about when they discuss the utilization of social research by policymakers. An illustration from higher education would be an analysis by legislative staff of the costs and benefits of alternative student financial aid programs.

Political Feasibility Analysis : This is applied research directed to the policy process, and perhaps the least developed of any of the research foci displayed in the paradigm. In one sense this is less a formal analysis than an informal, intuitive activity generally performed by practitioners, their immediate advisors, and, to a lesser extent, policy analysts. The term is borrowed from Arnold Meltsner, who argues that in order for analysts to have an impact on policy, their policy formulation must be preceded by a political feasibility analysis which identifies the relevant actors, motivations, beliefs, resources, and the opportunities and constraints of the given policy site. This almost parallels policy analysis, except that the focus of applied research is on political variables rather than policy variables. To illustrate, political feasibility analysis would involve an assessment of the political environment, the influential policy actors, their political dispositions toward policy alternatives, and the identification of strategies to influence key decision makers toward a preferred policy alternative.

Disciplinary Research : Two forms of disciplinary research are suggested: policy research and process research. Policy research is the study of policy for the purpose of explaining the policy system. This is comparable to Thomas Dye's definition of policy analysis: "the systematic identification of the causes and consequences of government activity, the use of scientific standards of inference, and the search for reliability and generality of knowledge in the form of systematic theory." Dye goes on to describe the concern with the causes of public policy as "policy determination research" and the study of consequences as "policy impact research." Using an illustration from educational finance, policy research in Dye's sense could be an analysis of determinants of public expenditures for higher education, or more specifically, an analysis of the characteristics of low tuition states versus high tuition states.

Process Research : This is analogous to policy research, except that the focus is on the decision-making process the "how" of policy rather than the "what." This distinction can be illustrated by Spadaro's plea that we pay attention to policy as well as process:

If we are trying to explain a specific welfare policy, it is important to know why policy makers decided the way they did on that policy, how it was implemented, and how resources were allocated; but it is equally important to know or try to know also the impact and success of the policy, the symbolic or intangible results of that policy in perceptions and expectations, and the function of feedback for new welfare policy, which means not only new specific welfare policies but also the general policy environment.

Lawrence Gladieux and Thomas Wolanin's research on the passage of the Education Amendments of 1972 is a good example; it exhibits a balance between policy research and process research. With respect to policy research, the study explains the specific provisions of the federal legislation and how it shifted federal financing priorities toward student-based aid and away from direct institutional aid. They also analyze the impact on higher education during the first three years of implementation of the amendments.

Their discussion of the relationships at each stage of the policy process is an equally important contribution. They conclude, for example, that the policy outcomes were shaped by circumstantial factors, that the emergence of issues was a complex, social-political process, that there were diverse sources of alternatives for policymakers which tended to be narrowed to a small number of viable options, and that new policy tended to represent incremental adjustments to previous policy decisions.

Evaluative Analysis : The evaluative level includes the two activities of evaluation research and meta-policy analysis. Evaluation research is related to policy analysis and policy research in that they all share a focus on policy per se. Evaluation research attempts to apply the methodology and relevant theory of social research to an analysis of the extent to which the implementation of policy achieved its objectives. It is often more rigorous and systematic than the policy analysis which supported the program's initial implementation. To the extent that program revision or improvement is a by-product of evaluation research, this research may serve a similar function to that of policy analysis.

Meta-Policy Analysis : Primarily concerned with evaluating policy analysis through an examination of the policy process, meta-policy analysis is specifically concerned with the nature and extent of the utilization of policy analysis in decision making, its impact on policy and, ultimately, upon the policy system. It relies extensively on process research but takes it one step further by examining the influence of the policy process on the character of decisions made.

Linda Ingeson provides a description of policy research that reflects several elements in our matrix. She notes that relatively little is known about "(a) the linkages among the organizational structures involved in the policymaking process and their functions in respect to one another; (b) the relationships between these structures and processes and the implementation, evaluation and review of policies; and (c) the role of research in informing both sets of processes." Points (a) and (b) fall within our conception of process research. A concern with the role of research in informing those processes (point c) is an apt description of what we mean by meta-policy analysis. According to Weiss, the key research questions regarding the utilization of research in policymaking all focus on the policy process: "How do policies get made?" and "What information do decision making groups seek to pay attention to?"

There is a growing body of literature on the influence (or lack of it) of policy analysis in the policy process. Robert Andringa found that policy research and studies ranked ninth out of ten among factors influencing federal education legislation, according to an informal survey of congressional staff. G. E. Sroufe suggests that evaluation research is itself a political act: "What to evaluate, how, when and by whom, and who decides the criteria are all tied to outcomes which are political resources in the allocation of stakes." David Florio indicates that different types of analysis and information are useful at different stages in the policymaking process, and the need for specific information targeted on the issues increases as the process moves from issue identification to deliberation and decision. Wirt and Mitchell describe a multifaceted dynamic process of interaction between policy and research: "Knowledge alternatively describes, explains, criticizes and forecasts a world where policy maintenance and change interact constantly."

Meta-policy analysis can be useful in giving as a broader understanding of the nature of the policy process and the broader societal and historical forces which give rise to policy concerns. Jerome Murphy speaks of a "paradox of state educational reform," meaning that each set of solutions to an existing problem brings with it the seeds of a new set of problems. He argues that many of the efforts of the 1960s to broaden participation, strengthen decision-making structures, and to introduce analysis have resulted in overloaded communication channels, increasingly complex decision processes, and in the mobilization of narrow constituency groups which have fragmented the social consensus needed to support educational policy. Elizabeth Hansot and David Tyack point to the cyclical pattern of fundamental educational reforms, suggesting that if we can find patterns in the historical issue-attention cycle this may help policymakers discover the underlying causes of educational reform.

In summary, a better understanding of the policy process and its relationships to broader societal conditions and trends is relevant to our understanding of public policy and the role of analysis in influencing that policy. Thus meta-policy analysis should become a very important part of the research agenda for social scientists concerned with educational policy and public policy.

The Question of Complementarity

According to Spadaro there is a certain ambivalence within the political science community regarding a fuller immersion in the public policy area for fear that "public policy could swallow all of political science." One implication of the analytical paradigm discussed above is that process research is a necessary complement to policy research. Furthermore, since process research calls for many of the same skills and perspectives associated with political science, this discipline can make a needed contribution to policy research without becoming absorbed into an undifferentiated policy science.

Second, findings from studies in the area of higher education politics can be brought to bear on more general questions of policy research. To cite a specific example: A dissertation on the appropriations process for higher education in Minnesota identified many legislative strategies and behaviors that are highly consistent with Aaron Wildavsky's findings on the congressional appropriations process. Thus research on the policy process for higher education can contribute to our understanding of policy processes in general.

Third, research across subject matter areas can be complementary and synergistic. Owen Porter's study of the determinants of influence in the Michigan legislature suggest that legislators take their cues from legislator colleagues who are viewed as "experts" in a policy area. Actors outside the legislature exert their influence through a two-step information flow in which the legislative expert becomes the target in the effort to influence the legislature as a whole. This finding could be relevant to questions of legislative influence for higher education as well. According to Porter, "Our knowledge of how the process of deciding differs among different fields within the same legislative body is still quite limited."

This complementarity of political analysis and policy research goes both ways; higher education policy research also strengthens the field of higher education politics. For example, as noted earlier, much of the literature on higher education policy is largely commentary. However, even this literature focuses attention on relevant issues for more systematic research on the policy process. Finally, attention to meta-policy analysis or the study of how research influences policymaking contributes to our understanding of both the policy environment in which this research must be carried out, and also the character of the policies themselves and their impact upon the higher education system.

Summary

On one level, this is directly attributable to the diversity of topical foci. Our taxonomy of politics and policy in higher education helps illustrate the range and boundaries of the field: It defines three institutional loci of politics and five substantive policy domains. In addition, there are five forms of accountability; in other words, five general areas in which higher education systems are influenced by public authority.

A second explanation for the current state of the literature on higher education politics is due to its multiple research agendas. Research may legitimately focus on any of six distinct realms: policy analysis, political feasibility analysis, policy research, process research, evaluation research, and meta-policy analysis. This analytical paradigm suggests that politics and policy, while integrally related, are in reality quite distinct. At the same time, applied, disciplinary, and evaluative research in each area can be complementary and synergistic.

The implications of this discussion for the broader field of policy research may be that a focus on policy processes (which has been the traditional domain of political science) is a necessary and complementary adjunct to the policy sciences. For the field of higher education research this may mean that a consensus on the concepts and theoretical perspectives is unlikely in the near future. Such a paradigmatic closure may not, however, be necessary. In fact, it should not be expected in light of the broad domain which this field currently addresses and the multiplicity of functions which the politics of higher education literature can be expected to serve.

2

Quality and Equality in Higher Education

Introduction

The academic community, heretofore highly autonomous, has become increasingly concerned about growing government influence over matters pertaining to academic conduct and freedom: the right of the academy "to determine for itself on academic grounds who shall teach, what may be taught, and who may be admitted to study." Concurrently, the institutional, system-wide, and national retrenchment forecast for the 1980s has significant implications for government efforts to maintain and improve both the quality of higher education (training programs and research capacity) and the equality of higher education opportunity.

The transition from elite to mass to universal higher education in the United States during the years following World War II is the result of an expanded governmental presence in the higher education arena. This transition has been marked by a major shift in governmental roles. At the federal level, the role of government has shifted from that of purchaser and consumer of university research to supporter and underwriter of expanded access to and participation in higher education. Similarly, the state role in higher education has changed dramatically from passive provider to concerned underwriter as public higher education has evolved from a limited, low cost, meritocratic system to one of open and potentially unlimited access to all citizens regardless of age, ability to pay, or previous educational achievement.

Education is not a specific federal responsibility. Both by constitutional design and conscious political choice, education is the responsibility of the individual states. While the federal presence may in some instances be more visible than that of the states, the federal government remains the junior partner albeit an increasingly influential one in higher education. The federal role in education is limited and specialized, usually takes the form of categorical grants, and aims to supplement state and local efforts "to solve particularly urgent problems or provide various kinds of assistance and leadership to help improve the quality of education." Because education is primarily a state responsibility, the federal presence has evolved as part of the larger, less explicit and at least in constitutional terms federal concern for the commonwealth. This commonwealth concern has led to federal education policy initiatives linked to a variety of areas: land and agricultural development; veterans' benefits (the GI Bill); scientific development; national defense; and economic opportunity. The Higher Education Act of 1965, part of the "Great Society" legislation, was thus the first major federal legislation to address higher education policy. Until then federal initiatives having direct and major impact on American higher education were linked to other, often peripheral, issues and outcomes.

The rapid growth of federal higher education programs since 1965 has tended to overshadow the historical state role and responsibility. The states still have primary responsibility for higher education; the states alone grant charters to both public and private institutions. With regard to funding, state expenditures for higher education continue to exceed those of the federal government. In the years following World War II, state governments carried the major burden of broadening college access by providing the bulk of the resources required for institutional and system-wide growth. During the twenty-five-year period beginning in 1950, the number of public colleges and universities, including two-year institutions and branch campuses, increased 228 percent; public institutions, which enrolled roughly one-half of all college students in 1950, accounted for better than 75 percent of all enrollments by 1975. This growth in the public sector occurred at the same time that total degree enrollments were increasing just over 400 percent.

In sum, national higher education policy has been based on two factors: state support for "mortar and brick" issues and federal "carrot and stick" priorities and program incentives.

Table 2.1. Sources of Income for All Colleges and Universities for Educational and General Purposes, 1939–1976

	Year			
Source	**1939-40**	**1959-60**	**1969-70**	**1976-77**
Federal Government	7.4%	24.1%	22.5%	16.4%
State Governments	28.7	32.0	36.6	41.6
Local Governments	4.6	3.5	4.8	5.1
Tuition and Fees)	38.1	26.8	26.8	28.2
Gifts, Grants, Endowment, etc.	21.2	13.6	9.3	8.7
	100.0	100.0	100.0	100.0
Total (in billions of dollars)	**$0.57**	**$4.34**	**$16.2**	**$32.28**

Responsibility for Quality

Until recently quality was largely the sole jurisdiction of the academic community. Accreditation and peer review were the major vehicles for identifying, assessing, and promoting quality within higher education. Government, with rare exception, was not an active participant. After a controversial attempt by the U.S. Office of Education to rate American universities during the early years of the twentieth century, the federal government ceded the quality issue to the states, the accrediting associations, and the professoriate: Eligibility for federal funding would be determined by state charter, program and/or institutional accreditation, and peer review of research proposals. The states, with rare exception, assumed academic values as their own. During the period of postwar expansion, the states generally viewed quality in terms of students with high test scores and faculty with doctorates, publications, and research grants.

The State Responsibility

D. Kent Halstead indicates that state planning agencies have generally accepted responsibility for providing the leadership to improve the quality of public higher education. Until recently, however, the states generally viewed program quality as depending almost entirely upon student and faculty characteristics. The traditional state perspective is exemplified in the following statement from the 1960 California *Master Plan for Higher Education*, a document that became the model for statewide higher education planning during the 1960s:

> The quality of an institution and that of a system of higher education are determined to a considerable extent by the abilities of those it admits and retains as students. This applies to all levels lower division, upper division, and graduate. It is also true for all segments, but the emphases are different. The junior colleges are required by law to accept all high school graduates (and even some non graduates under some circumstances); therefore the junior colleges must protect their quality by applying retention standards

rigid enough to guarantee that taxpayers' money is not wasted on individuals who lack the capacity or the will to succeed in their studies. If the state college and the university have real differences of function between them, they should be exacting (in contrast to public higher education in most other states) because the junior colleges relieve them of the burden of doing remedial work. Both have the heavy obligation to the state to restrict the privilege of entering and remaining to those who are well above average in the college-age group.

As this statement makes clear, the California master plan is based on a meritocratic model of program and institutional excellence. Many states have recently moved beyond this traditional perspective, expanding their list of concerns to include educational process issues as well as student and faculty characteristics as manifestations of quality. This new perspective, motivated by a growing demand for accountability and reflected in the state program review process, has encouraged the states to look beyond traditional measures of quality in evaluating their support for and investment in higher education. Prior to 1970, during the period of growth and expansion, state program review was concerned primarily with assessing the resources required to develop new degree programs; by the mid-1970s, however, the scope of such activities had expanded to include the review of both proposed as well as existing programs.

While state program review has yet to replace accreditation as the primary means of quality assessment and review, accrediting associations and the academic community they represent (and protect) are under growing pressure to cooperate with state and federal agencies. The Division of Institutional Eligibility of the U. S. Department of Education has established requirements for the evaluation criteria of accrediting associations. And in at least one state, Maryland, the state board of higher education and the regional accrediting association have agreed to cooperative efforts in the evaluation and accreditation of public colleges and universities.

A pragmatic acknowledgment of the potential for tension between the state program review process and accreditation is found in the recent Sloan Commission on Government and Higher Education report. The commission's call for the "periodic review of quality of educational programs at every public college and university to be conducted by academic peer groups, not state employees," recognizes the fiscal realities and political climate in state capitals, yet is also sensitive to the academic community's traditions and concerns. Program review is a fact of life for many public (and some private) institutions. The commission's view that program review is consistent with and complementary to institutional needs and state planning purposes, and that it should make use of existing accreditation structures, may disarm critics who fear uninformed and insensitive governmental intrusion into academic matters. At the same time, the commission's recommendation for periodic review may placate those state officials who demand greater accountability and who might support more drastic and less academically responsive methods.

The Federal Interest

Although the states are primarily responsible for issues pertaining to the quality of education, the federal government too has a major interest and investment in the quality of higher education. Commonwealth concerns for national defense, scientific and technological capacity, human resource development, and competent social/medical services provide a rationale for federal R & D expenditures, graduate professional fellowship programs in specific fields (medicine, public health, physical sciences), plus other programs. The proliferation of student aid programs since 1965, culminating in the entitlement provisions of the Basic Grant (now Pell Grant) program of the Educational

Amendments of 1972 (as amended), has contributed to federal concern for degree and program quality and integrity, particularly at the undergraduate level and in proprietary institutions. The federal government also funds and coordinates a number of programs to improve the quality of higher education focusing on "national educational problems" beyond the scope and resources of state and local governments (e.g., basic skills programs, international education). While the list of federal quality concerns seems long, no doubt the major focus and impact of federal interest (and funding) has been in the area of university-based R & D capacity and ancillary issues such as scientific and medical training.

Responsibility for Equality

Just as education is the primary domain of the states, so too it would seem that the states are primarily responsible for assuring and providing equality of educational opportunity. Yet the primacy of the state in education and the constitutionally dictated balance of powers among levels and branches of government have inevitably led to conflict over priorities and programs.

Frances Keppel, former U.S. commissioner of education, states, "The conventional wisdom acquired during the 1960s and 1970s suggests that the federal government has set the right agenda on such issues as civil rights, poverty, and policies for minority groups and the handicapped issues which state governments have generally neglected." Observing that the history of the past two decades shows an "uneasy relationship between federal purpose and state performance" on such educational issues as equal opportunity and desegregation, Keppel notes that policymakers and educators often forget that "the states' willingness to administer a program electively is the key to success of federal programs."

The tensions implicit in the gap between federal priorities and state performance are not new. The growing significance of the federal role in higher education adds to the current tensions and highlights once again the distinct nature of federal and state roles. These tensions are not likely to recede because of the priority/performance gap and because litigation remains the primary form of redress for the perceived failures of state and local governments to meet espoused domestic priorities in the area of equality of educational opportunity.

The State Responsibility

State support for "mortar and brick" issues during the postwar years implicitly addressed the issue of educational access and opportunity long before these concerns were part of the federal policy agenda. Patrick Callan states:

> *The primary and financial responsibility for meeting the educational needs of the American people resides with the states. For the last two decades state energies and resources in higher education have focused on the expansion of opportunity in response to rapid growth of the college-age population, higher proportions of high school graduates, and increased participating rates. Since the 1960 California Master Plan for Higher Education, the first formal state commitment to provide education after high school to all who had the desire and motivation to benefit, the states have been at the forefront of the national movement to improve access. The state master plans developed during the sixties and early seventies were essentially blueprints for increasing access, and they led to dramatic increases in the numbers of programs and institutions of postsecondary education. The approaches used by the states have varied but generally have included some combination of ensuring geographic proximity, enlarging institutions, developing new institutions and programs (most notably community colleges and vocational programs), providing student financial assistance, and increasing institutional support.*

Callan adds that, while the federal role has become increasingly important and financially significant, the states are primarily responsible for "the task of linking factors related to access student aid, various forms of institutional support, and articulation between high schools and colleges ideally working in collaboration with campuses." He notes that although the goal of equal access and opportunity has yet to be fully realized, the progress of the past two decades has been significant.

Not all observers would agree with this assessment. Although the states and their education agencies and institutions are concerned about expanding educational opportunity, a number of other issues appear to have a much higher priority, at least as indicated in annual agency reports. And, although the states did create the structures required to accommodate increasing numbers of postsecondary students, many critics argue that they have not been as successful in dealing with the real heart of the issue of educational opportunity increasing the entry and retention rates of non-traditional (i.e., low-income, disadvantaged, minority, handicapped) students in public higher education. Federal incentives and aid programs have been responsible for much of the movement of non-traditional students into public colleges and universities. And the *Adams* case, pertaining to the role and mission of historically black public colleges in state systems, serves as a lingering reminder of the discriminatory impacts of previous state policies and practices.

Public policy generally has focused on the issue of access to any postsecondary institution, assuming approximately equivalent impacts and benefits of college attendance, an assumption not supported by nearly three decades of research on college students and institutional impacts. The meritocratic criteria frequently found in state master plans have a policy impact clearly reflected in expenditure patterns across levels of public higher education. Financial resources are concentrated at the top of the institutional hierarchy, in the universities. University expenditures for educational and general (E & G) items perhaps the best measure of an institution's investment in its students are more than 40 percent higher than in public four-year colleges and almost 60 percent higher than in the community colleges. The extent to which public institutions subsidize their students also varies significantly: Universities have a mean FTE subsidy that is nearly 50 percent greater than that of other institutions. These figures suggest that one important aspect of the equality issue relates to the distribution of educational resources and the concentration of resources in the "least accessible" or more selective institutions.

The expenditure figures reflect, in part, perceptions of the differing costs of equality (at the two and four-year colleges) and quality (in the universities). Clark Kerr was among the first to describe the quality versus equality debate from the standpoint of the states, warning that they would find it difficult to satisfy the academic community's heightened expectations for program expansion and quality improvement and at the same time accommodate the increasing numbers of high school graduates with degree aspirations. Indeed, the states' interest in and responsibility for educational access and opportunity at all degree levels, and for all citizens not just recent high school graduates may well conflict with traditional notions of academic quality. However, as previously noted, state perceptions about the attributes of quality are changing. This shift in perspective is in large part a response to the demands from a number of constituencies for an accounting of (1) the resources allocated to public postsecondary education, and (2) the availability and distribution of educational opportunities to various clientele. State program review, with its focus on accountability, equality, and quality accountability and efficiency in the use of resources, equality of educational opportunity, and quality of education programs also contributes to a new awareness of the nature of the state responsibility for higher education.

The Federal Responsibility

Since 1965 first blacks and American Indians, and later others Hispanics, the poor, women, and the handicapped have been the implicit if not specific beneficiaries of a range of federal programs intended to expand educational opportunity. Both legislation and litigation have contributed to federal concern for equality of educational opportunity.

Table 2.2. Mean Expenditures in Public Institutions, Academic Year 1977 (Per Full-Time Equivalent Student)[a)]

	Institution[b)]		
		Four-Year	Community
Expenditure Item	Universities	Colleges	Colleges
Educational and General	$4,816	$3,358	$3,019
Library	163	136	108
Subsidy[c)]	4,334	2,928	2,190
a) Adjusted to include higher FTE costs of graduate education.			
b) Classification based on Carnegie Council typology.			
c) Subsidy = (Education and General Expenditure) + (Financial Aid) – Tuition.			

Prior to 1965 federal forays into higher education were generally linked to areas often only marginally related to higher education. This led to what might be called a contextually defined "quality/equality cycle" in federal higher education policy. Specific "equality" concerns were explicit in the legislation; underlying egalitarian principles were often implicit, and in time would become dominant.

In the 1860s the Morrill Act provided federal incentives for the growth, development, and curricular focus of public higher education. The practical and agricultural curricula stipulated by the legislation reflected egalitarian interests in an era marked by more aristocratic priorities.

By accident or intent, the GI Bill was largely responsible for the immediate surge in college enrollments following World War II. More than two million veterans of the Second World War used their educational benefits to pursue some form of postsecondary education. It brought to the nation's college campuses thousands of former servicemen who otherwise would not have attended college and thus contributed to a tremendous increase in upward social mobility. It is not clear that Congress had such goals in mind when, in 1943, it first passed legislation intended to assist disabled veterans' return to postwar jobs. The scope of the legislation was expanded in 1944 as much to reward returning veterans as to assist in postwar economic recovery.

Harry Truman was the first postwar president to encourage federal support for equality of educational opportunity. Conscious of the traditional state responsibility for education (and of congressional opposition to a federal role in education), Truman advocated using federal funds to reduce inequalities in state educational expenditures. He also appointed the first federal commission charged with the task of examining the goals and functions of American higher education. The 1947 report of the President's Commission on Higher Education espoused a broad set of egalitarian goals and policy objectives, not all of which were warmly received by the higher education community. The commission called for an end to racial and religious discrimination in higher education and advocated the expansion of the public sector, particularly two-year colleges, as an effective way to expand and equalize educational opportunities for all citizens. Truman's public statements and the commission's recommendations underscored growing federal concern for an end to discrimination and for the expansion of educational opportunity.

During much of the postwar period litigation rather than legislation helped to define a federal responsibility for equality of educational opportunity. A series of U.S. Supreme Court decisions, ultimately leading to the historic 1954*Brown* decision, helped give form and focus to the federal concern for equality.

Beginning in 1964 three sweeping pieces of legislation the Economic Opportunity Act of 1964, the Civil Rights Act of 1964, and the Higher Education Act of 1965 radically transformed the federal role and presence in higher education. Disadvantaged youth, a major focus of the Economic Opportunity Act, found two federal programs to support their college aspirations: Upward Bound was designed to help them gain college entry, and the College Work-Study program provided them with subsidized, on-campus, part-time employment. The Civil Rights Act prohibited discriminatory practices in federally supported programs, and used federal funding as a "carrot and stick" to enforce compliance. And the Higher Education Act espoused a broad set of egalitarian objectives for American higher education.

Table 2.3. Government Outlays for Higher Education, 1976-1977

		Amount (in billions of dollars)	**Percent**
Federal Government :			
	Research	$2.717	9.9%
	Student Aid	$6.482	23.7%
	Other	$2.532	9.2%
State Governments :			
	Institutional Support	$13.426	49.0%
	Student Aid	$.589	2.2%
Local Government		$1.631	6.0%
Total Government Outlays		$27.378	100.0%.

The federally funded student aid programs, first begun in 1965, perhaps best reflect the extent of federal concern and responsibility for equality. The decision to aid students, rather than institutions, clearly placed the federal government on the side of equality of student access and educational opportunity. The change in federal policy as manifested in the "all who can benefit" focus of the Higher Education Act of 1965 led eventually to the entitlement provisions of the Basic Grants program established by the Educational Amendments of 1972.

The changing federal role in higher education is reflected in the rapid expansion of student aid and related support programs, coupled with the leveling off of constant-dollar federal R&D funding. These two trends resulted in a dramatic shift in the allocation of federal higher education expenditures; thus in 1967, 65 percent of the expenditures went for institutional support, largely R & D funding, and student aid allocations amounted to only 35 percent of the total. By 1975 student aid totaled 72 percent of federal higher education expenditures, and institutional support dropped to 28 percent.

Table 2.4. Total Outlays for Student Aid, 1976-1977

	Amount (in billions of dollars)	Percent
Federal	$6.482	80.2%
State Programs	$.589	7.3%
Institutional Funds (a)	$.659	8.2%
Private Sources (b)	$.350	4.3%
Total Student Aid Outlay	$8.080	100.01.

a) Total institutional aid expenditures, which may originate from both public and private sources.
b) Estimated.

In the 1976-1977 academic year federal student aid expenditures accounted for almost one-fourth of total (federal, state, local) government expenditures for higher education and for just over 80 percent of total government student aid outlays.

The postwar change in federal policy defines the broad context of government concern for equality. Government, and particularly federal government, roles and responsibilities increased, prodded by both litigation and an expanding definition of government responsibility for the commonwealth. During the 1960s and 1970s the academic community, "enthusiastically sharing in the national fervor for equal opportunity and social mobility through education," responded to a combination of government directives and incentives designed to expand educational opportunity and promote equality.

Summary

The growth of government support for higher education has also affected the government responsibility for quality and equality in higher education. Litigation and legislation have established the federal role and defined the nature of state responsibility for equality; government interest in and concern for quality have been linked implicitly to the federal commonwealth concern and to growing public and state government demands for accountability. The likelihood of changing federal education priorities as part of an effort to control the federal budget signals the end of the concurrent state and federal support for both improving quality and expanding equality in higher education. The declining level of real-dollar support for higher education seems certain to increase the implicit competition for funding among the constituencies representing "quality" and "equality" factions.

Higher Education in India is one of the most developed in the entire world. There has in fact been considerable improvement in the higher education scenario of India in both quantitative and qualitative terms. In technical education, the IITs, and in management, the IIMs have already marked their names among the top higher educational institutes of the world. Moreover the Jawaharlal University and Delhi University are also regarded as good higher educational institutes for doing postgraduates courses and research in science, humanities and social sciences. As a result, students from various parts of the world are coming today for higher education in India.

Higher Education system in India: Higher education in India starts after the higher Secondary or 12th standard. While it takes 3 years for completing a B.A., B.Sc or B.Com pass or honors degree from a college in India, pursuing an engineering course would take four years and five years (with six months of additional compulsory internship) for completing a bachelor of medicine or bachelor of law degree.

Postgraduate courses generally are of two years duration. But there are some courses like Master of Computer Application (MCA) that are of three years duration. For those who cannot afford to attend regular classes for various pre-occupations can pursue correspondence courses from various Open Universities and distance learning institutes in India.

Higher Education Institutes in India: Universities and its constituent colleges are the main institutes of higher education in India. There are at present 227 government-recognized Universities in India. Out of them 20 are central universities, 109 are deemed universities and 11 are Open Universities and rest are state universities. Most of these universities in India have affiliating colleges where undergraduate courses are being taught. However Jawaharlal University is a remarkable exception to this rule. Apart from these higher education institutes there are several private institutes in India that offer various professional courses in India. According to the Department of higher Education, government of India, there are 16,885 colleges, 99.54 lakh students and 4.57 lakh teachers in various higher education institutes in India.

❑❑❑

3

Evaluation Politics of Higher Education

Introduction

Politics has to do with the distribution of stakes within a society or group. "Stakes" means jobs, money, prestige, influence, status, or even acceptance of ideas. People care enough about such stakes to try actively to influence their distribution. To this end they develop and husband their influence, and seek to use it wisely to affect the distribution of stakes. "Politics ain't bean bag."

When the above concepts are applied to evaluation, its political nature becomes apparent. Evaluations are derived from biased origins, in the sense that there are often political motivations behind the decision to evaluate something. Moreover, the choice of which program is evaluated is often a result of politics, insofar as politicians create and fund programs to address certain problems and please constituencies. Evaluators themselves have basic political orientations that can influence their conduct during evaluations. Political forces can dictate the kinds of populations sampled place limitations on the data collected, and influence the design, procedures, and reports of evaluations, as well as affect the impact that evaluations can have. These forces are so prevalent that ultimately methodological considerations are inextricably tied up with political ones so that the evaluator cannot simply be politically neutral in his use of evaluation approaches. In short, from the beginnings of an evaluation to its completion, politics is inescapable at every step.

Yet it is not enough to say merely that external political factors intrude upon the process of evaluation or that participants in evaluations are politically active. Conceptually, the reality of the relationship between politics and evaluation goes even deeper to the very core of what evaluation is. Lee Cronbach points out that, although evaluation does have a substantial and growing scientific tradition, science is only a subordinate aspect of evaluation: "If evaluation is not primarily a scientific activity, what is it? It is first and foremost a political activity, a function performed within a social system." This political nature of evaluation is based upon a central notion of politics; i.e., politics can be defined as those interactions involved in the authoritative allocation of valued commodities (e.g., money, education) for a society. Since evaluations produce judgments of worth about things or people, such judgments involve the potential or real reallocation of existing "stakes" that people have in various goods and services. Consequently, evaluation is part of the "process of who gets what in the society."

The relationship between evaluation and politics can be depicted in three general ways. One way might be called "politics in evaluation." Within this general category would be included any number of power struggles, conflicts, and the like that occur during the actual evaluation process. Such politics usually directly involves the participants in the evaluation (e. g., evaluator, client, staff of program being evaluated, the program's immediate constituencies), and the politics of these participants is often directed at influencing the processes and the outcomes of the evaluation. Attempts by a program staff to socialize or influence the evaluator of the program would be an example of politics in evaluation.

A second general category might be labeled "politics *and* evaluation," which refers to the interactions that occur between an evaluation process and various societal political systems. The main political systems that often interact with evaluation processes are the federal government and the governments of individual states. To the extent that these governments, through their officers and agencies, affect and are affected by evaluations, politics *and* evaluation are in evidence. An example would be the federal government's mandate that programs funded by Title I of the Elementary and Secondary Education Act be evaluated.

The third general category, "the politics *of* evaluation," is the foundation of the other two. Since one root meaning of politics is that it involves the authoritative allocation of values for a society, evaluation is political insofar as it is involved in making authoritative allocations. A judgment of worth, i.e., an evaluation, necessarily entails support or lack of support for an allocation of resources. Consequently, an evaluation has at least the potential of affecting the existing and future stakes of various competing interests. For example, I recently was a member of an evaluation team whose responsibility it was to evaluate several projects and to choose one for refunding by the state. In this case, the politics *of* evaluation referred to the allocative nature of the evaluation. In sum, evaluation is highly political in at least three logically distinct but interdependent ways. Participants in the evaluation attempt to influence the evaluation in directions consonant with their self-interests (politics *in* evaluation). Governmental bodies interact with evaluations (politics *and* evaluation). And evaluation judgments potentially or actually reallocate stakes (the politics *of* evaluation). Each of these kinds of evaluation politics is evident in higher education, though the unique nature of academic institutions affects the ways in which politics is manifest.

Organized Anarchy, Autonomy and Messy Pluralism

Three aspects of American higher education are especially noteworthy for an understanding of evaluation politics in academe. Higher education institutions operate quite differently from most organizations in our society. Also, academic institutions have traditionally exercised a great amount of independence from external control. And finally, higher education is noted for its diversity. Each of these characteristics warrants some discussion. Higher education institutions (specifically universities and colleges) exhibit neither the bureaucratic structures and processes of most other large organizations nor the collegiality that many academics have often claimed. Rather, academic institutions usually fit the patterns of a more political model, one that Victor Baldridge and others term "organized anarchy." Their model entails the following elements, the combination of which makes higher education a unique arena for evaluation politics:

1. Goals are normally vague and multifaceted; highly specific goals are usually highly contested.
2. The people served by higher education institutions often demand influence over institutional decision making.
3. There is no one "correct" way or technology to accomplish goals.
4. Higher education institutions are dominated by academic professionals who demand considerable autonomy and expect performance reviews to be done only by peers.
5. Academic professionals are not a cohesive group, often having closer ties and more loyalty to

colleagues within the same discipline around the world than to colleagues of different disciplines within the same institution.

6. Within an institution conflict is normal, participation by academics in institutional decision making is highest among those who vie for such power, formal authority is relatively limited, and external interest groups and agencies have a growing influence over institutional decision making.

Since many evaluation approaches focus pointedly upon goals, the inability of higher education institutions to define goals clearly means that academic evaluators are likely to meet considerable resistance. Likewise, the absence of agreement regarding the appropriate means or technologies for meeting goals probably makes the evaluation of the success of any given technology highly controversial. In addition, it might be expected that individuals and interest groups within academic institutions (including professors) would vie for the power to evaluate; at the same time they would resist being evaluated. And the widespread presence of fragmented groups and intra-institutional conflict implies that any potential weapon, such as evaluation, could be employed in the struggles to determine who gets what. Such a political atmosphere cannot help but reinforce the political nature of evaluation.

This organized anarchy exists along with another characteristic feature of academic institutions their traditional autonomy. As Robert Berdahl has indicated, institutions of higher education have traditionally exhibited three kinds of independence. Intellectual independence (known as "academic freedom") means that faculty have a degree of autonomy from external pressures (especially of the government) in matters related to the exploration, discussion, expression, and teaching of ideas. Faculty tenure is seen by some as a device that insulates academic freedom from political influences. Academic independence ("substantive autonomy") refers to the relative autonomy institutions and facilities have traditionally had in dealing with substantive academic matters such as institutional goals, admissions standards, grading policies, and other concerns at the heart of the academic mission. Most states have adopted through constitutions or legislation some form of a self-denying ordinance, whereby states have agreed to provide funding to higher education while at the same time limiting their own control over how the institutions govern themselves and use those funds. Administrative independence ("procedural autonomy") refers to the degree of autonomy that institutions of higher education have enjoyed in determining the administrative procedures used to meet institutional goals. The extent of each of these three kinds of autonomy has varied from state to state.

Particularly pertinent to this discussion are these facts: (1) the greater the autonomy of an institution of higher education, the less vulnerable it is to outside influence (such as external evaluations by governmental agencies); (2) autonomy usually implies that any evaluations that do occur will be self evaluations and peer evaluations; and (3) as several authors have noted, the traditional autonomies are being eroded by external pressures, especially as states demand more accountability for their dollars of support, as consumer protection and student protection movements grow stronger, and as the impact of specific governmental mechanisms such as "sunset" legislation, right-to-privacy and confidentiality regulations, and public disclosure mandates are more widely felt. Many of the sources of these external pressures use evaluations as a means of gaining more control over the once autonomous institutions of higher education.

A third characteristic feature of higher education is its diversity. What Berdahl calls a "messy pluralism" is a whole range of profit and nonprofit, public and nonpublic institutions. Baldridge and others classify the many higher education institutions into the following categories (while recognizing that there is considerable intra-category variance): private multiversities, public multiversities, elite liberal arts colleges, public comprehensive institutions, public colleges, private liberal arts colleges, community colleges, and private junior colleges. Moreover, there has been some pressure recently to replace the term "higher education" with a more comprehensive term, "postsecondary education." The latter refers to "an expanding variety of institutions, programs, and delivery systems in many different settings and under various forms of sponsorship."

This "messy pluralism" is particularly evident in the vast array of state, regional, and national coordinating bodies, postsecondary systems, governmental agencies, professional associations, accrediting bodies, and lobbying groups, and it has major consequences for any attempts at evaluation. There is a great deal of competition at all levels of higher education, a competition that often uses evaluation as a political weapon to further certain interests. And there is likely to be a great deal of disagreement regarding appropriate goals and means to attain those goals at the levels of individual institutions, statewide systems, or within higher education as a whole.

By way of summary, organized anarchy, autonomy, and messy pluralism characterize higher education. Whereas evaluation is by nature a political process, the specific political forms manifest in higher education are in large part dependent upon these three characteristics. These specific manifestations can be categorized in three general ways: politics in evaluation, politics *and* evaluation, and the politics of evaluation.

Politics in Higher Education Evaluation

As is true of most evaluations, evaluation in higher education often involves relationships among three key parties: the evaluator (or evaluation team), the decision maker or sponsor for whom the evaluation is made, and a constituency composed of those who have a stake in what is being evaluated. This conceptualization does not preclude self-evaluation, which conceivably could join all three roles in the same individual or group. For the sake of analysis, these parties are viewed here as existing in different individuals. The particular issues involved in self-evaluation are addressed later.

Politics in higher education can be said to comprise the political interactions among these three parties. Evaluation participants attempt to maintain or increase personal or group stakes by influencing the evaluation. For example, one evaluation in which I was involved found the evaluators virtually besieged by letters and phone calls ranging from testimonials in favor of the program being evaluated to veiled threats about possible consequences if the program received an "unsatisfactory" evaluation. Those phoning or writing letters had a stake in the program, and they were trying to secure a favorable evaluation by means of raw political power.

Since the organized anarchy model would lead us to expect political activity, one question that needs to be answered is: In what ways do evaluation participants exhibit political behavior? The answer lies in the nature of the evaluator, the decision maker, and the constituency and the propensity of each to act politically when interacting.

The *evaluator* is a political animal to the same extent that anyone else is. Though she may strive to be objective and rational, her role as evaluator has several political dimensions when she interacts with the decision maker and a constituency. As Carol Weiss notes, the evaluator's basic inclination is reformist. Since social scientists in general tend to be concerned with shaping the future, and since the dominant political orientation of college and university faculty is liberal, those evaluators who are also faculty members may be expected to have a general pattern of political leanings. It is unclear to what extent such leanings actually affect evaluations, but from the viewpoint of political analysis such a general orientation has at least the potential for influencing evaluation results.

One way in which the general political orientation of the evaluator could enter into an evaluation is the evaluator's choice of an evaluation approach. Ernest House describes the political assumptions underlying eight different evaluation models. The choice of one of these models (e.g., accreditation) necessarily involves a choice of certain political assumptions (e.g., the government should have a relatively minor role in evaluating). Similarly, a choice of a given approach to evaluation usually carries with it an implicit assumption about how goals are determined within an institution. The evaluation of a program's success by comparing outcomes with goals implies that the goals have already been set rather than that goals are being constantly renegotiated. In the organized anarchy of higher education, such an assumption might operate to the detriment of certain factions engaged in negotiating institutional goals.

In addition to general political orientations and assumptions, the evaluator also has political motivations of her own that may affect the evaluation. Higher education's organized anarchy necessitates the accumulation of power in order to affect policy decisions and to maintain organizational status. In institutions that pride themselves on respect for knowledge, the accumulation of knowledge has a certain amount of power, and increased power is needed to gain more knowledge. Aaron Wildavsky makes just this point in his commentary on the evaluator (evaluative man): "Evaluative man seeks knowledge, but he also seeks power. His desire to do good is joined with his will to act powerfully. Evaluative man is well off when he can pyramid his resources so that great knowledge leads to enhanced power, which in turn increases access to information." One manner in which the evaluator who is also a faculty member pyramids power in Wildavsky's sense is to be promoted and tenured. Since evaluation is a relatively new field, any evaluator who wishes to establish academic legitimacy by means of the standard criteria associated with scholarship, teaching, and service may find herself forced to emphasize "more respected" lines of scientific inquiry (such as experimental research designs and sophisticated statistical analysis) in evaluations. Yet such research designs, because of the nature of scientific inquiry, may have an inherent conservative bias. The evaluator's attempts to enhance her personal power and prestige may, therefore, result in the rejection of potentially useful solutions to problems because of overly stringent designs or tests. Similarly, findings are often published when they are generalizable to larger populations. Yet evaluations almost always deal with phenomena that are situation-specific and rarely transferable to other settings. It is conceivable that the evaluator could find her need for legitimacy in the eyes of colleagues in conflict with the dictates of the evaluation.

The *decision maker* or sponsor is also a source of potential political activity. In many cases he sponsors the evaluation and takes such action as he sees fit on the basis of the results. In the academic world, the decision maker is often a faculty member who rose to the heights (though many faculty might say fell to the depths) of administration. In the context of organized anarchy, where power is relatively fluid and diffuse, the administrator is regarded as a colleague or peer on temporary assignment rather than a permanent boss. For this reason, the administrator who wants to exercise his authority needs to bolster it by building power coalitions and wielding information. Evaluation thus becomes a source of data as well as a means for building support for a position. It has been my experience that the administrator's decision to evaluate something is frequently more politically motivated than disinterested, and often a means of testing the waters to determine what political support someone or something might have. A comment by House is particularly apropos here: "Evaluation is always derived from biased origins. When someone wants to defend something or to attack something, he often evaluates it. Evaluation is a motivated behavior."

It should not be surprising, therefore, when a decision maker conveys to the evaluator his expectations about what he hopes the evaluation results will be. The evaluator, who is usually hired by or in some way responsible to the decision maker, is then under at least subtle pressure to produce the desired evaluation results. One colleague of mine tells how she was hired to evaluate several campus programs and how the decision maker told her beforehand that he hoped she would find that such a program was indeed the most successful of all. Of course, any evaluator worth her salt, as she was, would not be consciously influenced by such remarks. Interestingly, she did admit she was at least a little relieved when the data clearly indicated that the expected program was the most successful. There is no telling, however, what the unconscious effects of the decision maker's suggestion were.

Just as the decision to evaluate is political, so too is the making of the decision on the basis of the evaluation data. There are many reports of cases in which action was taken on findings that fit academic decision maker's preconceived conclusions, while contrary findings were simply ignored. In such cases, evaluations serve to legitimize beliefs already held, such a legitimization being a very important resource to an academic decision maker in need of a political weapon.

Yet the academic administrator operating in an organized anarchy often does not have the power to act unilaterally. The fluid nature of academic power often demands that a group of faculty (aka a committee) be a decision point for action. Anyone who has worked with committees knows that the group dynamics inherent in committee work can preclude substantive action. Alexander Astin conducted a study in which a sample of higher education institutions was provided with evaluation data. Task forces in each institution were charged with taking whatever action they deemed appropriate given the evaluation data. The results were what Astin termed "academic games," that is, defensive tactics that committees used in order to avoid coming to grips with the data. Such games included "passing the buck" (i.e., leaving the substantive decisions to another committee), "rationalization" (i.e., arguing that bad data are really good if only seen in the proper perspective), and "displacement/ projection" (i.e., shifting the attention to some outside source). Such tactics should be anticipated in an environment in which the locus of power is often shifting and power coalitions need to be fashioned continuously.

In addition to an evaluator and decision maker, evaluations often involve a *constituency* for what is being evaluated. In the case of a program that is being evaluated, the constituency would include the program staff and those who derive some benefit from the program. Generally, the constituency tends to view the evaluation as a threat. After all, it is merely human nature that people resent being evaluated.

The very nature of the funding of special projects almost demands that the project writer cite goals that are not fully attainable. These ideal goals are needed to secure funding, but they never translate into action exactly as written. And once funded, the project takes on a life of its own. Project staff believe the project to be good, and as it matures a myth of success develops. The evaluator, analyzing performance vis-a-vis ideal goals, is bound to identify some degree of lack of fit. The project staff reacts strongly for two reasons. First, their belief system has become very strong. Second, project staff members, especially the director, are usually upwardly mobile entrepreneurs. They realize that they personally need unblemished records if they are to advance. Yet the structure of a university is such that, because the people in the top positions are not more competent than those at the bottom, job contenders are more often excluded because of blemishes on their record than are chosen because of true merit. The evaluator's least hint of failure for a project could potentially damage the entrepreneur's reputation. As House concludes, the case of the evaluation of special projects exemplifies the fact that universities are ill-equipped to handle critical evaluations.

Since constituencies are reluctant to be evaluated, a counteroffensive against the evaluation can be anticipated. This usually comes in the form of either trying to prevent the evaluation or attacking the evaluation if it produces results perceived to be negative. If the evaluation has been sponsored by an academic administrator, he is barraged with appeals to call it off. Copies of these appeals are sent to his superiors or supporters. Data are brandished in keeping with the constituency's belief system that the project is good. Since vocal power blocs are usually powerful within the organized anarchy of higher education, every attempt is made to create an inflated image of the power of the constituency. If the evaluation is mandated by an external funding source or if the tactic of prevention is not successful, then criticism of the evaluation itself (if it is perceived to be negative) is the next tactic. Politically, this can be effective for two reasons. Since evaluations must deal with relatively short-term deadlines and are situation-specific, their methodologies are never pure, in the textbook sense of ideal designs. Also, since the staff of the program being evaluated is probably conversant with research methodology and more knowledgeable about the program than the evaluator, attacks on the evaluation can be both scholarly and comprehensive. These attacks can serve as a rational basis for the political activities of constituencies.

Finally, not all evaluations are necessarily negative. Attempts can be made early in the evaluation to socialize the evaluator into the belief system of the program staff and wider constituency. The evaluator, once socialized, can emphasize the intangibles that the program is affecting and the enthusiasm of staff and constituency. In higher education the likelihood of socialization may be enhanced to the extent that the evaluator and the program staff view themselves as colleagues and peers. And the staff and constituency can use a positive evaluation as a political weapon to increase the image and power of the program.

In brief, politics in higher education evaluation can surface in many forms. The evaluator's general orientation, assumptions, and motivations have political bases. The decision maker's decision to evaluate and his prior expectations can influence the evaluation, while his action or inaction affects the impact of the evaluation. The constituency of what is being evaluated is reluctant to have an evaluation occur, and thus tries either to halt the evaluation, attach a negative judgment, or socialize the evaluator into the staffs views of the positive sides of the program.

Politics and Higher Education Evaluation

Whereas "politics in higher education evaluation" refers to the attempts by participants to influence an evaluation, "politics and higher education evaluation" entails the interrelationships between governmental political systems and the process of evaluation. More specifically, this term emphasizes the ways in which federal or state politics affects evaluations or is affected by evaluations. To analyze "politics *and* higher education," three relationships need to be addressed: the relation between the academic evaluator and the political decision maker, the influence political systems have upon evaluation processes, and the effect that evaluation has on political systems. These relationships are especially complex in higher education because of its long tradition of institutional autonomy and messy pluralism. Government actions are often viewed as intruding upon the academic environment and tending to impose uniform standards that constrain the diversity of higher education institutions.

Evaluators and Decision Makers : To understand the relationship between the academic evaluator and the political decision maker, it is important to realize that each operates on the basis of different values, assumptions, and objectives. Academic evaluators are essentially social scientists. In contrast to political decision makers they tend to be more egalitarian and libertarian, less attentive to the political and monetary costs of situations, more concerned with logic and rationality, and more inclined to support societal change. Moreover, academics are often out of their element in dealing with policy matters.

University researchers are used to choosing their own problems on grounds that derive from the state of their discipline and its theoretical development. They tend to select problems that fit the methods that they know and prefer. They like to take the time to do respectable research, win the plaudits of their colleagues, and gain academic rewards through publication in prestige journals.

But political decision makers do not have the luxury of doing exhaustive research. Because of elections, public officials have relatively short periods of time in which to launch initiatives and produce results. They look for immediate answers and are under too much pressure to gather evidence painstakingly or to conduct adequate assessments. Consequently, tensions and communication gaps develop between the political official and the academic evaluator, with the former trying to push the latter to develop concrete, value-laden recommendations for action and yes-or-no answers. These tensions are intensified by the nature of the political process; new social programs have political origins, embody political priorities, and have political consequences; therefore, any evaluation necessarily enters into the political arena of constituency politics.

Political Systems and Evaluation Processes : Because of the stakes involved, it is no wonder that the political system often influences evaluations. This occurs in many ways. The political system has funded numerous evaluation projects in its attempt to assess performance. Some evaluations are funded by grants from government agencies, the grants being awarded on a competitive basis to individuals after the proposals have been reviewed by a group of peers. Other evaluations are supported by government contracts, although academic investigators normally receive most of their support through grants. Some evaluations are mandated as part of a funded program. For example, a bilingual education resource center is funded by federal funds, but the center is required, or at least expected, to spend some of the money for evaluation purposes to see how well the center is accomplishing its goals. And still other evaluations are required by various pieces of federal legislation that include evaluation components. Thus, Title IX of the 1972 Education Amendments, which forbids sexual discrimination in any educational program receiving federal funds, includes a provision for self-evaluation by institutions to determine the degree of compliance with federal non-discrimination policies. No matter what the specific vehicle for support, the federal government has initiated, supported, or mandated a large number of evaluation projects, most of which probably would never have been undertaken without federal involvement. This involvement represents a major influence upon higher education institutions, insofar as they must comply with federal requirements or as they voluntarily redirect resources toward federal priorities in order to take advantage of the available funding. Similarly, such federal involvement has provided a great impetus for the evaluation as a whole.

Yet such funding rarely comes without strings, and through numerous strings the government's presence is felt at the institutional level. Forms that are used as part of an evaluation (e.g., to collect data) can be liable to review and clearance procedures by federal agencies, including the Office of Budget and Management. In one documented case, such clearance required in excess of 1,400 pages of paperwork at a cost of over $150,000 in preparation and materials, and months of waiting for federal approval.

Evaluation projects are subject to federal regulations regarding privacy, freedom of information, and protection of human subjects.

Because they involve judgments of worth, evaluations can also involve litigation. For example, in Delaware the dean of an institution that was being evaluated for accreditation sued a member of the accreditation team on the grounds that the latter made defamatory statements in his report. In addition, there have been a number of court cases regarding the evaluation of the performance of professors, especially where tenure and promotion decisions were involved. What emerges, therefore, is the image of a process subject to influence by the political system through an intricate maze of regulations and legal constraints. To the extent that evaluations are so constrained, the results of the evaluations are likely to be affected.

The word that perhaps best captures the notion that politics influences evaluation in higher education is "accountability." Traditionally, academic institutions have been relatively autonomous, even when they have been funded by state dollars. Increasingly, however, state officials have talked of holding higher education more accountable for its use of state funds. Accountability necessarily involves some level of assessment or evaluation of performance.

The first thing that needs to be said about accountability is that it is much more than an economic notion. In fact, accountability is best understood in terms of such political concepts as control, responsiveness, and power. The calls for accountability are essentially attempts to influence the control of higher education, i.e., who has the power to allocate resources, effort, and the like. Attempts to make higher education institutions more responsive imply that they are to be more responsive to someone. Whether that someone is the student, the government, the profession, or the public at large, power is the issue.

Attempts to hold higher education accountable to state government have increased over the last decade. One form of accountability is performance budgeting, which attempts to allocate resources on the basis of performance measure (i.e., outcome and impact measures). The attempts were made to institute performance measures for higher education in Hawaii and Washington, the higher education institutions vigorously resisted. Interestingly, after the performance measures were completed, those in the "poor" institutions argued that they needed more resources to improve, while those in "good" institutions countered that they deserved increased funding because of their fine performance. In short, performance budgeting as an evaluation of higher education institutions proved inherently political as institutions protected autonomy and diversity.

Another mechanism for state-imposed accountability is the performance audit (or post audit) whereby the effectiveness of an activity or institution in achieving its goals is assessed. Traditionally, such audits have been concerned principally with fiscal and management analyses, especially by quasi independent commissions. By 1975, however, thirty-six states had assigned auditing functions from quasi-independent commissions to the state legislatures, primarily through their staffs. Even more alarming for higher education institutions is the fact that states are indicating a willingness to go beyond traditional auditing concerns and touch upon academic programs in their audits. Such attempts are patently political insofar as the state government is involved (especially a partisan legislature) and a political purpose is being served (increase of legislative control over higher education institutions).

The problem of applying a performance-audit approach to academic programs is that legislative staffs, while expert in fiscal matters, are not attuned to the subtle nuances of academic programs within diverse academic institutions. For this reason, another mechanism has emerged, which holds institutions accountable but still respects the diversity and academic complexities of higher education. Known as statewide coordinating bodies, these agencies have varying degrees of control over academic institutions, depending on the authority invested by each state. These boards are responsible for program review, and the board members are normally quite knowledgeable about the specifics of higher education programs. Although there is considerable resentment by higher education institutions about the power of these boards over individual institutions, some noted authorities have urged the coordinating bodies to assume the key role in academic program review lest state legislative staffs fill the void and attempt to control academic programs under the guise of accountability.

Institutions of higher education have reacted to these attempts by state agencies to increase control over higher education through various evaluation mechanisms with the same political tactics used by other constituencies: prevent the evaluation or, failing that, attack their legitimacy. One way of preventing the external evaluations is to claim that the institutions are already accountable. This argument proceeds as follows. Institutions have claimed that (1) they must already operate within stringent legal and fiscal constraints; (2) they are evaluated regularly by accreditation agencies; and (3) students can vote with their feet by refusing to attend irresponsible institutions. State officials respond that (1) higher education institutions enjoy an autonomy that no other state institutions have; (2) accreditation procedures have questionable rigor; and (3) there are few examples of widespread student dissatisfaction being an effective accountability tool. Here is not the place to resolve this debate, but merely to point out that in essence it is a political issue, with control and power at stake. Such a confrontation influences both the kinds of evaluations employed and their quality. Ultimately, by affecting the means of evaluation, the movement for accountability can influence the nature of the institutions being evaluated. As Melvin George and Larry Braskamp have noted, "Accountability mechanisms can change the fundamental character of the institution being held accountable." If student credit hour production is the basis of a formula for allocating state funding support to individual institutions of higher education, it is likely that admissions standards will be changed to admit more students, course offerings to attract more, and grading policies and academic standards to retain more. These potential consequences alone make the politics of accountability a serious matter for higher education institutions.

Evaluation and Politics—Another View : Not only is academic evaluation affected by politics; at times the political system is itself influenced by evaluations in higher education. Potentially, information can be an instrument for power in politics, and evaluations can be a source of such information. For example, legislators are usually most eager for information about the success or failure of programs. The reality may be somewhat disappointing. There is evidence that although information plays an important role in policymaking, educational inquiry (including evaluations) has had relatively little direct impact on decision making. I suspect that some of the reason for this lies in the different perspectives of policymakers and evaluators: The outputs of the latter are not geared toward the political needs of the former.

The political system can also be affected by evaluation in another, less direct way. Evaluations are conducted by professionals who hope for financial support from state and federal governments for additional evaluation projects and have a stake in the kinds of legislation regulating the conduct of evaluators that is passed. It stands to reason, therefore, that evaluators will attempt to wield political power to lobby for more government funding and fewer governmental constraints. Recent attempts by the American Education Research Association to develop its political arm (the Government and Professional Liaison Committee) reflect such a growing awareness. From a political perspective, it can be expected that this will be a growing trend as evaluators and researchers in general attempt to counterbalance governmental influences by trying to influence government.

In sum, while there is a basic lack of congruence in the approaches of politicians and academic evaluators, the range of the relationships between the two is very wide. The processes and outputs of the political system influence evaluations through extensive mandates, regulations, and demands for accountability. In turn, evaluations have a strong potential for impact on the political system.

Politics of Higher Education Evaluation

The essence of politics is the authoritative allocation of values. Hence, the critical political issue in academic evaluation is how it affects the distribution of stakes, i.e., education, life chances, prestige, status, resources, and so on. This issue is at the heart of the politics of higher education evaluation.

Four common types of evaluation are examined below. Students are assessed by various tests for admission to institutions and throughout their academic programs. The performance of academic personnel is evaluated, especially for promotion and tenure. The institution itself and its academic programs are regularly reviewed. And any number of internal analyses and judgments are made to determine resource allocations within the institutions. Since these evaluations occur in the academic context, their forms depend upon the organized anarchy, autonomy, and messy pluralism characteristic of higher education.

Student Assessment : Professional autonomy demands that academic professionals have considerable control over which students are allowed into an institution and which can successfully complete their academic programs. Normally, this control is exercised through a series of tests and grades, with the criteria for success established by the professionals within each institution. This entire system of student assessment is largely constructed upon normative, competitive, meritocratic foundations. That is to say, the talented are selected and advanced through the system, while the less talented are not. In political terms, some win and some lose.

This win-lose assumption is built into the admissions policies of higher education. Since the various institutions are by no means equivalent, a student's future is determined not only by whether he attends college but also by which college he attends. Admission policies are generally directed at choosing the best students possible, because competition among institutions for status and resources is usually won by those with the best alumni, i.e., most successful and most prestigious. Thus, instead of admitting students they can help the most, institutions select those most likely to succeed. The outcome of such a system is obvious: "Students denied access to the universities and more selective four-year colleges, including a disproportionate share of low-income and minority students, receive substantially less public subsidy for their postsecondary education than students who enter the more selective public colleges and universities."

It is no wonder, then, that admissions tests have come under close public scrutiny recently and are in many instances bitterly contested. In 1979 New York State passed a truth-in-testing law requiring test companies to make public the validity studies on their tests, to inform those who took the tests of the meaning of those tests, and to give copies of test questions and correct answers to consumers after scores have been sent to institutions. And in 1980 the Ralph Nader Report on the Educational Testing Service (ETS) claimed that the ETS tests serve as "gatekeepers" for many of the rewards of society. The report also maintained that the tests have an effect upon students' chances to enter 50 percent of all U.S. colleges and 75 percent of all U.S. graduate programs. The report concluded:

The ETS test system has operated for years as a large, powerful, and entrenched mechanism that served the interests of its managers; offered convenience, prestige, and political justification to its clients; and, as long as consumers were not organized, made no powerful enemies. ETS has an overwhelming economic and political interest in maintaining the current test system.

Such language indicates that testing has entered the political arena, and the contest is not about the educational value of the tests themselves, but about those valued things to which tests provide a measure of access.

Much the same can be said about the use of student evaluations in general, including grading. Some argue that the effects of grading and other evaluations endure for years. And there is some evidence that student evaluations influence student motivation and performance. The main objection to current grading practices is that they are usually relative, i.e., ranking students in relation to each other rather than indicating the amount any one student has learned. One authority has argued that gain scores (indicative of learning and development) should be emphasized more than relative grades. This reduces the emphasis on winners and losers, on the sorting function of colleges in society.

Clearly, there is a growing awareness that student assessment affects many important outcomes. As the *Bakke* case exemplified, admissions procedures can be highly political precisely because some individuals and groups gain at the expense of others. Those who lose are relegated to inferior institutions that offer less opportunity for later success in certain professions and fields. The understanding of this fact should make us much more careful and conscious about the assumptions underlying any particular assessment approach.

Personnel Evaluation : Just as student assessment affects the distribution of stakes in society, so too does the evaluation of personnel in higher education. In any evaluation, since the issue of control is involved, three questions are most important: Who controls the evaluation? What is evaluated? And by what criteria does the evaluation occur? It is instructive to ask these questions about the evaluation processes involved in the promotion and tenure of higher education faculty, since these are central to the institution of higher education.

Academic organizations place great emphasis upon the professional autonomy of faculty. Professionals have traditionally demanded that they be evaluated only by their peers. This professional control is the result of a lengthy struggle over who has control in academic institutions. As one researcher has noted: "One of the long-term developments in American higher education has been the gradual accumulation of professional power plays, both inside a given institution and outside in professional organizations and unions." In institutions that emphasize graduate study and research, peer influence is most strongly felt in promotion and tenure decisions. In undergraduate institutions and especially community colleges, peer pressure is less strong, and administrators have a stronger role in evaluation. Whoever evaluates has a large measure of control in the institution, since academic organizations are labor-intensive. To the extent that evaluations are determined by peers, external influences upon the academic mission can be minimized, and professionals (particularly tenured ones) can be afforded a degree of insulation from non-professional interference. Moreover, through peer evaluation tenured professors have a powerful voice in determining who their long-term peers will be.

What is evaluated has serious implications for the nature of an academic institution. Evaluation is part of the reward system, and the principal rewards for academic professionals are promotion and tenure. Evaluation is thus a means of distributing effort, for those activities that receive the highest priority in the evaluation are likely to be most valued in terms of actual effort. Traditionally, activities that have been evaluated include undergraduate teaching, graduate teaching, research, institutional service, and professional service, though never in equal proportion. In most institutions of higher education, undergraduate teaching has highest priority, followed by research and graduate teaching. However, in large public and private multi universities (e.g., Harvard) research is accorded the highest priority. There are some indications, though, that the reward system associated with evaluation can be affected by the national economic situation and by pressures for accountability, that it is not totally in the control of academic professionals. One study found a growing emphasis upon on-campus, student-oriented activities such as teaching and student advising, presumably as a result of economic pressures. If this is true for all of higher education, if professional control over what is evaluated is subject to external forces, then peer evaluation may become a mediating influence between powerful forces and allocations of academic effort.

The criteria for evaluation in cases of tenure and promotion are mainly subjective. This is not to say that no data are employed, because a candidate for promotion and tenure typically submits extensive materials documenting his specific achievements. Rather, the criteria are subjective in the sense that in the final analysis quality of contribution is the crucial criterion. Since there is no agreement in academe regarding the best ways to conduct research or teach, peer judgment of the worth of a candidate's achievements is the final arbiter. This subjective peer judgment represents the means by which professionals control the evaluation process. And since the stakes are high, that is, control over who attains the status of tenured professor, the power of peer judgments is carefully protected. The literature (as well as the personal experiences of myself and many colleagues) is replete with instances of bitter struggles involving faculty, students, and administrators regarding who receives tenure in an institution. University administrators have been driven from office on just this issue. And, since the faculty member who is denied tenure is often terminated in an institution within a given number of years, there have been countless court cases to decide whether or not a given faculty member was denied promotion or tenure legally. The stakes are indeed high.

Yet, because the criteria and judgments are subjective, they can be influenced by the political motivations of various individuals and groups. Indeed, one case study of promotion and tenure procedures at select academic institutions found that there were many complaints about departmental politics and other such factors dictating evaluation results. For this reason, there have been numerous attempts to increase the objectivity of the evaluation process. One growing movement is the use of student ratings of teaching performance. There is evidence that such ratings do have some validity. Yet there are warnings that dependence on such ratings may emphasize the wrong faculty characteristics (e.g., entertaining students). In any case, as the control of students over evaluation outcomes increases, control by the faculty decreases. This could be alarming to those who wish professional peers to have maximum control over which activities are to be emphasized in higher education.

Program and Institutional Review : Two evaluation methods are most common in the area of program and institutional review; accreditation and self evaluation. Though both are aimed at making judgments about academic quality, the former makes use of a visiting accreditation team, while the latter employs an internal evaluation team.

The stakes involved in accreditation are eligibility and respectability. By federal law, accreditation helps academic institutions become eligible for federal funding. Accreditation is not the only means for eligibility, but it is a central one insofar as other prerequisites to eligibility (e.g., state licensing) often directly or indirectly depend upon accreditation. At the same time, most people place a great deal of faith in the accreditation system:

Operationally, . . . state and local governments, hundreds of employers, trade associations, and individuals rely on accreditation. The concept is firmly embedded in our language and thought patterns. We tend to use "accredited" as if it were synonymous with good, respectable, and acceptable which in fact it is, more often than not.

When the stakes are as considerable as these, the political question becomes: Who controls the distribution of these stakes? In the case of accreditation, the control lies in three sources: the academic peers who serve on the accreditation teams, the member institutions of the accrediting body, and the organizations seeking to control any given accreditation agency. The peer accreditation team has operational responsibility for site visitation, review of the institution's self-study materials, and development of a report. The actual decision on whether to grant accreditation to a program or an institution is made by the accrediting agency based upon the data reported by the review team. But, since the accreditation agency is usually supported by member institutions (i.e., those reviewed for accreditation), since the agency makes its accreditation judgment on the basis of criteria voted on and adopted by these member institutions, and since each institution has a measure of veto power over who will serve on its accrediting team, one could not characterize the accreditation body as a totally impartial, outside party with no stake in the accreditation results. In fact, peer influence and the ties that exist between an accreditation body and its member institutions strongly suggest that current accreditation procedures may be characterized as an internal evaluation rather than an external one. Certainly this is so in comparison with the classic Flexner accreditation study, in which a non-medical professional evaluated medical institutions as an external evaluator.

The third source of control over accreditation is not as obvious. Control of accreditation bodies at times involves a struggle among special interest groups. It is exemplified by the case of accreditation for teacher education programs. The appropriate accreditation body is the National Council for Accreditation of Teacher Education (NCATE). The National Education Association (NEA), primarily a teacher organization, has recently been actively attempting to gain control over teacher certification. Such control would mean control over entry to the teaching profession, much as the medical association controls entry into the field of medicine. Specifically, NEA hopes to develop field-based, apprenticeship programs for new teachers, controlled by the NEA. On the other side, the American Association of Colleges of Teacher Education (AACTE) counters that NEA's position operates to the detriment of campus-based, more scholarly approaches to pedagogy, i.e., what might be offered by higher education institutions. Total victory by NEA would mean elimination or at least curtailment of teacher education by colleges and universities, which gives an idea of the stakes involved in accreditation.

Determining Resource Allocations : A fourth kind of evaluation worth examining further highlights the manifestations of the politics of higher education evaluation. Every institution must develop a budget to distribute revenues among subunits. Various forms of evaluation serve to provide data for such distributions. As Wildavsky has said, "The budget lies at the heart of the political process."

Needless to say, evaluations associated with the internal budgeting of institutions are highly political, because they concern the allocation of scarce resources. An example would be an actual attempt by a major university to make the budgeting process more rational. Two formulas were used, both based upon changes in total student credit hour production within each subunit. One formula calculated the average "productivity" of subunit faculty by dividing total student credit hours by total number of full-time equivalent faculty (FTE) within each subunit. The result was a ratio expressing how many student credits hours per faculty member each subunit averaged. This ratio was calculated for each of five previous years. The second best ratio during that time was considered the criterion. Since trend analysis could "predict" the total number of student credit hours a subunit would have five years in the future, the number of faculty that unit would need in the future could be determined merely by applying the criterion ratio to any given year. The second formula involved a complex relationship of previous cost per credit over five years, projected student credit hours, and use of a criterion cost per credit ratio based on the subunit's historical pattern of costs and credits.

By going to some length explaining these formulas, emphasis is placed on how rational they were (i.e., proceeding from objective data) and how relatively fair (i.e., each subunit was compared not with other units but with its own historical patterns). Even though these formulas seem rational, in fact they were highly political. As can be imagined, the responses of subunits were not rational. The historical data were attacked as fuzzy and inaccurate, the formulas themselves as favoring certain subunits over others, and the future projections as hopelessly simplistic. What in effect had occurred was that rational formulas had invaded the academic autonomy of various subunits. As with any allocation, there were some winners and some losers. The losers quickly coalesced and formed an effective power bloc within the institution. Academic professionals rallied around the cry that no simple formula could capture the nuances of academic programs. In the end, the formulas fell because the countervailing power, under the guise of academic program, proved stronger.

The allocative nature of evaluation is apparent in the way higher education assesses students, evaluates faculty, reviews programs, and makes budgetary analyses. The politics of evaluation represents both the distributions that occur as well as the impact those distributions have on those with a stake in the institution. Because there is a politics of academic evaluation, there is also a politics in academic evaluation and a politics and academic evaluation.

Implications

The implications to be drawn from the above analysis are numerous; three merit special note. First, those who participate in evaluations must recognize their political aspects. If knowledge is power, then the recognition that politics is involved could be valuable. Take the case of the formulas for resource allocation discussed above. If those putting forth such formulas wish to have an effect upon budgetary allocation systems, they must recognize the political nature of what they are doing. They can most assuredly expect a political response, and such a response should be recognized as reasonable and appropriate to the situation. Anticipation of such a response should lead to the development of plans for how to deal with it when it occurs and for possible counter responses.

Second, this chapter implies that we all can (and need to) become more precise in our use of the term "politics." Most people use the term disparagingly and thoughtlessly. It can in fact be used in a more rigorous fashion. Politics in evaluation is not the same as politics of evaluation, though they are related. Each may indeed demand different skills. And neither necessarily means anything bad or dirty. Conceptual clarity is both worthwhile in its own right and potentially useful in actual situations.

Finally, it needs to be stressed that just because evaluation is inherently political does not imply that it does not involve rational inquiry. House puts it especially well: "Arguing that all evaluations proceed from biased origins does not necessarily invalidate the study. All knowledge is biased but some of it is also true." Evaluations, when properly and intelligently conducted, are invaluable in increasing our knowledge about various phenomena. The fact that an evaluation is political should be viewed as an asset, not a detriment, to its knowledge value. An evaluation that is both scientifically and politically well conceived and conducted can be a valuable tool for increasing our fund of knowledge and in building political support for the application and use of that knowledge.

4

Higher Education Administration and its Development

Introduction

Some of these individuals belong to identifiable groups now protected by a system of laws and regulations related to the provision of equal educational opportunity. The body of case law that deals with the provision of equal educational opportunities for all American citizens is already large and is steadily growing. As more of the individuals who belong to the so-called protected groups begin to understand their rights under the existing laws, there will be increased pressure on educational institutions to provide additional services and facilities which will ensure an equal access to all important learning experiences.

Underlying the movement toward the provision of equal opportunities for education at the post-secondary level is a set of important assumptions which may be said to permeate the entire fabric of American life. The notion that equality is a necessary factor in the American democratic experience and that such equality is an appropriate and achievable goal for the American society is not of recent origin. The notion that the American political experience can provide an environment in which the majority of its citizens might experience a fundamental degree of equality is not to be found with any certainty in the works of the founding fathers. At the same time, the thrust of the American experience toward the development of basic equality for all American citizens was so great that the Frenchman Alexis de Toqueville, writing in the early part of the nineteenth century, was able to affirm that the fundamental quality or aspect of the American political experience was a basic equality among all of the citizens.

In addition to the philosophical problems involved with the possibility of achieving any real measure of equality in a diverse population, the educational administrator in the coming decades is confronted by many interfacing and at times contradictory rules and regulations which restrict the free operation of the college or university in the achievement of its goals. There is no doubt that some federal laws and regulations relating to equal opportunity are confusing to both educational administrators and the educational public. There is a tradition of judicial response to questions involving equal opportunity in education, but, for the most part, this tradition deals with the primary and secondary education setting, not with higher education. The development of measures providing equal educational opportunity for all Americans may be seen as a logical outgrowth of programs that were developed for primary and secondary schools.

Definitions

Affirmative action— A series of positive measures to make opportunities available to individuals belonging to groups that have been discriminated against in the past.

Anti-nepotism— Restrictions against more than one member of the family being employed by the college or university within the same work team, division, or department. If this law discriminates against a woman or minority by denying employment it can be termed unfair.

Discriminatory conditions—Conditions that are the results of unintentional biases which have been reflected in certain personnel policies; or, they may be the reflections of personal biases on the part of individual administrators, faculty members, and the college or university as a whole.

Equal educational opportunity—The development of measures and procedures providing equal educational opportunity for all Americans without considering race, creed, color, or national origin.

Feudal patronage—Discrimination in job placement preferring those persons who graduated from particular colleges or universities or were related to or closely associated with college or university alumni for the purpose of job prospecting.

Minorities—Specifically defined by the Department of Labor as Negros, persons with Spanish surnames, American Indians, and Orientals.

Non-discrimination requirements—These requirements apply to all persons including citizens of the United States and those who enjoy the benefits of citizenship through legal or temporary residence. No discrimination shall be placed upon these persons though not members of a legal minority.

Positive action— The process employed to overcome the systematic exclusion of members of various minority groups from access to career opportunities and advancement tracks available to other citizens.

Systematic exclusion—A process of systematically excluding particular persons from professional or occupational advancement or training because of race, creed, color, or national origin.

Following is a discussion of major concerns of the academic administrator relating to laws and regulations involved in equal opportunity.

Higher Education Guidelines

In 1972 the Director of the Office for Civil Rights of the Department of Health, Education and Welfare issued a set of guidelines to college and university administrative personnel in the matter of compliance with Executive Order 11246, "Non-discrimination Under Federal Contracts." This document was a major source of information on the concepts of equal opportunity and affirmative action as they apply to higher education.

Non-discrimination and Affirmative Action

As explained in Executive Order 11246, the obligations facing institutions of higher education and the administrators who are responsible for their activities fall into two categories: non-discrimination and affirmative action. Non-discrimination requires the elimination of all existing discriminatory conditions. These conditions may be the results of unintentional biases which have been reflected in certain personnel policies, or they may be the reflections of personal biases on the part of individual administrators, faculty members, and the college or university as a whole. In the light of the law and of the executive order, the origin of the alleged discrimination is not of prime importance, although the moral factors involved in discrimination practiced by an educational institution cannot be completely ignored. A college or university contractor, that is, an institution that receives federal funding must "carefully and systematically" examine its employment policies to insure that they do not hinder the opportunities of any persons on the grounds of race, color, sex, or national origin. The contractor must also ensure that the practices of those who are in a position to make recommendations for employment, and to supervise the activities of employees, and to make recommendations for advancement are non-discriminatory.

Affirmative action, on the other hand, requires the college or university to take positive measures to make opportunities available to individuals belonging to groups that have been discriminated against in the past. These measures may involve a variety of actions, including additional efforts to identify, employ, and promote qualified members of groups formerly excluded. The premise or concept behind affirmative action is that positive action must be undertaken in order to overcome the difficulties of "systematic" exclusion of members of various minority groups from access to career opportunities and advancement tracks available to other citizens. The college or university administrator should realize that this obligation is imposed without regard to whether there has been any active discriminatory activity on the part of the institution in the past. Affirmative action implies a positive approach to the problem of inequity through inequality of opportunity; the assumption is that unless positive action is undertaken to overcome the effects of systematic exclusion and discrimination, the status quo will tend to prevail, even if it is deplored by administrators and other members of the academic community.

In considering the protection of certain individuals under the law as implemented by Executive Order 11246, a distinction is made between the nondiscrimination requirements of the law and the affirmative action requirements which are dependent upon the law. The nondiscrimination requirements of the executive order apply to all persons, including citizens of the United States and those who enjoy the benefits of citizenship through legal temporary residence. This presumably would include foreign nationals with student visas. The individual need not be a member of a conventionally defined minority group.

Affirmative action programs which require assessing needs in the form of estimates of underutilization of individuals in target groups, setting goals, and establishing time-frameworks for the achievement of goals are directed in particular towards minorities and women. Minorities are specifically defined by the Department of Labor as Negros, Spanish-surnamed, American Indians, and Orientals. Other groups may consider themselves to be minorities, and it is clearly against the law for colleges and universities to deny consideration for employment or advancement within employment on the basis of membership in any particular ethnic or religious group. But affirmative action programs as such are directed at specific elements within the general population.

What is to be done to Comply?

Part of the establishment of affirmative action programs involves the establishment of goals and timetables for minority and female employment. It is necessary to determine if women and minorities are underutilized within the work force of a particular institution, and if that is the case, specific timetables and goals must be developed by the organization to remedy that underutilization. The term underutilization means that there are fewer members of minority groups or women present in the work force than would be expected in light of their availability in the employment marketplace. If, for example, the ratio of available men and women with doctoral degrees is 40 percent female and 60 percent male, the expectation would be that approximately 40 percent of a university's professional staff with that academic credential should be female. This particular conception has been the subject of controversy and can cause difficulty within the academic community and the imposition of obstacles to the success of the affirmative action program in a college or university. Nothing in the executive order or the law which it is intended to implement requires that a college or university contractor eliminate or dilute standards that are necessary for the conduct of the institution's functions. The affirmative action concept does not require that an institution hire an individual who is unqualified. But a particular burden of proof is placed upon the employer. The employer must prove or demonstrate that a selection for employment is made on the basis of legitimate job related qualifications.

The development of an affirmative action plan is similar in several ways to the development of various forms of Management by Objectives programs. The college or university contractor must set particular goals for the recruitment and hiring of minorities. The achievement of these goals is not considered to be the sole measurement of compliance with the executive order and the law concerning equal employment opportunity. But as in the case of other systems or programs in which goals are set and used as a means to determine performance, failure to meet a goal requires a determination of the causes of such a failure. If the educational institution falls short of an affirmative action goal that it has set, this does not automatically mean that a conclusion of non-compliance with the executive order would be reached. Failure to reach the goal does require, however, a statement from the institution as to why the goals were not reached.

If, on the other hand, it appears that the cause for failure of the affirmative action program was a lack of attention to the non-discrimination and affirmative action policies and procedures set by the institution itself, then the institution (contractor) may be found to be out of compliance with the law and the provisions of affirmative action. Goals are required, but quotas are not required or permitted by the executive order. Goals are designed to be a means of evaluating progress and achievement, not a rigid measure of legal compliance.

Executive Order 11246 should not be construed to mean that standards should be lowered or diluted. It is recognized that standards must be set and maintained in order to retain the integrity of the college or university and the excellence of its academic programs. The affirmative action concept does not require the promotion or hiring of unqualified personnel. What it does do is to require a serious effort at making opportunities available to qualified individuals who may be targets of discrimination. The institution is required to demonstrate its good faith in setting goals for its own behavior and to demonstrate accountability in reaching those goals. In this regard, the type of activity required for the establishment of a program of affirmative action and the maintenance of compliance with such a program is similar to activities in developing and maintaining a Management by Objectives program in a university or college administration, or the setting of learning goals and objectives in any course of instruction. The concept of equality of opportunity requires that any standards or criteria for employment or advancement that may have had the effect of excluding women or minorities or of limiting their access to opportunities must be eliminated, unless it can be shown that such criteria are conditions of successful performance in the particular position involved.

In order to comply with the provisions of Executive Order 11246, the institution involved must establish procedures to be used in employment and related practices which govern all procedures involved with the employment of individuals in particular units. This includes a description of any tests which may be used to evaluate preparation for the position and the criteria by which a candidate is considered either for initial employment or for promotion. It is up to the contracting college or university to demonstrate that the standards and criteria to be used in employment selection are valid predictors of job success. These criteria must be demonstrated to have some direct relation to the duties of the position involved.

The requirement that only performance related criteria be used in the selection of candidates for employment or advancement in employment brings up several related questions. For an occupation such as college teaching, the requirement of an appropriate academic degree seems to be a reasonable prerequisite. But is the holder of an advanced degree granted by an external degree program as well prepared for service as an instructor who graduated from a public or private university of the traditional type? Should a minority candidate with an advanced degree from an external degree program be given equal or preferential consideration in comparison with those who hold degrees from programs requiring on-campus residence? The answers to such questions will be based upon the goals and responsibilities outlined in the school's affirmative action plan. It is a fact of academic life that all programs and all degrees are not equal in quality. On the other hand, competent educational leaders have traditionally looked for the proper person to fill a particular position, with the source of academic credential being of secondary importance. Because the principal commitment of colleges and universities traditionally has been to the individual student, institutions have been primarily interested in obtaining the services of the best qualified individual for a particular position. It is generally accepted that the process of selection of applicants for academic positions has in many cases in the past been discriminatory toward women and minorities. This situation has resulted in an imbalance of composition of the staffs of American colleges and universities in favor of white males. In light of the condition of over supply in the academic job market of today, there is little excuse for administrators to claim that qualified women and minority applicants are not available. In any case, the executive order makes it clear that institutions must take the initiative in identifying opportunities that may be highly desirable to minority job candidates and in seeking applicants from minority groups who are qualified to fill such positions.

What about Recruitment?

In the past, universities and colleges may not have expended much effort to recruit females and minorities as employees. According to Executive Order 11246, universities and colleges now must recruit both women and minorities as actively as they have recruited white males in the past.

If, for example, some universities have tended to recruit primarily from a few schools which traditionally produce mostly white male candidates, they must take measures to insure contacts with other schools which may be producing minority and female candidates who are qualified for the available positions. Advertising in media that reach female and minority candidates is another step that can be taken to insure compliance with the law and the executive order. Traditional methods of staffing in the academic areas, principally the reliance on the word of mouth system for advertising position vacancies, and the buddy system, in which department chairpersons and administrators rely upon external professional contacts for informal recommendations in the matter of hiring professional personnel, have come under especially severe criticism. Before enactment of the civil rights legislation that has been directed toward reducing and eliminating inequities in the composition of university and college faculties, a standard practice was to allow department chairpersons to recruit and select personnel for their own departments. Often these individuals would utilize contacts at the universities from which they graduated or to which they felt the strongest ties. An informal advertisement of the position or positions to be filled would be made by letters or perhaps by telephone calls to a select number of friends and associates at other institutions. These individuals often would be able to recommend qualified candidates for the position under discussion or make a referral to another source. This was a type of feudal patronage system which had both limitations and advantages for maintaining academic quality control. Although there have been some positive results from such a system, in many cases women and minority candidates are not in the same word of mouth channel, and their candidacies may not be advanced with the same effectiveness. On the other hand, in some cases the word of mouth system was able to serve as a control mechanism, since colleagues felt that their personal reputation was involved in each endorsement. Under the present laws, however, the word of mouth system is clearly precluded as a major means of recruitment. The university or college contractor must examine the activities and policies of each unit that has responsibility for recruiting and hiring. If the applicant pool reveals a significantly lower number of women or minorities than would reasonably be expected from their availability in the work force, the contractor must modify or supplement its recruiting policies. This supplemental action may take several forms. Where there is evidence of any practice that is discriminatory against qualified women and minorities, these practices must be eliminated. It is recommended that an expanded search network include not only the traditional avenue through which candidates have been located (for example, letters to academic departments at other institutions in the case of academic appointments, and advertisements in newspapers in the case of other jobs, often termed "classified positions"), but whatever non-traditional means are liable to produce results. Some means and areas of recruitment are:

a. Advertisements inappropriate professional journals and other periodicals which list openings for the professional positions of the type or types required.
b. Unsolicited applications or inquiries.
c. Women and minorities teaching at colleges and universities which aim at serving minorities or women as a special student target group. (So-called Black or women's colleges.)
d. Minorities or women who have professional preparation and status but who are working in other areas—that is, areas other than the area of post secondary education. These areas include government, industry, law, hospitals, etc.
e. Professional minorities and women who have received grants or professional recognition.
f. Minority and female doctoral recipients from the contractor's own institution and from other

institutions who are not presently utilizing their professional training.

g. Women and members of other protected groups who show what seems to be outstanding promise for achievement in the future. Some institutions have set up programs where an opportunity to work on a terminal degree is provided for these individuals, along with a promise of possible employment related to the completion of the degree. While such a program may be useful in providing candidates who reflect the philosophy desired by a particular institution, the practice would seem to leave the institution open to problems at a later date. Such problems relate to a perceived "guarantee of employment."
h. Minorities and women who have been listed in data banks, especially those which have made a conscientious effort to locate minority and women talent.

Specific Areas of Responsibility

Under the provisions and directions of Executive Order 11246, the institution is required to make explicit its commitments to equal opportunity employment in all recruiting announcements or advertisements. It is not permissible for a prospective employer to eliminate from consideration any individuals on the basis of sex or minority group status. It is a violation of the executive order for an employing institution to state that only candidates from minority or protected groups will be considered.

One of the alleged problems which has been encountered in the recruiting of faculty members from institutions that employ primarily minorities or women is the problem of so-called raiding of these faculty members by more prestigious, predominantly white universities and colleges. By and large, the executive order does not take this problem into consideration. The needs of so-called minority colleges and universities would seem to be considered as secondary to the overall process of education in the public sector. It would thus appear permissible for predominantly white public institutions to use their advantages of prestige and ability to offer economic incentives to secure the best talent from the faculties at minority institutions.

The availability of large numbers of unemployed or underemployed academics may mitigate this problem to a degree. Many individuals are willing to accept positions at a relatively low rate of pay in order to secure an academic appointment in a market in which oversupply conditions at times exist. Unfortunately many of these individuals are not of the first rank in academic preparation and scholarly skill. There is a possibility that minority students attending institutions who employ these persons are thus being shortchanged since they are not able to come into contact with appropriate standards and criteria of excellence. The perception that the predominantly minority institutions are second rate and inferior is accordingly enhanced and perpetuated.

Discrimination in the Hiring Process

After a suitable talent pool of applicants for relevant positions has been established, standards for selecting candidates from that pool and assigning specific salary levels and positions must be established in a non-discriminatory manner. Specific procedures must be formulated and made explicit in order to insure non-discrimination. Since a major complaint among female academic professionals has been that they have been assigned to and kept at lower ranks than their male counterparts, care must be taken to avoid this practice. Assumptions often were made that female employees, regardless of their professional preparation and stature, would be likely to marry and raise a family. It was thus assumed by personnel officers that these individuals would see their work at the university or college as secondary to their family career responsibilities. This assumption often produced an attempted justification of lower salaries and restricted job advancement opportunities offered to female applicants and employees.

It has been the policy of some major universities and colleges to discourage applications for instructional positions from individuals who have received their terminal degrees at that particular university. Executive Order 11246 precludes the restriction of women and minority candidates on this basis if they are otherwise qualified. Unless the institution does not hire any of its own graduates at all, it must give equal consideration to its own students who are women and minorities. In other words, the fact that they are graduates of a particular institution should not be used to justify excluding qualified women and minority students from positions at that same institution on the pretext of avoiding "inbreeding."

Official commentators on Executive Order 11246 point out that in the area of academic appointments a non-discriminatory selection process does not require or permit a process of "reverse discrimination" through which unqualified individuals will be given the preference over qualified individuals. Employees are not to be fired, demoted, or displaced on the grounds of race, color, or national origin in order to fulfill an affirmative action goal. It is theoretically not permissible, for example, to refuse to renew the contract of a qualified white male instructor after the first year merely in order to replace him with a female with equal qualifications. It is possible that replacement with a female or minority faculty member with superior qualifications would be permitted, however, on the grounds that the institution has the right to plan for its own future development. Such a substitution might be made if the particular faculty member to be replaced did not meet performance requirements, or did not meet tenure requirements. In any case, principles of justice and equity should be guiding forces in all personnel decisions.

Replacement of competent individuals is not the intention of the executive order.

There is nothing in the law or in Executive Order 11246 that justifies dismissals, job transfers, alterations of job descriptions, or changes in line of promotion or fringe benefits on the basis of achieving a particular quota of women and minorities in a particular institution. Administrators may adopt such practices and attempt to justify them in light of the executive order, but this is clearly a contradiction of both the letter and the spirit of the law.

Several other areas of the personneling process that may be troublesome to the administrator formulating and implementing affirmative action policies include:

> *Training to ensure that employees receive opportunities to upgrade their skills and work potentials without reference to their sex, race, or religious faith. Training programs should be constructed and designed so as to assure opportunities for staff development and effective human resources utilization. This is especially important in light of the emphasis which will be required in the future on the upgrading of skills of professional workers. In the college and university setting, training programs for academic workers are often confined to occasional opportunities to attend conferences and meetings of professional groups and associations. Naturally, there must be no discrimination in allocating these opportunities to qualified individuals.*

An equally important aspect of a training program established by a college or university should be classes and opportunities provided for non-teaching personnel. Secretaries and other employees, including janitorial and maintenance personnel, should have opportunities for developing their skills. Institutions of higher education are in a particularly advantageous position in providing these opportunities to their staff members. Tuition waivers for so-called classified personnel may allow workers with modest incomes to attend classes during their free time. Some institutions allow staff members released time during the day in order to attend particular classes that are related to job advancement and job skills. If an institution has democratic ideals, it is not inconceivable that employment in a non-professional capacity might be a step on the path to eventual professional qualifications. Unfortunately, employers are not accustomed to think of staff development in terms of value produced for the operation of the institution. Usually, the sole criterion for job performance assessment utilized by those who are in charge of employment at colleges and universities is whether or not an individual performs his present task. Little thought is given to what the potential of the individual within the organization might be if sufficient opportunities were provided for developing skills and personal resources. This narrowness of vision is wasteful of the energies both of the individual and of the organization.

Institutional Antinepotism Policies

In order to correct certain abuses in the control and distribution of employment opportunities, some colleges and universities established so-called antinepotism practices or procedures. Because of employment patterns in the past, stated or implied restrictions against the employment of more than one member of the same family by the institution or within the same academic department tends to limit opportunities available to women. If an antinepotism rule has led to the denial of opportunity for employment of a minority individual, that restriction is discriminatory and not permitted under the terms of Executive Order 11246.

Placement and Job Classification

Certain job classifications have tended to include a disproportionate number of women and minorities. In institutions of higher education, these categories include secretarial positions in the case of females and janitorial positions in the case of black and Hispanic females and males. Care must be exercised by the administration of colleges and universities to insure that where no valid or substantial differences in duties exist, artificial classifications are not made that tend to segregate employees by race or sex. An example is the classification "administrative aid" or "administrative assistant." If there are no valid distinctions in the duties performed the classifications should be combined so as to avoid a two tiered structure.

Promotion and Termination

One major requirement of all personnel policies and practices which may be expected to stand a test of justice under the law is that policies must be made explicit and administered in such a way as to insure that women and minorities are not subject to discrimination. In the case of promotion, Executive Order 11246 implies that an employer must make every effort to insure equal promotion opportunities for women and minorities. It is important to note that special efforts must be made to provide such opportunities where required. Job training and job counseling are two ways in which such requirements may be met.

One area related to affirmative action programs and the legislation behind Executive Order 11246 involves actions to be taken when terminations of employment are necessary. In situations in which terminations are necessary, the employer must be able to demonstrate that the decision to terminate is unrelated to race or sex, religion, color, or national origin. Seniority may be used as a basis for making decisions on terminations. But if it can be demonstrated that an individual would have had more seniority had it not been for discriminatory actions, seniority must be eliminated as a consideration, or the individual must be presumed to have the seniority required or which she or he would have had if there had been no discrimination.

An example may be helpful. Let us suppose that because of a drop in student enrollments and poor administrative planning it is necessary for a particular department at a major university to reduce its staff by two individuals. Naturally, thc dcpartment chair and the dean of the college will be reluctant to attempt to make a decision on particular individuals whose contracts will not be renewed. But since they know that they cannot avoid doing so, they establish a decision-making process based on an assessment of the following characteristics. The order of the list does not necessarily reflect priority: (1) Holding of tenure; (2) length of service with the institution; (3) productivity in scholarly publications and research efforts; and (4) teaching effectiveness, as evidenced by student and chairperson assessment of teaching skill.

In order to make the selection of individuals who must leave the institution more equitable, the university president and the dean of the division affected by the reduction in strength decide to establish a special task force to make recommendations. After suitable deliberation, this task force narrows its selection to two individuals. Both have attained the rank of assistant professor and, naturally, both have earned the terminal degree. While there is some difference in the publishing and research histories of these two individuals, the task force has determined that there can be said to be a "rough parity" in their achievements in research and publication, and also a "rough parity" in their ratings by students, faculty members, and administrators in the area of teaching effectiveness and overall performance. Professor Johnson, a woman, has held the rank of assistant professor for one year, while Professor Adamson, a man, has held the rank of assistant professor for two years. Each of the two faculty members has served at the university for five years. Professor Johnson, however received her appointment as assistant professor one year after Professor Adamson. On the basis of these facts, the special task force or group appointed to determine which faculty member should be terminated recommends that Professor Adamson be retained on the basis of longer service in the rank of assistant professor. It should be remembered that both individuals have identical overall time in service with the university.

After the task force has submitted its recommendation to the dean and president, Professor Johnson contacts the University Faculty Grievance Committee to indicate that she will contest the decision. It is her contention that she was not elevated to the rank of assistant professor at the same time as Professor Adamson because the university administration had discriminated against her on the basis of sex. She indicates that if consideration is not given to her case at the university level, she will consider filing an action with the Office of Civil Rights of the Department of Education. If her argument is upheld, Professor Johnson may be successful in removing time of appointment to the rank of assistant professor as a consideration in determining which of the two faculty members will be subject to severance of employment, and another criterion for making the decision will have to be found.

Conditions of Work and Related Benefits

The terms of Executive Order 11246 and the provision of the law require that employers, including university and college employers, insure non-discrimination in working conditions for all employees. Aspects of work that may be especially pertinent to the university situation include the opportunity to do research, selection of assignments, and training opportunities in the form of in service training and professional conventions. Assignment of office space and access to clerical and paraprofessional services also may be included in these considerations.

For all employees, access to eating facilities such as dining halls or faculty clubs must be open to all individuals within grade of employment. No discrimination on the basis of race or sex may be permitted. In addition, where any services are a part of the ordinary benefits of employment for certain classes of employees, no members of such classifications can be denied on a discriminatory basis. A strong argument could also be made that as a part of the democratic structure a publicly supported college or university would not feel comfortable with its mission while denying access to service facilities to any member of its work force, regardless of job classification.

In the past, members of minority groups have been denied access on the basis of race or sex to housing made available to faculty members at a reduced rate. Such practices are openly discriminatory and may not be continued.

Executive Order 11246 also requires that college and university employers adhere strictly to the concept of equal pay for equal work. A university or college must set forth in sufficient detail guidelines for determining the pay scales within each job classification, and these guidelines must be made available to present and prospective employees. The applicant's level of pay must be determined on the basis of capability and record of performance, not former salary. If a minority or female applicant applies for a position as an associate professor at a state university, and the starting salary range for individuals entering employment at that level is $24,000 to $30,000, the fact that at her former institution she earned significantly less for a similar position can not be used as a reason for denying her equal pay with others at her new institution who hold similar rank.

Back Pay

Under the Civil Rights Act of 1964 (Title VII), the Equal Pay Act, and the National Labor Relations Act, universities and colleges may be required to make up discrepancies in pay to female and minority employees in the form of back pay. Evidence of discrimination that requires back pay as a remedy may be referred to the Office of Civil Rights for negotiation of a voluntary settlement. If this effort is not successful, the appropriate federal enforcement agency may be involved in a dispute involving back pay.

Leave and Fringe Benefits

Women are afforded particular protection from employment discrimination in the areas of leaves related to pregnancy and childbirth. Basically, Executive Order 11246 specifies that women may not be penalized in their working conditions on the basis of requiring time away from work for the purpose of childbearing. Pregnancy and childbirth are to be considered reasonable causes for a leave of absence for all female employees, disregarding marital status, and following childbirth they must be reinstated without loss of benefits. Leave for reasons related to pregnancy must be treated in the same way as other medical leave, without additional conditions. Mandatory lengths for leaves should not be stipulated, since the principle is that the leave should be related to the medical need involved. The length of time required for such leaves should be dictated by individual health, not by arbitrary policy. Following the end of a leave related to childbirth, a female employee must be reinstated to her position or one of similar status and pay without loss of seniority and benefits. Any leave related to pregnancy must be in accord with the employer's general leave policy.

Grievance Procedures

In hearing complaints of matters dealing with discrimination in employment in universities and colleges, the Office of Civil Rights and the Equal Employment Opportunity Commission (EEOC) share responsibilities.

The EEOC has jurisdiction over individual complaints of discrimination by academic as well as non-academic employees of educational institutions. As a result of a formal agreement between EEOC and the Office of Civil Rights, individual complaints of discrimination are investigated by EEOC, while class complaints and information involving possible patterns of discrimination for example, a consistent policy of excluding Spanish-surnamed applicants from employment consideration—are within the jurisdiction of the Office of Civil Rights. In general, the Office of Civil Rights of the Department of Health and Human Services is concerned with patterns of discrimination, and the EEOC is the appropriate agency to deal with individual complaints. However, institutional grievance procedures which are written and effectively promulgated remain the first step in discussing alleged discrimination.

Developing Affirmative Action Programs

The following points are suggested for consideration as part of an affirmative action program:

1. **Development or reaffirmation of the equal opportunity employment policy.** This is a necessary first step, and involves goal setting by each organization and subunit. The statement of goals should take into consideration the mission of the college or university as well as its overall commitment to eliminate discrimination in employment on the basis of sex, race, religion, or national origin.
2. **Dissemination of the policy.** This step is vital to the effective formulation and administration of all policies. It is essential that all individuals with responsibilities in relation to employment and promotion understand their responsibilities in light of the law and the institutional policy. The policy should be made available to all employees.

3. **Responsibilities for implementation.** An administrative procedure must be set up to organize the institution's efforts and to monitor progress. It is suggested that an individual be delegated to direct EEO programs and that this individual be given the requisite top level support to execute the assignment. Some colleges and universities combine EEO functions with other duties, while others create a special office at the directorial or vice-presidential level. Some institutions appoint the director of personnel to oversee this function. This would seem to be a less suitable approach than appointing a special officer who is free to devote major efforts to the success of the program. In some institutions the EEO officer has been assisted by one or more task forces comprised primarily of women and minority faculty members. While such a task force may aid in the identification of problems and the establishment of positive goals, it also may lead to factionalism and lowered morale within the institution.

4. **Internal audit and reporting systems.** An integral part of the affirmative action program of each institution must be a system for auditing and monitoring progress. Systems will vary from institution to institution. It is important, however, that all such systems be sufficiently planned and developed so that a proper evaluation may be made. The institution must report at least once per year to the Office of Civil Rights on the results of its program. In the majority of cases, an effort to locate and appoint women and minorities must be in evidence. Reporting systems should include a method of evaluating applicants, referral and retention rate, and a system for retaining and evaluating applications.

5. **Publication of affirmative action plan.** Affirmative action plans that are accepted by the Office of Civil Rights are subject to disclosure under the Freedom of Information Act, 5 U.S.C. 552. Certain areas of an affirmative action plan may be exempt from disclosure, however. Any information about employees that may be considered an invasion of privacy, information that may be considered to be a part of trade secrets, and certain confidential commercial and financial information may be excluded from disclosure. The major point to remember is that the bulk of the institution's affirmative action plan is subject to disclosure.
6. **Development of an affirmative action plan.** Because responsibility for personnel decisions may be more decentralized at many colleges and universities than at the majority of private businesses, the chief administrator of the institution will need to enlist cooperation from a broad spectrum of individuals and subunits within the campus organization in the formulation and implementation of an effective affirmative action plan. It is suggested that administrators attempt to involve faculty members as well as other administrative personnel in implementing the provisions of an affirmative action program which will involve individuals throughout the institution and the entire academic community. It is especially important that those individuals who have responsibilities in personnel function areas including such "first-line" leadership personnel as department chairpersons be involved as much as possible not only in enforcing the provisions of an affirmative action program, but in formulating the strategies for implementation. It is also important that all members of the administrative

team and the academic community understand the philosophic and legal background and implications of the affirmative action program so that they can cooperate fully with it.

Non-discrimination on the Basis of Handicap

The responsibilities of college and university employers with regard to handicapped individuals deserve a separate treatment from a discussion of the federal regulations that preclude discrimination on the basis of sex, race, or national origin. The regulations issued by the federal government, governing non-discrimination on the basis of handicap are designed to implement Section 504 of the Rehabilitation Act of 1973, 29 U.S.C. 706, as amended. Section 504 states that "no otherwise qualified handicapped individual shall solely by reason by his handicap, be excluded from the participation in, be denied the benefits of, or be subject to discrimination under any program or activity receiving federal financial assistance."

Unless proof of undue hardship can be furnished, recipients of federal funds must make reasonable accommodation to the handicaps of both applicants for positions and employees. In addition, universities and colleges must make efforts to provide equal services to handicapped students. In order to provide such services, administrators must make sure that new facilities which are constructed are accessible to handicapped individuals and that all programs are operated in a nondiscriminatory manner. The administrator in higher education should remember that the major principle is that no agency or institution receiving federal funds may discriminate against a person solely on the basis of a handicap. The essential concept here is that the discrimination must not be only on the basis of the handicap. It is not necessary to offer employment to individuals who are unable to perform work at a desired level, but it is illegal to refuse consideration for employment in a certain position to an individual merely on the basis of a particular handicap.

While the concept of affirmative action does not apply precisely to the actions that must be undertaken to insure non-discrimination against handicapped individuals, institutions are nontheless required to take positive steps to insure that programs and facilities are made accessible to handicapped students, and that handicapped individuals are not discriminated against in employment or promotion on the basis of their handicap.

Definition of a Handicapped Individual

Section 84.30(j) of Section 504 of the Rehabilitation Act of 1973 defines handicapped persons as those who fall under the following categories:

1. Individuals with physical or mental impairment which substantially limits one or more major life activities (i.e., walking or speech).
2. Individuals who have a record of such impairment or who are regarded as having such an impairment. For example, an individual who has been in the past committed to an institution for the mentally impaired would be covered under the provisions of the Act, even though the person has never actually been mentally impaired.

To insure that recipients of federal funds are aware of the law, they are required to submit a letter of assurance to the Director of the Office for Civil Rights. Some of the types of disabilities covered by the law include visual, speech, and hearing impairments; diseases such as cancer and diabetes; mental retardation; and alcohol and drug addiction. The inclusion of individuals with histories of drug and/or alcohol addiction in the category of those who are considered as handicapped individuals is troubling to some administrators and faculty members. The concern is that the law may require individuals who are unable to perform the needed tasks to be hired in place of individuals who can and will perform. The spirit of the law is, however, that no job should be denied to an individual merely because that individual has a handicap unrelated to job performance. If the individual cannot perform the work to a satisfactory level, the job need not be offered.

The major fact for administrators to remember is that their prime goal remains the filling of positions with qualified personnel. The purpose of the federal legislation is to insure that there will be no discrimination against qualified individuals who are able to perform the job functions simply because of a handicap or disability that does not affect job performance. Administrators in colleges and universities cannot afford to be ignorant of the provisions of the law regarding equal opportunity in employment and services provided to individuals with handicaps.

Because of the function of higher education within the fabric of American society, administrators must be aware of their responsibilities with regard to the laws affecting equal opportunities in employment and education for women, minorities, and the handicapped. In addition, administrators should be aware that it also is illegal to discriminate against persons between the ages of forty and seventy in terms of employment. The laws and regulations which relate to equal opportunity are sometimes perceived by educators as restraints upon the ability of the institution in the making of personnel decisions. In addition, some administrators may utilize federal regulations in an unethical manner to achieve goals and ends that are not related to the intent of the law. College administrators may restrict hiring of full-time instructors, for example, claiming that the laws relating to equal opportunity require the filling of certain posts with minority applicants. In this way, instructor overloads and part-time instructors may be utilized at a considerable savings to the institution in salaries and fringe benefits.

It seems essential to rely upon the principles of justice and equity in all the operations of an institution dedicated to public service. The administrator who can view the application of the principles of equal opportunity and affirmative action as challenges requiring positive action will aid the institution in meeting its leadership obligations in society.

❒❒❒

5

Student Development Administrative Models

Introduction

The administrators most affected, and therefore most in need of being in the thick of things, are the chief student personnel and instructional administrators. It is upon their shoulders that the tasks of dealing with these partnership demands will fall. They will be charged with finding ways of interfacing students with the institution in its various forms.

Several questions need consideration: Are these the same college students in different clothing or a new breed? Do they require the same institution in a new form or a truly changed institution? Do these questions require traditional ways of thought restated anew, or do they require new and therefore radical ways of thought?

A body of literature which portrays a quandary in the student personnel area has come into existence in the past decade. This literature generally questions and points directions for the future. This process is a necessary evil yet undoubtedly a healthy state of affairs. However, student personnel and instructional administrators and professionals alike must begin to act on these questions and recommendations, thereby setting their houses in order and providing leadership for the college as a whole.

Definitions

Bureaucratic paradigm—Budgeting, facilities, design, and intra administrative relations.

Counseling paradigm—Humanizing one-to-one relationships; administrative credibility based on personal credibility

Curriculum paradigm—Curriculum development with the student in mind.

Environmental paradigm—Helping students interface with their universe.

Ombudsman paradigm—Student and faculty problems facilitated.

Emergent Philosophy of Student Development

Post-World War II philosophy in student personnel was based on a student services point of view. It anticipated and attempted preparation for individual student differences, it viewed the student as a whole person, and it started with the student where he was at any given moment. While no one would quarrel with these tenets, it is instructive to see that they grew more out of expedience and coincidence than out of a true philosophy. As needs were haphazardly uncovered, they were assigned to whomever had time for them, would accept them, or could be coerced into accepting responsibility for them. This last thought is essential. This coincidental approach leads to a philosophy of hindsight, an analysis that underwent periodic updating.

Even though these three tenets were sound, they were not interrelated in any way because of the nature of their development. Dispersion of student personnel tasks by expedience precluded input of a coordinated nature from the various divisions of the institution. The student personnel worker thus became a regulator, a serviceman, or a therapist. The student went to student services much as a patient goes to a doctor or pharmacy to have the appropriate remedy to his particular ill dispensed. With the advent of the 1960s, and an awakening student, the "doctors" started running out of diagnoses and prescriptions. The resulting quandary, which still exists, made us all uncomfortable, but it did bring about the start of a search for a real philosophy for student personnel. The student development point of view has been the result.

Student development assesses the student in terms of goals and objectives rather than needs. This is radically different from the student services point of view and requires new ways of thought. Student development brings the student to interface with the entire campus and involves all parties in developing objectives for the student. While student services is a service station, student development moves outward, is emergent; attempts to go to the student, not to wait for the problem to arise and then dispense a service. This requires a separation of the nature and attitude of the duties and functions involved. Students at an institution with a student development program will be free to choose the direction of their learning and will be responsible for those choices. This will remedy one of the major problems student personnel administrators faced with the student awakening of the 1960s. By its very nature, student services trapped student personnel staff into accepting responsibility for the student. When students began to develop on their own and student services were still dispensing prescriptions, the trap was sprung. Student service areas are generally thought of as: guidance and counseling, financial aid, placement, health, follow-up, student inventory, student activities, veterans' affairs, housing, intramurals and extra murals and various other services.

Students now enter into interpersonal relations with a development facilitator, a relationship that includes: challenge, stimulation, confrontation, and excitement; warmth, caring, understanding, acceptance, and support; and appreciation of individual differences.

Student Development and Administrative Philosophy

What existed prior to student development was an involvement with student regulation or therapy. Student development calls for a behavioral climate of learning. This requires a new student personnel professional, one who is catalytic what has been called a facilitator by counseling psychologists. This approach, which is still in transition, requires decentralization in some form of various student learning and counseling activities. It also requires support services from learning resources and business affairs.

Student services lacked integrative, institution-wide input. Student development strives to involve the whole campus community. The chief student personnel administrator must consider organization in a period of transition. Attitude is of utmost importance in this respect. Attitude will undoubtedly affect the success of this task of involving the institution with the student. Just as student personnel organization tends to be traditional and its staff passive, so other institutional areas most likely will be benign at best and myopic at worst in their attitude toward student development.

An emergent philosophy would require a similar style of administration, never status quo but always changing, taking on new shape to meet new challenges. To begin with, the student personnel and instructional administrator must be offensive, as this yields complexity of control as well as rigidity of structure in direct proportion. He must have the strong self-concept necessary for effective leadership. This yields trust in subordinates and gives those levels of information interchange which frees an organization from the cycle of advance and decline. Open mindedness will allow instructional and student personnel adr. inistrators to influence rather than control. The student personnel and instructional administrator must learn that effective management involves the movement of resources to dynamic organizational units which obtain their objectives to the satisfaction of the student while providing a sense of accomplishment for the instructional and student development professional.

Some parallels in the world of business management merit consideration. Rensis Likert of the University of Michigan has conducted extensive research showing that the more participative the approach, the better the results, except for the autocratic type of leader.

System 1 is described as "Exploitative Authoritative," system 2 as "Benevolent Authoritative," system 3 as "Consultative," and system 4 as "Participative Group." They range from complete lack of trust to complete trust. Interestingly enough, Likert reports that when managers were asked what action was taken when costs were cut, increased productivity resulted, and improved earnings were desired, the answer was a move toward system 1, a system proven to achieve the opposite results. Likert suggests that faulty accounting procedures do not represent increased earnings in their true light; that is, cash income derived from even greater liquidation of business assets. All administrators must avoid falling into this trap.

Student Development and Administrative Action

The administrator must view the tasks before him through a theory or philosophy, a way of thought, that has an emergent nature. People's relationships are the guiding nature of student development. People affect people in varied ways; they communicate both formally and informally in varied ways. Student development is the membrane of interface between the student and the institution, and the

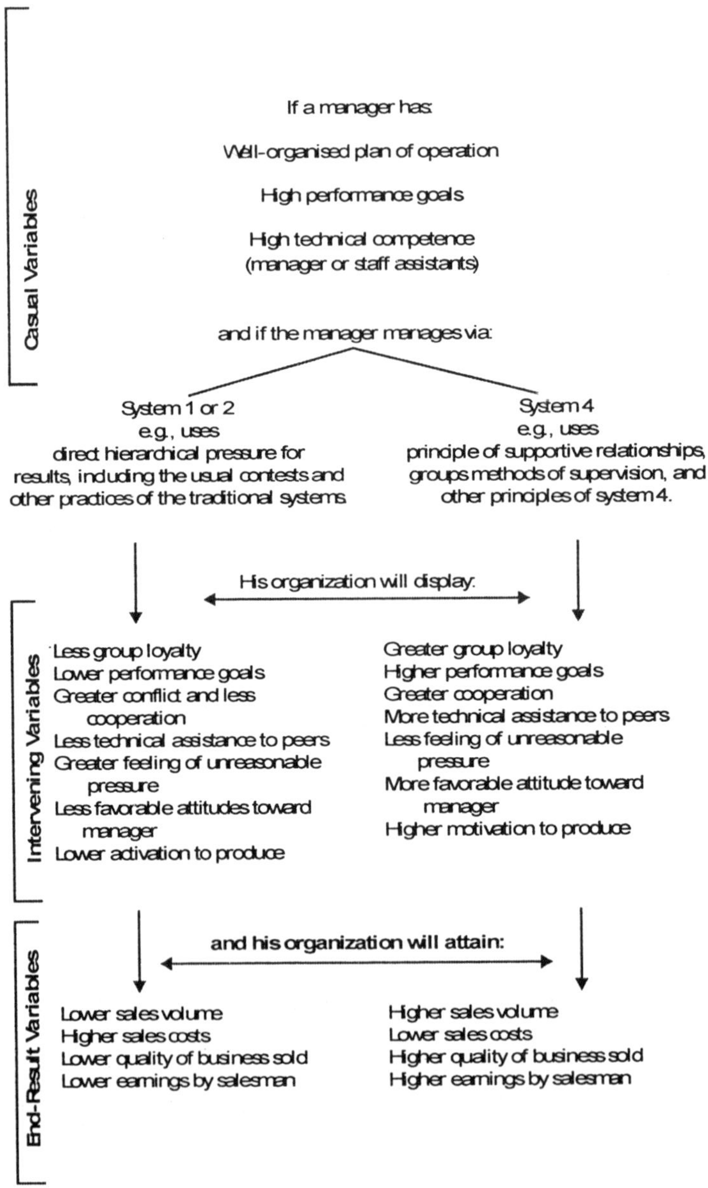

Figure 5.1. The Manager and his Organization

student personnel and instructional administrator can begin to imagine organizations which bring institutional goals and objectives into focus in ways that are mutually supportive, compatible with the institution's character, and integrative. This integration includes not only student personnel and instructional programs, but all support areas as well, such as business service and learning resources.

The administrator's first action then is to consider; what point of view, what way of thought sees an organization that is most responsive to the student development viewpoint. The administrator must imagine what the clientele, competencies, and roles in that organization will be.

Student Development and Administrative Organization

In the organizational process the administrator will go from expansive conception to specific models in setting up an emergent organization.

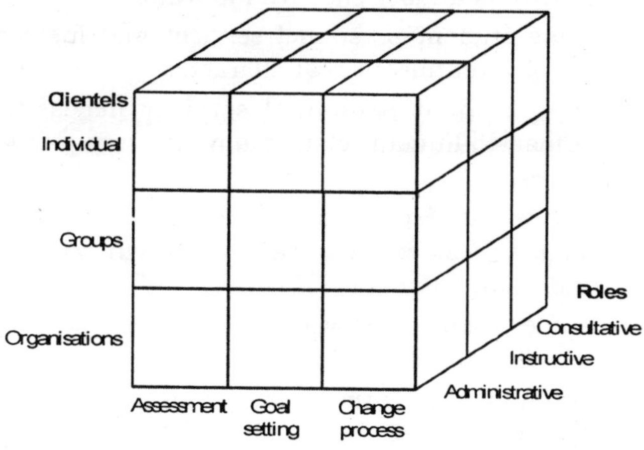

Figure 5.2. Personnel Work: An Emerging Model

While this may seem contradictory, Figure 5.2 shows this concept more clearly. It is not a constricting process but an emerging one; and when various clientele, roles, and competencies enter the universe of thought, it is integrative and liberating. In analyzing the work to be administrated, three divisions appear: (1) the jobs to be done, (2) the optimum time for doing those jobs, and (3) the roles and relationships of the personnel employed to do those jobs. Jobs fall into categories of routine services best done by clerical staff, developmental functions performed by professional staff, and activities with students. Time analysis is a standard component of any organizational structure which is to function effectively. Roles and relationships must be organized in a dynamic, high trust manner. Student development will then become part of every job on campus. The following ideas must be kept in mind as the organization is built.

1. Effective student personnel work and instruction takes time and costs money.
2. Active involvement by students and faculty in an activity is a most effective motivator.
3. Some student personnel services and instruction are of a routine clerical character.
4. Most student personnel services necessitate a human-to-human relationship, or a group-to-group process.
5. Effective student personnel services and instruction require clear communication through both formal and informal channels.
6. Student control by rigid regulation and policy leads to evasion and rebellion.
7. The high trust principles of wide participation in decision making, face-to-face relationships, mutual confidence, open communication, and internal control of performance make for good management.

Once the administrator has a grasp of functions and roles, models can become more specific. One possibility is to break down the organizational structure by functions and roles. This suggests the separation of development functions from those of a managerial or service nature.

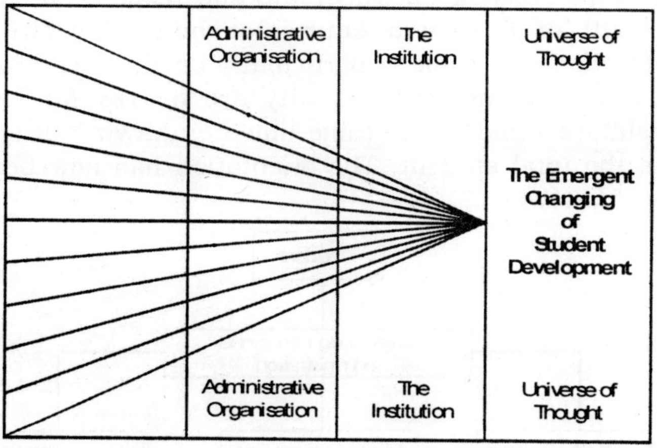

Figure 5.3. Shows this breakdown

The student development administrator will be a professional practitioner trained in the development area. (Such programs are now starting to develop in higher education.) The managerial services administrator could be a person of business/legal background adept at the managerial, control, and, most likely, disciplinary functions of his role. The student services managerial administrator must be familiar with the latest technology in data storage and retrieval. This model frees the student development personnel to be full-time educators. This model applies only in the student personnel area.

Student development now is in a position to engage in the decentralization of both counselling and advising. The counselor will no longer be in a cluster of offices. He or she may be in the learning resources center, the student center; or may be found in each instructional division office or in the cafeteria. Individual counselling now takes on a supermarket approach. As the student goes up and down the institutional aisles, the counselor is there to guide his educational purchases. As institutional involvement with the individual grows, the counselling professional can become involved with group counseling, where students help each other, taking on leadership and responsibility. The thought of having a counselor housed within an instructional division is particularly enticing in terms of academic advisement. Faculty are nearby for expert consultation and at the same time are drawn to interface with the total student. The orientation has now become "how," not "when."

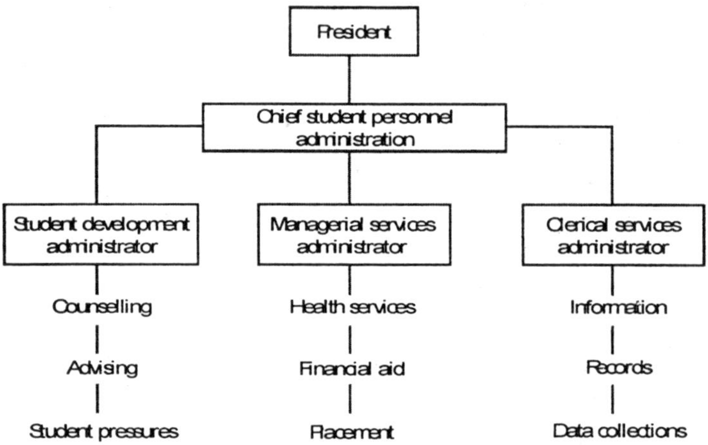

Figure 5.4. Student personnel organization chart Bob Miller

With decentralization student personnel administration begins to merge with instructional administration. As employment time decreases continually in the development of society, leisure activities and quasi volunteer activities will increase. Students must be prepared for this future. With the concept of in loco parentis dead for all practical purposes, student personnel can help higher educational institutions replace it with a concept of a vuncularity, from parent to uncle as it were. This is especially possible with the faculty boom over. For this model to be realized, student personnel workers must be open to redefinition, scholars in the field must maintain a link with their professional heritage and develop desirable future alternatives for developmental programs, and education must anticipate needs and create student development practitioners with professional expertise and administrative skill. Student personnel workers must master a body of knowledge, acquire skills and techniques, and pursue development and integration. With goals now well clarified, the chief personnel administrator can involve his staff in a sound organizational technique. Management by Objectives, which has been proven sound in business, industry, and government, can easily be converted to administration by objectives, or administration by results. The administrator now has a system which will bring the emergent philosophy of student development to life. This may be seen in the following list of advantages :

1. Communication is improved.
2. Evaluation is stressed.
3. The importance of the student is emphasized.
4. Institutional objectives are clarified.
5. Relevant items are brought into focus.
6. Accountability is established.
7. Merit pay is objectified.
8. Planning is brought into focus.
9. Supervision is lessened and influence expanded.
10. Morale is improved.

There are, however, some disadvantages to administration by results or objectives. Administration by objectives does not measure methods (these are activities), and the administrator must insure the ethical accomplishment of objectives. Administration by objectives takes time, costs money, and is hard work. Arbitrary decisions must be made, so the administrator must have a positive self-concept. Last of all, administration by objective can be little more than paper shuffling without real commitment on the part of all concerned. This concern must start with the chief administrator and involve low level managers.

Administration by objectives has obvious ramifications for budgeting given the current rise of program based budgeting systems and Zero Based Budgeting. A student development program in an emerging posture and objective oriented program will be ready for these budgeting systems when they arrive. They may indeed be instrumental in the institution-wide development of these systems given the increased cost of student development, as opposed to student services, in dollars and cents. Student development budgets already will have been well justified. The institution's business manager must be cooperative and supportive if these budgeting processes are to work effectively.

Student Development Administration, Students and Faculty

Higher education faces a new student today as the open door becomes the accepted admissions practice throughout higher education. This new student is characterized all too often by lower persistence, a lower degree of parental support, financial problems, a preoccupation with survival, poor self-image, and a nonacademic perception. The new student calls for new administrative designs and administrators who are willing to consider the possibility that traditional higher education could be wrong in some aspects.

"In loco parentis seems to have gone the way of the academic gold standard." Administrators must strive for student development to help students enter into a shared search for values and value systems. The new student must be helped to accept uncertainty, to realize that values will be matters of import that will claim his attention and utilize his basic energies. He must learn to choose freely from alternatives, taking into consideration the consequences of those alternatives. This means that the student must become well versed in the problem-solving or decision making process. As those choices are affirmed and cherished, they will form a basis for action and a pattern of social behavior by their repetition. This process must occur as the student encounters the real world through contemporary history, and most of all through the process of dealing with people.

Student development faces several challenges in interaction with the new student. One is overcoming affective testing. Education is moving from cognitive to integration with the affective domain, and testing can be a useful device. The student must be assured that testing will not be used to pigeon-hole him.

As student development progresses, the student may experience emotional problem in leaving his environment and heritage. We are still working with elements of future shock where many students are not ready to face a world of change. Co-curricular activities can be of help here in bringing the student's heritage to new light. Special studies, courses in human development, and so forth, are possible solutions. Co-curricular activities can also help alter an anti intellectual posture. Low finances can be the cause of a surface appearance of lack of seriousness. Education must be made inexpensive, not cheap, for students. No student with academic or occupational abilities should be deprived of educational opportunity because of lack of financial support. Plural admission criteria probably need to replace the "gold standard." This is not to be taken as a lowering of standards but as a new view of the possible competencies that traditional views may have ignored. The question might be asked, "Are we educating for the right things in life?" Bringing students into the college community is perhaps the most difficult challenge. Minorities, foreign students, varied ages, commuters—how can these diversified elements be brought to some sort of unity? How can we provide an effective education to meet the needs of society?

Student Roles and Faculty Roles

The college community should strive to be a microcosm of society. Faculty involvement in the student development process is a prerequisite for this. Who does the student come in contact with more often, excepting his peers, than the faculty? They must be the front line of any successful development program, suggesting again a need for the merging of student development and academic administration. In addition, this merging must occur up and down all levels and all ranks concerning student/faculty roles. While these suggestions are offered within a community college format, they are equally applicable to the four-year college or university.

"Toward Improved Involvement"

1. Each community college should have a student organization with defined powers and responsibilities and an established place in the machinery for the development of institutional policies.
2. To improve communication between the student organization for policy formulation and the faculty organization for policy formulation, there should be representatives of each sent as observers to the other. It would be the responsibility of such observers to comment on the point of view of their organization upon request and to keep their organization informed of the activities of its counterpart.
3. Joint faculty-student standing committees should be established to deliberate and make recommendations to the faculty and student policy-formulating bodies. Faculty members should predominate and there should be a faculty concern. Student members should predominate and there should be a student chairman of those committees involving matters of primary concern to the students.
4. An attempt should be made to ensure the representativeness of student policy formulating organizations by the election of candidates from defined constituencies as opposed to the at-large elections which are frequently the case at present. It is suggested that the division or department might serve as a basic reference point in defining constituencies.
5. Divisions and departments should be urged to consider students majoring in their disciplines as viable sub-groups of the college and to create student advisory

committees that would meet with faculty members in these areas to foster communication and planning for improved student life. These advisory groups might also be involved in faculty meetings of the department or division whenever possible.

Several areas should be primarily or totally under student governance.

1. Student publications such as newspapers, bulletins and yearbooks.
2. Allocation of student activity fees to various students.
3. Assisting in student conduct and discipline unrelated to the classroom situation. (Example: student courts.)
4. Recognition of campus student organizations through chartering and approval of various clubs, fraternities, etc.
5. Approval of a variety of guest speakers invited by students.
6. Approval of distribution of student-initiated literature on campus.
7. Approval of distribution of off-campus literature on campus.

Areas which should be considered for some degree of student involvement are as follows:

1. Faculty reappointment, promotion to higher rank and tenure through faculty personnel committees.
2. Recommendations on admissions standards for curricula and courses.
3. Recommendations on class size.
4. Input into allocation of instructional funds.
5. Leadership given to curricula or course revision, addition, or deletion.
6. Ad hoc committees or task forces on administrative structure of the college.
7. Recommendations to the administration on staff salaries, fringe benefits.
8. Input on teaching loads.
9. Provision of services to the community.

10. Requirement for degrees and certificates.
11. Input and recommendations on the selection of a president.
12. Input on selection of college officers directly related to student life.

Student responsibilities include:

1. Compliance with and support of duly constituted civil authority as an individual student.
2. Respect for the rights of others and cooperation to ensure that such rights are guaranteed, whether or not the views of those exercising such rights are consistent with the views of the majority. Student documents should provide for both responsibilities and rights.
3. Cooperation to ensure that the will of the majority is implemented after due consideration has been given to contrary points of view. Such cooperation, however, does not include the suppression of minority points of view. The minority must be protected as well as the majority.
4. The exercise of dissent within a framework compatible with the resolution of difference. Constructive criticism is always helpful in improving an institution.
5. Knowledge of college regulations established through the joint efforts of students, faculty, and administration. Handbooks should be written in student language where students are involved.

Faculty advising in the traditional sense is out of date. Faculty must be brought to an understanding of the complexity of human relations and aspirations needed to advise the new student. They must realize that all education does not happen in the classroom. Student personnel professionals need to realize that a great deal of learning does occur in the classroom. In student development, there should be a team aspect for advisement involving faculty, student development professionals, and paraprofessionals.

They must help the student take an active part in his own educational experiences and assist the student in the synthesization and integration of those experiences. They must be concerned with the growth as well as the performance of students with whom they come in contact. Faculty must allow student personnel to assist them in a catalytic way with appropriate counseling and testing services. This again calls for faculty to hold a favorable opinion of student development and of their own teaching, for qualified student development personnel, and for student development administration organized for campus-wide permeation. Both groups, faculty and student personnel workers, must assist each student in a teaming process which involves learning in the affective, psychomotor, and cognitive domains.

Considering student personnel professionals as educators in an administrative structure which allows for delineation of roles or paradigms holds great potential for catalytic activities. The student development professional is best suited to relate the cognitive and affective domains. He or she can aid in divisional organization and in scheduling, can serve as an inter-disciplinary liaison, and teach developmental courses. Also, they can aid in the training of student assistants, work-study students, and paraprofessionals. In this educator role, they can be invaluable in bringing student development to life for the student and faculty to the benefit of both. Student development must be emergent, dynamic, and organized in a climate of trust and support. It must permeate the institution, utilize all its resources, and thereby motivate it to become integrated in an interface with the student. Student development must be catalytic, a permeable membrane between the student and the institution. Student services must decentralize, seek out the student, anticipate his needs, and share in his hopes, goals, dreams, and joys. The faculty member will continue to be the content specialist but will team with the student personnel specialist in bringing the affective and values domains to the student.

What is the nature of the person who becomes involved in this field? That is perhaps the last remaining key to bring student development to fruition. Programs that attempt to train professional practitioners in the student developmental areas are now coming into being. These people oriented educators are the student development administrators of tomorrow, yet they generally have little administrative skill. To improve the system, there must be specific education for faculty, student development professionals, and administrators. Yet a combination of counseling and administration is probably not a sufficient base either. Chief student personnel administrators, when surveyed, suggested the following areas in some combination as making up a student personnel curriculum.

1. Courses in Psychology and Sociology
2. Counselling principles and techniques
3. Practicums in student development work
4. An overview of student development work in higher education
5. A study of college students and their experiential background
6. Social psychology, anthropology and human relations
7. Higher education, the university, college and community college

Not enough is known at this juncture to bring the behavioral and social sciences to the practitioner state. Therefore no foundation exists for the training of a student development professional as a behavioral scientist who is a student personnel practitioner. However, what is known is being passed along, and programs are moving in the professional practitioner direction.

The student personnel administrator should constantly work toward the goal of eliminating his existence, for as student development reaches new heights, his services are needed less and less, if he does an effective and efficient job as student developer.

❒❒❒

6

Techniques and Strategies for Higher Education Evaluation

Introduction

It is difficult to generalize a model for the various possible programs that might be developed in all of the public and private universities, junior/community colleges, and post-secondary technical schools, common elements and accepted techniques are useful in most developmental situations. The first of these is the institutional examination and information-gathering technique necessary to preplanning. The second involves the development of the program itself, the marshalling of resources and personnel leading to the writing of program elements of curriculum. The third component of program development involves the implementation of program elements, usually in a pilot phase.

A fourth, and often neglected, element of program development focuses on evaluation. This element emphasizes an objective examination of the program elements and outcomes. From this evaluation answers can be found to questions such as, Should this program be integrated into the institution in its present form? Are the outcomes congruent with the stated objectives of the program? And, most important, Do students benefit from this program?

Program development and implementation is a systematic process involving analysis of the key elements of need, desirability, and the ability to carry out the program. This is an intensive development and implementation phase with evaluation and assessment forming the final step in a process leading to the adaption of a particular program.

The following in-depth examination of the steps outlined in this chapter will necessarily cite particular examples, incidents and details regarding what various educators have said about program development and evaluation. However, it is important to note that although professional educators are in general agreement on the major elements involved, the order that these elements take and the weight given to the elements vary to a considerable degree from situation to situation and institution to institution.

Definitions

Cost analysis—A process which may be employed through three kinds of costs: research and development, investment, and operating costs. These are placed on physical qualities such as time, space, equipment, and supplies.

Free choice model—A planning model to develop projections predicated on the number of students expected to exit from a particular discipline and the number of faculty expected to teach in that discipline. Manpower planning model—Projects manpower needs, then develops projections of the number of individuals needed to fill those requirements.

Program development— A systematic process involving analysis of the key elements of need, desirability, and the ability to carry out the program.

Identifying Educational Needs

The impetus for developing educational programs can arise at virtually any level in an institution from the individual instructor through the president or board of trustees. It also may arise from regional, state, or federal suggestions or mandates, or from community or student pressures. Among these multiple points for generating possible program development, Dorothy Knoell and Charles McIntyre cite a natural division between those programs that operate on a laissez-faire or free choice philosophy and those that operate on the manpower planning model. In general, the free choice model includes general education, non vocational programs and attempts to "supply the right amount and kind of education predicated upon existing and anticipated student demand." The manpower planning model projects manpower needs and then develops projections of the number of individuals required to fill those needs. For example, if you allow too many dental programs in one state you can quickly flood the market. The point of departure in these two models is the relative role the state or federal government plays in determining the need for specific programs. The two governmental agencies greatly influence programs of colleges and universities, especially in connection to funding. This concept is within its basic right since "education is a function of each state and since the federal government gets involved in the matter of 'educational welfare.' " In general, the manpower planning model derives from extensive surveying of manpower needs in broad geographic areas and in numerous occupations. This type of surveying goes beyond simply determining the demand for manpower to also estimate the supply. D. Kent Halstead identifies the following formula for supply-demand analysis for developing manpower needs through state surveys. Manpower Planning Model (Demand — Supply = Manpower Requirements).

Demand for manpower is created by: (1) New jobs due to growth and technology; (2) Death and retirement; (3) Transfers and promotions to other occupations.

Supply for manpower is created by: (1) New entrants from training programs; (2) Unemployed workers seeking work in the occupation; (3) Entrants from other occupations; (4) Immigrants.

Obviously, this type of extensive and intensive surveying is beyond the scope of individual institutions. From these and numerous other state surveys, however, broad areas of need can be identified as possible areas for program development by individual institutions. The size and mission of the institution will determine whether further surveying is necessary to answer questions concerning the development of a new program. For example, a major university drawing students from across the nation might contemplate developing a program if multistate regional manpower needs dictate. A community college, however, with its localized clientele, would have difficulty in identifying which programs would be needed in its restricted geographic area by using state and regional surveys alone. In order to determine local manpower needs it is necessary for community colleges to turn to more localized assessments of manpower needs. A community college usually has several sources for local surveys. The U.S. Census Bureau is a major source which maintains statistics for area industries as well as detailed demographic data. In addition, many cities and counties maintain extensive data concerning occupations, including projections for future growth. Chambers of commerce and business organizations are also sources for information about growth and need in a community.

Most institutions, however, would not rely solely on surveys conducted by outside agencies. Instead, these surveys are indicators which tend to focus the institution on areas most likely to be candidates for program development. N. Dean Evans and Russ L. Neagley identity six components, including several local surveys that should be conducted to determine needs for new colleges. These include (1) County or regional population projections for the area to be served by potential colleges; (2) County or regional resources and development surveys; (3) Business industry surveys; (4) Professional surveys; (5) Student-parent surveys; (6) Enrollment studies to predict potential student enrollments in the college. Although these are cited as elements of a feasibility study, the same considerations must be taken into account when developing new programs or expanding existing programs to encompass new elements. As with the manpower planning model, the free choice model can be analyzed in terms of need. It is interesting to note, however, that the free choice model is based not solely on the numbers of students expected to exit from a particular discipline, but also on the number of faculty expected to be employed to teach that discipline. Halstead states that "the two most critical assumptions—because they vary and are subject to error are the expected student-faculty ratio and the trend in total enrollment." The problem of projecting total enrollment is highlighted by Donald Norris when he cites several competent but varying projections for enrollments through the year 2000. The extremely complicated, and admittedly imprecise, process identified by Halstead for determining student-faculty ratio in the free choice model at the state level is illustrated as follows. *Free choice model.*

1. Obtain for at least the past 5-year period the number of student credit hours classified by level of instruction (lower division, upper division, master's and doctor's), type of institution (junior community college, senior college, university), and field of study.
2. Convert the number of student credit hours in each field of study and at each level of instruction to

percentages of the total instruction at each type of institution. Thus for one year at all senior colleges, 10,000 credit hours of English instruction at the lower division level might equal 5 percent of the total instruction (200,000 credit hours) offered.

3. On the basis of past trends and stated assumptions, project the future share (percentage) of total instruction expected in each field-level combination. For the example in step 2, the past trend in lower division English instruction may warrant a 6 or 7 percent increase in the future.
4. For each type of institution, project total enrollment during each year of the projection period. Convert to full-time-equivalent [FTE] students and, in turn, to total instructional load in student credit hours (one FTE student is usually equal to 12 to 15 credit hours).
5. To determine projected instruction loads, apply the projected share percentages in each field-level combination (as determined in step 3) to projections of total instruction load.
6. For each type of institution, subject field, and level of instruction, determine planned future student-faculty ratios in terms of student credit hours or instruction per FTE teaching faculty member.
7. The number of FTE teaching faculty required in each discipline, by level of instruction and type of institution, can now be determined by applying the student-faculty ratios to the number of student credit hour instructional loads predicted in step 5.
8. New annual staff requirements can be expected to equal new additional staff requirements based on enrollments as calculated in step 7, plus replacement of yearly staff losses through resignation, retirement, or death.

The above process is useful for determining statewide enrollments in general studies free choice curriculums at the state level. This process would apply especially to senior colleges and universities. However, individual institutions can gain much useful information from conducting student-parent surveys as identified by Evans and Neagley, and by analyzing population trends in areas and target populations served by the institution.

Although external stimuli provided by need surveys are a major factor in program development, they are by no means the only influences that stimulate development. A commentary by experts in the field concerning internal influences that affect curriculum change of universities, lists (1) academic departments, (2) the college or other academic division, (3) the president and academic deans, (4) individual faculty members, (5) the students, and (6) the extra curriculum. These are major areas within the college or university that generate curriculum change, and with slight modification they may be applied to community colleges as well.

Additional internal forces that spawn curriculum change and modification are discussed by Lewis Mayhew and Patrick Ford. They state that analysis "suggests that discussion, political actions, judgement of experts, and search for social needs are the prevailing methods of curriculum analysis and development." Among the specific methods discussed, and the most used for analyzing curriculum, is administrative review. The administrative review process is defined as the ongoing process of accepting new courses into the curriculum on an annual basis. Generally, this is an organized process of review and expansion of existing programs. A more in-depth review of curriculum is gained through self study. The process of self-study may be a product of the accrediting process or may arise from the desire of an institution to examine its curricular offerings. At times a modified study will be used to examine the curriculum. This type of self-study is done by using a short-lived committees that recommend changes to the administration and faculty for consideration. These changes in curriculum usually involve state agency and regional accreditation association approval.

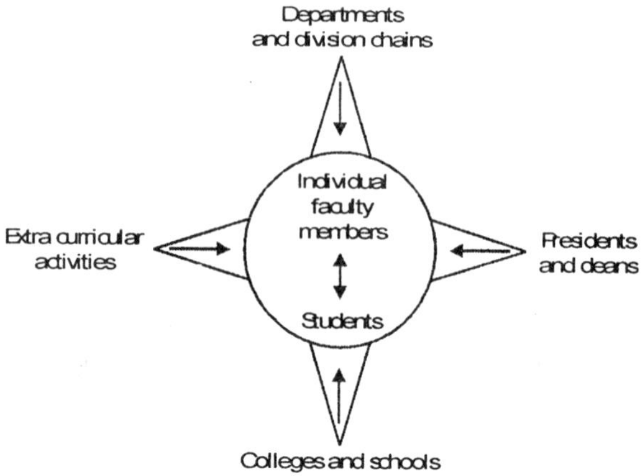

Figure 6.1. Internal changes that affect curriculum

In community colleges the role of advisory committees in curriculum change is important. Advisory committees are comprised of representatives from business and industry who may be considered experts in their respective fields. Their input is valuable because they can assess curricula, identify that which is outdated, and suggest modifications. Advisory committees are now utilized at senior college levels and in general education programs. This process likely will expand in the future. Other less frequently used methods involve the use of a consultant or group of consultants to analyze an institution and suggest curriculum changes. Finally, in isolated cases, a governing board may form committees with the assistance of selected resource persons to review and suggest changes.

It is readily apparent that the identification of the need for curriculum change and the gathering of information to effect that change is a complex process. Dependent on the type of program to be developed and the scope of the institution, it may involve federal, state, and local educational groups as well as outside sources of information and expertise. The result can profoundly affect an institution's offerings, both immediate and long-term. All too often, however, much red tape is involved. An institution should have enough checks and balances to provide quality control in curriculum development.

Factors in Program Development

In a generalized system of development, needs assessment, goal setting, resource analysis, and evaluation are closely allied. It is useful, however, to analyze each element separately to form a clear understanding of the relationship each of the various elements has to the other. Perhaps the most comprehensive work in this area of analysis has been done by the Western Interstate Commission for Higher Education (WICHE) Planning and Management Systems Program. This program is designed to develop common data elements and terminology in a number of planning areas across a variety of institutions of higher education. These elements may then be used by an individual institution for the purpose of program planning and resource allocation. Ben Lawrence discusses the numerous systems developed or being developed by WICHE.

Within this framework, systems for developing goals and objectives, for calculating resources, for identifying alternative programs, and others are explored. Although it is outside the scope of this chapter to examine in-depth the WICHE program, it is suggested that the WICHE planning manuals be considered for use in program planning and development.

Role of the State in Planning

The role of the state in planning has been previously mentioned in the area of needs analysis. The state also plays a large role in the actual development of programs. Halstead identifies eight areas in which the state has a planning function.

1. Delineating sharply and concretely the generally accepted broad educational objectives of the state

and determining through analysis and assessment those objectives which should receive highest priority over a given period of time.

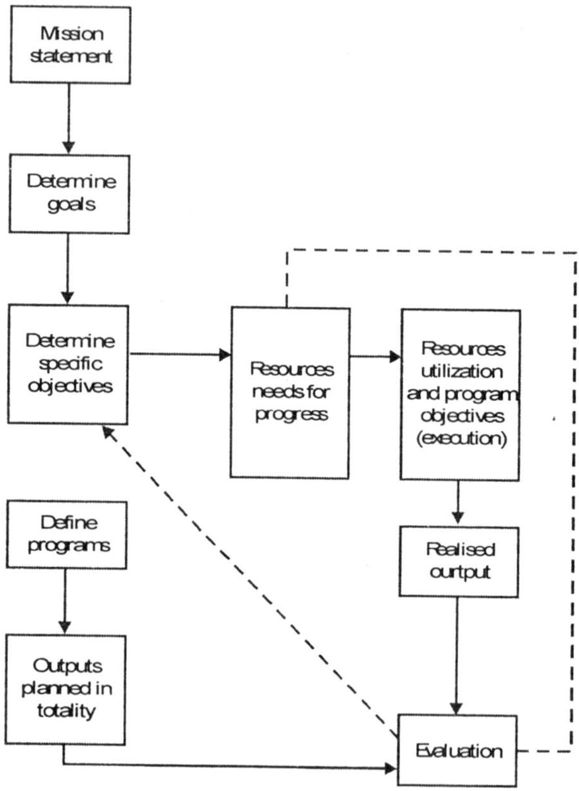

Figure 6.2. A model of Higher Education Management

2. Preparing multiyear comprehensive plans designed to integrate the curriculum, research, and services of statewide higher education, to correct inadequacies, and to attain educational objectives.
3. Developing various program alternatives and, by systematic analysis and comparison, presenting for review specific recommendations.

4. Studying continuously and evaluating thoroughly existing state programs in order to determine their adequacy and compare benefits and costs.
5. Examining state and other sources of financial support in order to determine the potential for additional revenue, and developing legislative and other proposals which will take advantage of identified opportunities.
6. Collecting, interpreting, and managing descriptive and quantitative educational data in the state and nation data which relate to and have implications for educational planning then applying such data to the development of plans.
7. Conducting and supporting research activities to determine cause-and-effect relationships, testing and analyzing the effectiveness of specific plans proposed and adopted, and developing assessment instruments and techniques.
8. Establishing coordinated working relationships and effective communication with all organizations and individuals directly concerned with planning.

These are broad areas of responsibility which in most cases do not extend to specific program elements. There are, however, exceptions in individual states. Texas, for example, controls individual curricular offerings through two state-level agencies. The Texas Education Agency has the primary responsibility in post-secondary education to approve instructors and courses in the occupational area. The Coordinating Board of Colleges and Universities, although it does pass on occupational programs, has the primary responsibility for approval of courses in the universities and in the academic offerings of community colleges.

Both agencies, as is the case in most states, fund occupational and university parallel programs; thus they influence courses and programs to a high degree.

On the institutional level, a great deal of work has been done relating to program development using simulation models. One application of simulation was PRIME, Planning Resources in Minnesota Education, as described by David Cordes. This particular application took place at three educational institutions in the state of Minnesota. The three institutions, a state university, a community college, and a public school, utilized a computer simulation, CAMPUS, to analyze factors in program development that impact the development, implementation, and ongoing activities over a several-year period.

The data elements needed to run this simulation include: (1) staff and staff support, (2) space, (3) teaching equipment, (4) type of course, (5) staff specialization, (6) schedule time, and (7) success factors for students enrolled. This very sophisticated simulation was used to project program needs and cost factors for up to a ten-year period. In institutions with sufficient resources, this type of analysis has a distinct advantage and, though costly, provides invaluable planning information. For institutions unable to implement the sophisticated design characterized by CAMPUS, the problems of analysis are more difficult; however, the elements to be considered remain the same. Planning and projecting by institutions should constantly attempt to approach precision while remaining aware of the imprecise nature of these activities.

Analyzing Program Costs

Cost analysis, one of the areas identified in WICHE documents, is explored in a different manner by Emil J. Haller. In his discussion Haller identifies "four basic types of resources that any administrator has available for allocation. The four types are: (1) Time (2) Space (3) Equipment and (4) Supplies." To these four types of resources Haller couples the three categories of "(1) Research and Development costs-necessary to develop a program to the stage it can be introduced into the system. (2) Investment costs—costs necessary to implement the program, and (3) Operating costs—costs necessary to operate the program" to form the following cost input structure.

R & D Costs	Investment Costs	Operating Costs
1.1 time	2.1 time	3.1 time
1.2 space	2.2 space	3.2 space
1.3 equipment	2.3 equipment	3.3 equipment
1.4 supplies	2.4 supplies	3.4 supplies

It can readily be seen that research and development costs do not reflect the long-term expenses of operating a program. The same can be said of investment costs to a lesser extent, with replacement of equipment and retraining of personnel being the prime factors of continuing expense in this area.

Through the systematic development outlined, educational institutions attempt to approach precise measures of cost to implement new programs. The complexity of the factors involved has so far made precise measure elusive. Paul Dressel states that because of the number of complex variables involved "no institution or school system has carried out a systems analysis to the point of allowing and applying fully satisfactory models of prediction and control. The fact remains that both short- and long-range projections of cost factors are important in curriculum planning.

Program Evaluation

Program or curriculum evaluation, as with other steps in the overall development and implementation model, must find its root in the mission of an institution, its goals and general objectives, and the specific goals and objectives of the program. Many types of measures are available; however, the organization of these measures into a coherent framework is necessary if the institution is to have a retrieval base for making decisions about the successful individual program. This model deals with three variables of behavior, instruction, and population.

This particular model has advantages because it does not dictate the level of sophistication in evaluation, but instead provides a conceptual framework that can be used to provide evaluation information across a broad range of programs and program elements. With this framework an institution can address the key components of a program and utilize individual measures to address specific program elements. The Carnegie Foundation identifies measures that can be used by an individual institution as measures of effectiveness.

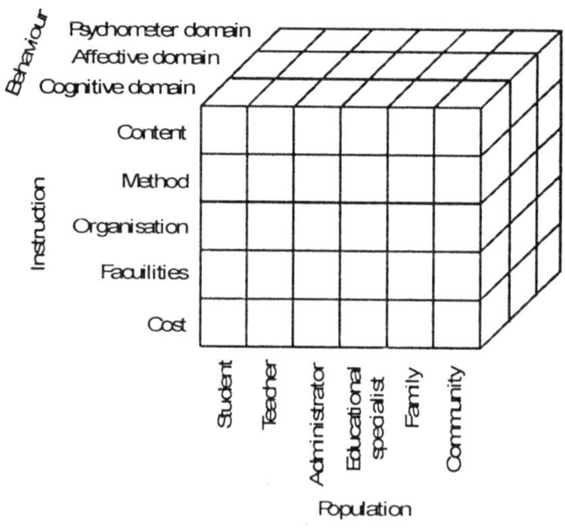

Figure 6.3. The Epic Evaluation Model

Program development in post-secondary education is an extremely important and complex process. Complicating the process is the imprecise nature of projecting needs, enrollments, and finances beyond the short term. In order to approach program development with a semblance of certainty, it is necessary to employ systematic data-gathering techniques and scientific projection methods.

This chapter has only touched on a few highlights and illustrations of the types of systems that might be employed. Each individual program development cycle will be constructed utilizing needs survey instruments, program models, and evaluative techniques that are unique to the institution and program. The selection of these elements must be done with clear understanding of the strengths and weaknesses of each and should be employed in a manner that makes maximum use of the information generated. Only through this method can educational institutions expand programs and at the same time maintain viability in educational offerings and stability in financial affairs.

Program development and evaluation is a most difficult area which requires team effort and cooperation to obtain quality control in the curriculum and instruction elements in a college. By utilizing appropriate techniques and strategies, the results achieved can be most gratifying for the institution, the administration, faculty, and, most of all, students.

The environmental context in which higher education may operate in the near future and to raise questions about how such contextual observations may be translated by the higher education industry and individual institutions into new strategic directions and programs. For this reason, this discussion is long on themes and short on recommendations. If the underlying premise that the convergence of technologies will enable new ways to fulfill higher education's teaching mission is true, then leading institutions have a range of strategic options that can expand both their geographical instructional reach and their sources of revenues. This range of options extends from achieving cost efficiencies by leveraging course offerings among existing university students to seeking new, potentially global, markets by franchising courses and information assets to students not currently served by higher education.

The first and primary recommendation is for our educational leadership to develop strategic frameworks for addressing the changing environment that is described here. Any institution's ability to exploit new instructional opportunities effectively depends on its establishing an "institutional" context for program development and institutional investments to "jump start" such development. Although Indian colleges and universities are prepared, for example, to create the data communications networks that will carry instructional content and information resources, is it appropriate (to their missions) for these institutions to "seed" the development of best-in-their-class technology-enriched instructional offerings? Many of our institutions have achieved academic recognition and excellence by localizing the responsibilities for curriculum development and execution as deeply as possible. The development of truly enriched, technology-intensive course offerings worthy of the reputation of Indian higher education will be costly and risky. The governance and organizational infrastructures for making such investment decisions are not well developed currently.

❑❑❑

7

Theories and Administration of Higher Education

Introduction

The approach to the study of management was functional rather than theoretical. Writers of that time spoke more of principles than of theories. The emphasis in management was first a task-oriented one, progressing to a manager-oriented one, and then to one concerned with the worker. Chester I. Barnard published his still-used organizational theory of cooperative systems in 1938. Barnard combines both of the major influences discussed in his concepts of effectiveness and efficiency.

Effectiveness had to do with achieving goals and getting the job done. Efficiency was person-oriented and had much to do with the satisfaction of the worker within the organization. Elton Mayo and Fritz J. Roethlisberger carried on the Hawthorne studies in the early thirties. The work of these individuals introduced into administrative thinking the importance of observing what managers do and analyzing these actions to determine the underlying theory of the administrative function. These works are viewed as scientific in nature. In addition, they illustrate an introduction of the behavioral approach to the study of management.

The concern over theory, research, and practice in administration gathered momentum in the post-World War II years. Research in the social sciences had increased very rapidly and was reflected in what has been referred to as the "New Movement in educational administration." Individuals such as Jacob W. Getzels, Herbert A. Simon, Daniel Griffiths, and Andrew W. Halpin became prominent as leaders in this movement. Its development began with dissatisfaction on the part of a group of professors of educational administration with the current methods of training administrators. At that time neither theory nor research formed the basis of instruction; personal experiences of the professors in school administration became the content of the courses. Getzels and his associates refer to the "trait" and "technology" points of view about administration as the "uncodified art" and "prescriptive" views. They describe a third view as one in which the focus of administration must be on "conceptualizations and theories not on simply directions to be followed but on complex relations to be understood." Simon was especially concerned that administrators be able to improve the decision-making process. Griffiths illustrates how social science contributes to the building of administrative sciences.

In 1947 a conference was attended by these "dissatisfied" professors who with the American Association of School Administrators secured funding for a research and development program from the Kellogg Foundation. In 1950 centers for this program opened at eight universities.

In a 1953 conference of professors of educational administration, there was a noticeable shift from concerns related to procedure, to concerns related to theory. Getzels made a strong plea for theory-oriented research at this particular meeting.

In 1954 a group of behavioral scientists met with professors of educational administration. At that time the scientists criticized the quality of research being done in education, indicating that it was "a-theoretical" in nature. This has been described as "the first real" confrontation between behavioral scientists and professors of educational administration.

James Thompson, a professor of sociology and business administration, described several advantages of administration theory: (1) preparing students for change with a view of the administration process as a "complex of simultaneously variable factors"; (2) offering a way of thinking "which would allow the administrator to incorporate knowledge produced by the several disciplines"; (3) alerting students to the results of research; and (4) preparing students for "growth through their own later experience."

As stated by Halpin, the leaders of the New Movement emphasized that (1) the role of theory be recognized and that nakedly empirical research be rejected in favor of hypothetico-deductive research in history; (2) educational administration not be viewed provincially, and especially not as distinct from other kinds of administration—administration as administration, without adjectival qualifiers, is a proper subject for study and research; and (3) because education can be construed best as a social system, educational administration must, in turn, draw heavily from insights furnished by the behavioral sciences.

Five research studies were considered as substantive achievements of the New Movement. One was on leadership behavior of superintendents (Halpin); another on administration as a social process (Getzels); a third on personality characteristics and administrative performance of principals (Hemphill and his associates); a fourth on place-bound and career bound superintendents in relation to effecting organization change (Carlson); and a fifth study was on the organizational climate in elementary schools. Out of these studies concepts and theories developed, although Halpin reflects pessimism in an article published in 1969 in which he indicates that the movement began to run down because the idea of theory in administration was oversold and because of lack of ability to attract enough quality manuscripts.

Although the movement for development of a theoretical base in educational administration lost its momentum, it left its mark. There is a developing theory, or theories, of administration, which is considered a discipline with a base that is scientific in nature. This statement is based upon the perceptions of most authorities in the area of higher educational administration. Drucker views management as being scientific in nature when he describes it as "a discipline, or at least capable of becoming one." It appears that management has become a field for the scientific study of how organizations and people in organizations do and can behave.

Organizations may consist of leaders who exhibit a variety of behaviors and traits, workers who display complex and constantly varying motivational patterns, and a structure that establishes tasks ranging along a simple-to-complex continuum. Administrative theory is a tool for systematizing the spirit of inquiry about organizations. It allows the administrator to rise above the unexamined assumptions he may have generated from experience alone or learned from fellow administrators.

Nature and Development of Theory

Understanding of the nature and development of theory must be based upon a common understanding of the involved terminology. Theory has two functions, one concerned with description and the other with explanation. In order to provide for a terminology which will not constantly involve a tangle of confusions, a definition of theory is presented; a "theory" is a set of assumptions from which can be derived, by purely logico-mathematical procedures, a larger set of empirical laws. The theory thereby furnishes an explanation of these empirical laws and unifies the originally heterogeneous areas of subject matter characterized by those empirical laws.

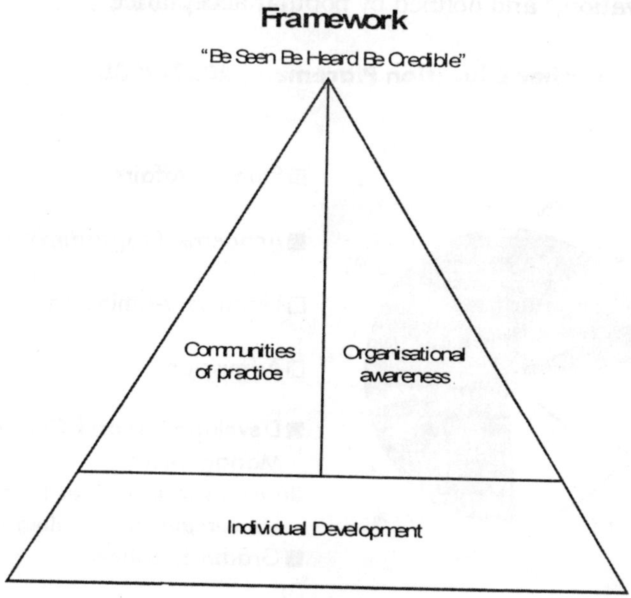

Figure 7.1

Getzels, James Lipham and Ronald Campbell list three functions of theory in the study and practice of administration—taxonomic, explanatory, and heuristic. Others define theory as a deductively connected set of laws. In general, a theory might be considered as a principle or assumption which serves to explain, predict, and question phenomena, and from which laws are derived.

Since theory is derived from a framework of concepts, it is appropriate to discuss the meaning of *concept*. According to Griffiths a concept is simply a term to which a particular meaning has been attached. The lack of appropriate concepts has made it very difficult to adequately describe administrative situations or administrative behavior. A concept is now considered to be operational if a link to other operational concepts can be clearly demonstrated. Concept has also been referred to as a "descriptive term, or observable." It is found in everyday experience, "susceptible to direct sensory observation," and defined by popular acceptance.

Higher Education Placement, 2002-2008

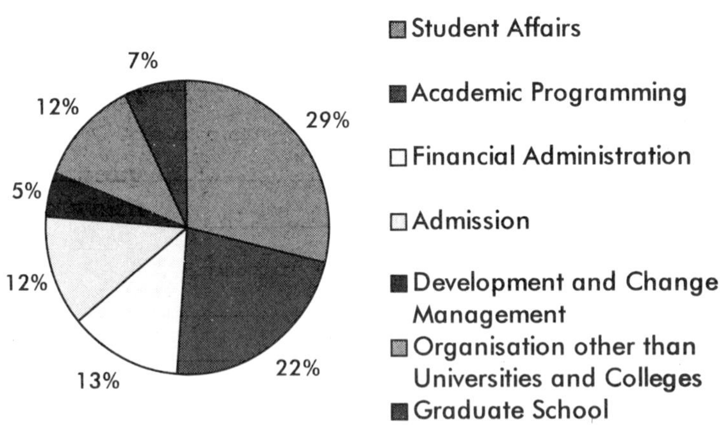

Figure 7.2

Griffiths refers to the steps in theory construction as stages in the development of a science. He describes his approach as the "level" approach, with sensitizing concepts at the lowest level, integrating concepts at the middle level, and theory at the top level. Sensitizing concepts are those which draw attention to specific behaviors associated with administrative activity. Integrating concepts order the relationships among a number of sensitizing concepts. According to Griffiths, the theory builder has useful thoughts, opinions, and ideas (presumptions), which he follows up by observation and description of the administrative behavior noted. Explanation of the observation is attempted on one of the three levels, but levels may be skipped or returned to from a higher level.

Rather than confronting the person directly, he controls by rules. This keeps the visibility of power relations down and thus lowers the interpersonal tension level. The lowered tension level increases the use of rules.

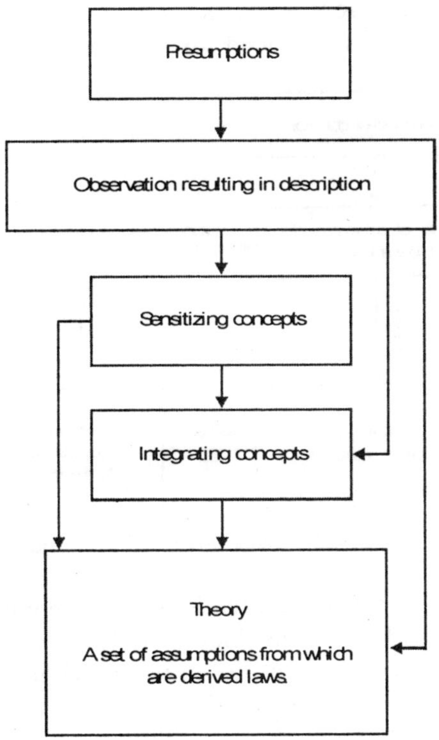

Figure 7.3. Paradigm for Theory Development

It depicts an example of a more complex integrative administrative act, where a consequence occurred which the administrator did not anticipate. When the general rule can only imply what is minimum acceptable behavior and only minimum behavior occurs, there will be an increased gap between the organizational goals and the attainment of the goals, resulting in closer supervision. Closer supervision leads to increased visibility of power relations, which in turn leads to an elevated level of interpersonal tension. The elevated tension leads to decreased effectiveness in the use of rules as a means of control. The more the organization is in a state of non satisfaction, the closer the supervision is likely to be. The more satisfactorily the organization is functioning, the less the need for supervision.

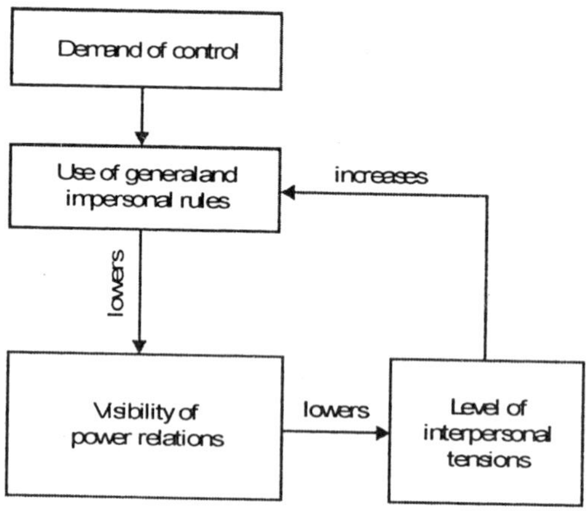

Figure 7.4. Anticipated consequences of demand for control

An analysis of the illustrated integrative concepts shows that their value lies in the fact that they order the less complex concepts and maintain an appropriate relationship between them. Thus the goal is still achieved by the administrative act of control. There is increased or decreased use of general and impersonal rules, resulting in lower or higher visibility of the power relations.

One must not assume that a knowledge of theory construction and a knowledge of standards for theory of educational administration insure that a complete body of knowledge called administration theory exists. Some say that it is in the initial stages of development, and others say that it does not exist. Most people will agree, however, that there have been and continue to be problems in the development of such a theory.

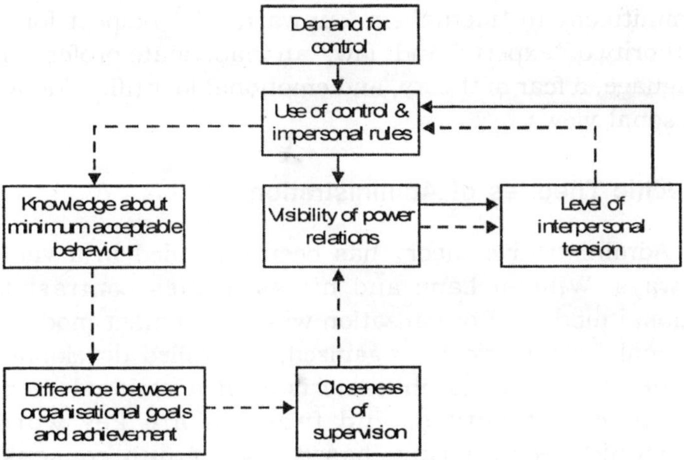

Figure 7.5. Unanticipated consequences viewed in the context of an administrator's anticipated consequences.

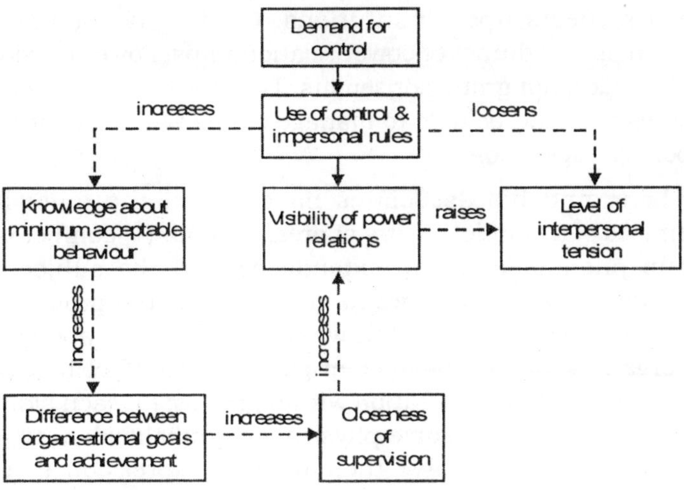

Figure 7.6. Unanticipated consequences of Administrative Act 19

Andrew Halpin and Arthur Coladarci have identified such problems as lack of a common understanding of the meaning of theory, a tendency to be too preoccupied with taxonomic methods, and a lack of certainty about the "precise domain" of administrative theory. Other problems identified are a commitment to "factualism," unwarranted respect for the authority of "experts" and "law," an inadequate professional language, a fear of theory, and emotional identification with personal views.

Specific Theories of Administration

Administrative theory has been classified in a variety of ways. William Lane and his associates contrast the rational models of organization with the conflict models. A rational, systematically organized, controlled development of the institution is characteristic of a rational model. Efficiency, structure, and function are key words. Harmonious equilibrium based upon group consensus prevails. That which disrupts the harmony is abnormal.

In contrast to rational models, the conflict models have as a common base the recognition of the presence of conflict and its effects upon institutions. Conflict is considered normal; is an adjunct of power relationships. Power provides social order, not group consensus. The effective and efficient manager should be able to manage conflict and turn it into a positive operation.

Lane and his associates have stated the following premises of a conflict theory of organization: (1) conflict is a group phenomenon and extends beyond the subjective attitudes of persons as group members; (2) the problem is not which side is "good," but what the fight is all about; (3) an organization is a balance of power; (4) conflict between groups promotes cooperation within groups; (5) each side in a conflict must have some physical or symbolic identity; (6) symbolic identities have their highest expression in the statements of ideologies justifying the group's position in the conflict; and (7) conflict nourishes a diversity of organizational goals and unplanned cleavages between departments which further compromise the original goals.

Conflicts are considered to be based upon group differences rather than individual ones. Differences may be racial, religious, goal-oriented, or even reflective of past group differences in viewpoint. Conflict does act as a stimulus, resulting in an effort to decrease the stimulus. Thus competition might occur with the ultimate result of achievement of institutional goals. Each group in the conflict must have an identifiable characteristic to give it visibility. When the characteristic disappears, the conflict disappears, even though it may not have been resolved. Conflict, in other words, must result in commonalities among members of the conflict group.

Griffiths uses a classification for administrative theory proposed by Frederick March and Herbert Simon which includes: (1) theories of conflict, that is, role conflict, personality conflict, and role-personality conflict; (2) theories of motivation in which the needs, drives, and motives of individuals are considered; and (3) theories of decision making in which man is considered as a rational being with certain limitations.

Motivational Theory

A specific theory of administration proposed by Chester I. Barnard considers organization as a cooperative system. This motivational type theory is representative of the rational model. It says that people act as they do because of their association with formal organizations, which may be defined as "that kind of cooperation among men that is conscious, deliberate, purposeful." Most cooperation fails because of factors outside the formal organization, and "survival of the organization depends upon the maintenance of an equilibrium of complex character in a continuously fluctuating environment of physical, biological, and social materials, elements, and forces, which calls for readjustment of processes internal to the organization."

The individual is a person and has properties which are: "(a) activities or behaviors arising from (b) psychological factors, to which are added (c) the limited power of choice, which results in (d) purpose." This individual has the choice of entering into a cooperative system based upon his own goals and the alternatives available to him. The organization is the key element in Barnard's theory of administration.

Barnard distinguishes between effective and efficient action by saying that an action is effective if it accomplishes its specific objective aim while it is efficient if it satisfies the motive of that aim. Individuals have biological characteristics which are limitations to be overcome by cooperation. From a sociological point of view, persons are regarded as "objects to be manipulated by changing the factors affecting them." Social factors in cooperation were identified by Barnard as (a) the interaction between individuals within a cooperative system; (b) the interaction between the individual and the group; (c) the individual as the object of cooperative influence; (d) social purpose and the effectiveness of cooperation; and (e) individual motives and cooperative efficiency.

The basic assumptions upon which Barnard built his theory are (1) the human being possesses a limited power of choice; (2) among the most important limiting factors in the situation of each individual are his own biological factors; (3) cooperation is a social aspect of the total situation and the social factors arising from it; (4) the persistence of cooperation depends upon two conditions, (a) its effectiveness and (b) its efficiency; (5) the survival of cooperation, therefore, depends upon two inter-related and inter-dependent classes of processes, (a) those which relate to the system of cooperation as a whole in relation to the environment, and (b) those which relate to the creation or distribution of satisfactions among individuals; and (6) the instability and failures of cooperation arise from defects in each of these classes of processes separately, and then from defects in their combination. The functions of the executive are those of securing the effective adaption of these processes.

There are two basic types of organization, formal and informal. A formal organization is a system of consciously coordinated activities of two or more persons. The elements of an organization are communication, willingness to serve, and common purpose. These elements serve to maintain internal equilibrium. Either effectiveness or efficiency is required for continued existence or maintenance of external equilibrium.

Informal organization is an "aggregate of the personal contacts and interactions and the associated groupings of people." Informal organizations are responsible for certain attitudes, habits, and institutions and also create conditions under which formal organizations may arise.

Informal organizations are made up of interactions between persons for personal reasons. They precede and arise out of formal organizations. An important function of informal organizations is communication. Other functions are cohesion and maintenance of individual integrity. In the informal organization there is usually a "Company Grapevine" for all types of communication which are not handled by the formal organization.

Barnard defines authority as "another name for the willingness and capacity of individuals to submit to the necessities of cooperative systems." Four conditions are to be met for the subordinate to assent to authority: (1) he can and does understand the communication; (2) at the time of his decision, he believes that it is not inconsistent with the purpose of the organization; (3) at the time of his decision he believes it to be compatible with his personal interest as a whole; and (4) he is able to mentally and physically comply with it. The whole aspect appears to be: will all of these fit within the mission of the organization?

Barnard explained that organizations would function under this theory of authority because of the concept of zones of indifference. Each individual has a zone of indifference for orders which are neither acceptable nor unacceptable. These orders will be accepted according to the degree to which inducements exceed the "sacrifices which determine the individual's adhesion to the organization."

Conflict Theory

A second specific theory of administration is Jacob W. Getzels's theory of administration as a social process. Getzels presents his theory in terms of a model of social behavior. This theory is representative of conflict theory.

Getzels views administration as the hierarchy of subordinate-super ordinate relationships within a social system. Functionally, this hierarchy of relationships is the center for allocating and integrating roles and facilities in order to achieve the goals of the social system. The functions are the responsibility of the super ordinate member of the hierarchy but only will be effective when accepted by the subordinate member. This interpersonal, social relationship is the core of the administrative process.

The social system is composed of two sets of independent but interacting phenomena: institutions with roles and expectations, and individuals with personalities and need-dispositions. The result of the interactions is called social behavior. Institutions, roles, and expectations comprise the nomothetic, or normative, aspect of activity in a social system. Individuals, personalities, and need-dispositions comprise the idiographic, or personal, aspect of activity in a social system.

Getzels uses the concept of selective interpersonal perception to account for the fact that some role incumbents understand very readily their mutual obligations and responsibilities, while others do so more slowly and sometimes not at all. When the two role incumbents understand each other, "their perceptions and private organizations of the prescribed complementary expectations are congruent." When the reverse is true, the term incongruent is used. Behavior, as seen in Getzels's model, is said to result from the individual's "attempt" to cope with an environment composed of patterns of expectations for his behavior in ways consistent with his own independent pattern of needs. The interpretation of the concept conflict is based upon the idea that sources of conflict in the model are role-personality, role, and personality. The entire concept that people are dealing with people generally forms the subordinate-superordinate relationships.

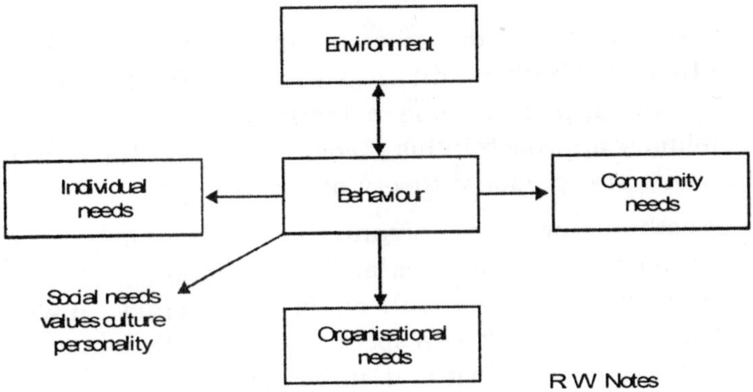

Figure 7.7. The interactions of behavior in a social system

Decision-Making Theory

The third specific administrative theory is identified as the decision making theory. Such theories often make up a part of theories placed in other categories. Decision making also is a concept in leadership theory. For the purposes of this discussion of administration theory, only a brief consideration will be given to decision-making theory.

Daniel Wren discusses Barnard's inclusion of decision-making theory under the "third executive function." He describes Barnard as viewing delegation as a decision involving ends and means to ends. The two facets to decisions are (1) analysis, or the search for "strategic factors" which would create the set or system of conditions necessary to accomplish the organization's purpose; and (2) synthesis, or the recognition of the interrelationships between elements or parts which together make up the whole system.

Several administration theorists equate decision making with the problem-solving process. Decision making is the process that one goes through in order to be able to pass judgement, solve a problem, and terminate a controversy. It is apparent that decision making can be called problem solving or other terms with the same connotation or relational meaning.

Robert Presthus describes organizations as miniature societies in which traditional social controls over the individual appear in sharp focus. He uses an inter-disciplinary approach in his theory, relying on Harry Stack Sullivan's interpersonal theory of psychiatry.

Presthus views large organizations as causing anxiety in their members. He defines large organization on the basis of Max Weber's model, the theory of bureaucracy, in which members tend to work with speed, precision, discretion, and technical know-how, without ambiguity or friction.

Presthus says that the large organization induces anxiety in its members simply because of its fundamental characteristics such as size, specialization, ordering by one's hierarchical position, attitude toward status, and amount of power in the hands of a few. Members accommodate the demands of the organization in three ways: upward mobility, indifference, and ambivalence. Those with upward mobility "enjoy organized life and have little difficulty making decisions in conflict situations because they accept the organization's values as decisives." The indifferent member does not compete for organization favors and develops his interests outside of the organization. His anxiety lessens because he is not involved in the "race for rewards." The ambivalent member cannot get along with authority and "cannot play the organization game." He gives priority to individual friendships above the good of the organization. This theory of organization considers man a rational being and discusses behavior within an organizational context. It includes consideration of conflict and motivation.

If a member utilizes much of his energies on the outside of the organization in a "moon lighting situation," there is little question about this activity being harmful to the organization; thus one of the administrative tasks is to analyze what is happening in the situation and try to avoid loss of important energies.

Systems Theory

A fourth theory of administration, the systems theory, is defined as a system of a complex of elements in mutual interaction. Systems theory is an organized manner of accomplishing objectives and goals. For example, in constructing a building one must start with the foundation before proceeding to assemble the walls and finally the roof.

Management theory deals with open systems which have many characteristics, including (1) having input and output; (2) having a tendency to maintain a steady state; (3) being self-regulating; (4) displaying equifinality (obtaining the same results from different initial conditions); (5) maintaining a steady state through "the dynamic interplay of subsystems operating as functional processes"; (6) maintaining a steady state partly through feedback; and (7) displaying progressive segregation. The system divides into a hierarchical order of subsystems which gain a degree of independence from each other.

A number of derived propositions regarding conditions affecting change emanate from the systems theory model. The major impetus for change in organizations is from the outside. The degree and duration of change is directly proportional to the intensity of the stimulus from the supra system. Change in an organization is more likely to occur if the successor to the chief administrator is from outside the organization than if he is from inside the organization. When change in an organization does occur, it will tend to occur from the top down, not from the bottom up. "Living systems" respond to continuously increasing stress first by a lag in response, then by an over compensatory response, and finally by catastrophic collapse of the system. The number of innovations expected is inversely proportional to the tenure of the chief administrator. This is one argument to change chief and other administrators over a period of years; for example, every five years. The more hierarchical the structure of an organization, the less the possibility of change. The more functional the dynamic interplay of subsystems, the less the change in organization.

Administrative Leadership Theories

A major component of administration is leadership. From the viewpoint of systems theory, leadership might be considered as a subsystem of systems administration. It could also be considered as a concept which becomes a part of the conceptual framework of administration theory. Leadership styles are definitely an important part of administrative theory.

Traditionally, the dimensions of leadership theory have been two in number, authoritarian and democratic. A third has been called laissezfaire. Authoritarian leadership is that which is associated with the bureaucratic organizational structure. Authority comes downward from the leader. He initiates decisions. He is the super ordinate and does not consult with the subordinates. The exact opposite dimension is the laissez-faire, or free-rein, type. This type is one in which the individual member is independent of the group and the leader. He makes his own decisions. He acts outside of the organizational structure.

The most favored dimension for some administrators is democratic leadership. This type is seen in a participative type of organization. Authority stems from the group. Group members participate in the decision-making process. Ralph Stogdill summarizes leadership types as follows: (1) "authoritative (dominator)," (2) "persuasive (crowd arouser)," (3) "democratic (group developer)," (4) "intellectual (eminent man)," (5) "executive (administrator)," and (6) "representative (spokesman)." The first three styles are extreme in nature, the more modern type of leadership style being that of situational leadership contingency management.

Stogdill surveyed the research done on leadership over the past forty years and categorized the definitions of leadership: (1) a focus of group processes, (2) personality and its effects, (3) the art of inducing compliance, (4) the exercise of influence, (5) an act or behavior, (6) a form of persuasion, (7) an instrument of goal achievement, (8) an effect of interaction, (9) a differentiated role, and (10) the initiation of structure.

A review of leadership theory indicates three phases in its development: scientific management, human relations, and revisionist. Three authors are named by Warren Bennis as revisionists—Robert McMurray, Chris Argyris, and Douglas McGregor. Although their specific approaches to leadership theory differ, "they all share a common concern for revising the naive, unsubstantiated, and unrealistic aspects of the human relations approach without sacrificing its radical departure from traditional theory."

Bennis describes McMurray's theory as one which indicates that "bottom-up management" is ideal but not possible because of the characteristics of managers as well as those of the "bureaucratic personality." "Benevolent autocracy" works and "is a method for making the best out of the worst." The individual's needs and the formal organization's demands (as they are presently defined) are basically incompatible. The outcome of this is frustration to the individual, manifested through defense mechanisms that ultimately lead to the attenuation of the organization's goals.

McGregor's theory, according to Bennis, contains two elements, "a collaborative relationship between superior and subordinate that takes full account of their interdependency and reality task considerations that focus on the work requirements.

Leadership theories may or may not be theories, but are attempts to gain an increasingly more sophisticated understanding of the nature of leadership. It is believed that characteristics of the individual and demands of the situation interact in such a manner as to permit one, or perhaps a few, person(s) to rise to leadership status. Groups become structured in terms of positions and roles during the course of member interaction. A group is organized to the extent that it acquires differentiated positions and roles. Leadership represents one or more of the differentiated positions in a group. The occupant of a leadership position is expected to play a role that differs from the roles of other group members. The expectancy reinforcement models seem best designed to explain the emergence and persistence of leadership in initially unstructured groups. They attempt to explain what leadership is and how it comes into existence. They do not explain who will emerge as a leader in any particular kind of situation.

Paul Hersey and Kenneth Blanchard have proposed a life-cycle theory of leadership in response to theories proposed by the Ohio State Leadership Studies of 1945 and in the "Managerial Grid" of Blake and Mouton. They feel that there is no one best leadership style, but that, since situations differ, so must leadership style. A three-dimensional model (relationship, task, effectiveness) was developed as a modification of the Ohio State two-dimensional model. The three-dimensional model illustrates the interaction between leadership style and the situation. When the style is appropriate to the situation, it is considered effective. Since effectiveness is determined by the interaction, there is no one best style, as the situation constantly changes.

The life-cycle theory of leadership attempts to provide the leader with some understanding of the relationship between an effective style of leadership and the level of maturity of one's followers. The emphasis will be on the followers. The theory states that as the level of maturity of one's followers continues to increase, appropriate leader behavior not only requires less structure (tasks) but also less and less socio-emotional support (relationships).

Two final points must be made. First, the domain of administration is considered general rather than specific. The theories discussed can be viewed from the aspect of administration in higher education as well as from the aspect of management in industry. Second, there is no one unified theory of administration at this time. Theories have been proposed from a variety of perspectives and, certainly, some are more scientific than others. At least theories are being suggested to provide a framework for the discipline of administration, thereby providing a research orientation.

Higher education has developed in numerous ways since the end of World War–II. Throughout the world, issues such as autonomy and accountability, the impact of technology, the growing role of markets and the privatization of higher education, the role of research and teaching, various efforts toward curriculum reform, and the massive expansion that has characterized higher education systems in most countries have all played important roles in the development of higher education. Universities are international institutions, with common historical roots, and at the same time are embedded in national cultures and circumstances. It is worthwhile to examine the contemporary challenges to higher education in comparative perspective, as most issues affect academe everywhere.

Expansion: Hallmark of the Postwar Era

Post-secondary education has expanded since World War–II in virtually every country in the world. The growth of post-secondary education has, in proportional terms, been more dramatic than that of primary and secondary education. Writing in 1975, Martin Trow spoke of the transition from elite to mass and then to universal higher education in the industrialized nations. While the United States enrolled some 30 percent of the relevant age cohort (18–21 year olds) in higher education in the immediate postwar period, European nations generally maintained an elite higher education system, with fewer than 5 percent of the population attending postsecondary institutions. By the 1960s many European nations educated 15 percent or more of this age group - Sweden for example, enrolled 24 percent in 1970, with France at 17 percent. At the same time, the United States increased its proportion to around 50 percent, approaching universal access. By the mid-1990s many European countries, including France, Germany, and the United Kingdom, enrolled around 50 percent of the relevant age group, and the proportion in the United States increased to three-quarters. While Europe and North America are now relatively stable, middle-income countries and countries in the developing world have continued to expand at a rapid rate.

In the Third World, expansion has been similarly dramatic. Building on tiny and extraordinarily elitist universities, higher education expanded rapidly in the immediate post-independence period. In India, enrollments grew from approximately 100,000 at the time of independence in 1947 to over 6.5 million in the 1990s – although India enrolls just 7 percent of the relevant age group. China enrolls a similar number, though this represents only 5 percent of its young people. China, especially, is engaged in a dramatic expansion program. Expansion in Africa has also been rapid, with the postsecondary student population growing from 21,000 in 1960 to 437,000 in 1983, but with growth stagnating in the 1990s as a result of the economic and political difficulties experienced by many sub-Saharan African countries.

❒❒❒

8

Systems Planning in Higher Education

Introduction

The process of systems administration is centered on a basic philosophy of administration, leadership styles and techniques, and mission of the institution. The process emphasizes that the institution will accomplish organizational goals by utilizing basic planning assumptions, objectives and goals, implementation processes, evaluation feedback, and modification or revision processes when necessary.

To initiate a systems approach to administration, an analytical approach must be utilized. This approach basically concerns analyzing the past and present strengths and weaknesses of the institution. A look at the past and present is necessary in order to plan effectively for the future. In addition, the process includes graphic portrayal (all items written or illustrated on paper) and checks and balances and is usually inter-disciplinary. Any given part of futuristic planning involves predictions and should be researchable, to determine if the planning and predictions are effective and efficient.

Further involved in the systems approach to administration are the following. The process should involve a "people approach" instead of a "mathematical approach," especially since administrators are working with students and individual professionals in an educational organization. The process will result in the teaming of people in the management leadership aspects. No one person has the expertise to do all of the planning for one organization. To accomplish planning processes, research, surveys, group meetings, interviews, and analysis of behavior of individuals will become involved. The process will require external and internal motivation of both subordinates and superordinates in planning, implementation, and evaluation tasks. The process of modeling, common flowcharting, PERT, and other graphic designs will be utilized to illustrate basic planning documents. The process will require continuous evaluation to determine effectiveness and efficiency factors of the plan, and "recycling" or modification where the plan has been inadequate. The process will include constant projecting and planning toward the future.

Definitions

Curriculum Flow Chart— An administrative flow chart for curriculum revisions. Suggestions gathered throughout the campus from students, department chairpersons, division chairpersons, deans, academic and administrative vice presidents form a planning cycle which imparts the system design to improve and assure proper operation and procedure. It keeps the process on target.

Quality Control Programs—A program of checks and balances along the system design to check the quality of the present administrative flow and project the quality of the future process. Brings the programs together for flow analysis.

Recycling— A function in systems design that returns the process to a given point in the system to pick up an inadequate procedure and cycle that procedure back through the flow of the system.

System— An analysis of the past and present strengths and weaknesses designed into an administrative flow developed on goals and objectives for the future success of the administrative procedure.

Systems Approach to Administration— A planning approach to administrative procedure that analyzes problems, organizes past and present processes, analyzes present priorities, writes general statements of goals and objectives in long-range terms, and states short-range objectives in order that long-range goals can be reached.

Initiating the Systems Approach to Administration

The important variables to initiate a long-range planning approach that involves quality control in an educational institution are: (1) analysis of past and present problems on a systematic basis; (2) analysis of the successes of past and present programs, concepts, individuals, groups, and organization; (3) analysis of past and present repetitions and omissions in any portion of the educational programs; (4) analysis of priorities for future planning in the educational organization; (5) writing general statements of goals defined as long-range priority items to be planned, implemented, accomplished, and evaluated; and (6) stating short-range objectives in order that long-range goals may be reached.

Historical Perspective on a Structure to Promote Planning and Implementing Changes on a Systematic Basis

During the 1970s, in a large college in the south-western part of the United States, an academic dean, who was the chief instructional administrator of the entire college promoted leadership when introducing his "Systems Approach to Administration." A model was first designed in connection with the campus and, more specifically, with the academic dean's position. This process was followed by involvement of division chairpersons, then department chairpersons, and finally involved faculty members.

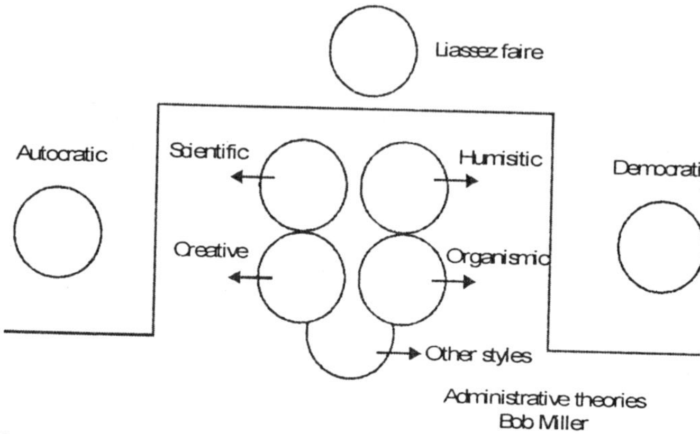

Figure 8.1. One-year objectives to accomplish long-range goals.

The dean had served in prior administrative positions in the college and on other campuses throughout the state and nation; he had given a great deal of thought and planning in regards to designing and implementing this Systems Approach to Administration model. Once the academic dean had been on the campus for about two months he began the process of putting the plan in action. Several systems approaches had been utilized previously in business and industry and had been implemented from the classroom teaching standpoint (a systems approach to instruction); however, such an approach had not been accomplished from an overall campus or administrative point of view. This specific college had not been involved in total long-range planning, which is a part of the systems approach. In fact, few systems approaches to administration are likely ever to be thoroughly completed in the educational domain. Generally speaking, administrative leaders are not well enough educated in management, not well enough organized, or will not take the effort to devise a complete system for planning. Until this type of process is accomplished it is doubtful whether most institutions will be successful in meeting organizational goals.

An aspect important to the entire Systems Approach to Administration is the need for flexibility at all stages of the process in order for programs to progress effectively. During initiation of the project the academic dean secured the services of a professional systems specialist. Together the two educators developed a model for an "Administrative Systems Approach." They felt that it was important to analyze the past in order to plan steps for the future. In addition, they must know how far they had progressed in order to project five or ten years in advance. Executives in business and industry believe that an organization cannot really be successful unless projections are made a minimum of ten years in advance. Although education institutions cannot plan to this extent, they can project a number of years in advance.

The concensus of recent administrative thinking is that if we project at least five years in advance, education will probably be moving in the right direction. There have been too many "hit and miss" programs in education. Somebody designing curricula or programs grabs an idea here and another there, never analyzing the overall picture of the educational program. This is what the Systems Approach to Administration and "Quality Control Programs" attempt to do. These approaches assist in bringing instructional items, concepts, generalizations, programs management, and organizational goals together. Several years ago at Cape Canaveral, Florida, the academic dean spent two weeks watching scientists construct space vehicles. On the campus of most modern colleges and universities there has been much discussion about long-range planning, quality control, development of priorities (especially for curriculum programs), staffing, facilities, financing, and innovations, as far as the five to ten-year approach is concerned. Unfortunately, there has been very little successful action or implementation. The aforementioned south-western college had, as an objective and goal, prevention of gaps or omissions, repetition, and duplication in the curriculum. Using the systems approach, or long-range planning, many attempts were made to influence students, instructors, department and division chairpersons, deans, the president, the chancellor and the community. If professionals are not familiar with the philosophy of the administration and institution, it is not likely that they will all be headed in the same direction to benefit the students. A complete analysis was attempted in this area or context of planning. Once educators and students know where they are trying to go and what they are trying to accomplish, they are more likely to reach their destination. Important to the "Systems Approach to Administration" are:

1. Assisting the instructor in the facilitation of learning with students. (Which is what the instructional program is all about.)
2. Assisting the faculty member with learning spaces for students.
3. Assisting the faculty member with learning resources. (What delivery system does it take to get the teaching job done effectively?)
4. Assisting the faculty member with instructional design.

Anything concerned with the Systems Approach to Administration should connect directly with the instructional design and learning of students, whether it be buildings, staff, budgets, or programs. A problem which exists in most institutions is the utilization of what is already on campus, for example materials, laboratory equipment, and technological devices. The use of community resources is also important. Educational institutions will probably never attain full utilization of all facilities and equipment on each campus and in the community; however, this is something that educators should constantly strive for in the systems approach.

Any project planned or implemented by a college or university should revolve around the student, whether it be evaluation, communicating program objectives, defining faculty responsibilities, resources and resource staff, off or on-campus facilities. Colleges should be organized to meet the needs of the community, state, and nation, whether they involve industry, business, education, culture, or recreation. Again, the number one concern should be the student. This concept cannot be over-emphasized.

Another aspect important to this philosophy is the correlation of instructional and student service programs. Programs under the academic dean and the dean of student services usually are not teamed together in most institutions. Both areas should integrate and complement each other. Complete correlation of instructional and student service programs is important for total educational development of the student.

Instructors should do their utmost to relate to the individual student. The instructor should know each student personally and *vice versa*. This prime objective provides for a most effective and efficient learning process.

This leads us back to the Systems Approach to Administration. The approach should involve people, not mathematical models. An effective and efficient administrator will delegate, trust, and hold accountable his subordinates. The program as stated previously was started by developing a model that took into account the past, present, and future of the college. For the past, the decision was made that the items of high priority were program analysis, content of subject area, organization of the institution, goals of the institution, individual faculty-administration conferences, departmental meetings, division meetings, and potential professional improvement areas. Need analyses of teaching techniques and resources employed, and need assessment for the students were conducted. Also analyzed to some extent were the resources available to the college. Several research studies had been made of instructional costs per student, per semester, and per year. Short and long-range objectives and goals were analyzed. Progress had been made in regards to instructional effectiveness, faculty evaluation procedures, and campus evaluation. None of these items were developed in any depth at that particular time.

The next task became, then, to analyze what was occurring at the present time in the educational process. A start was made by analyzing community and college programs, faculty objectives, division chairpersons roles, budgets, department chairpersons commonalities and relationships, faculty roles, materials requisitioned, materials needed, and materials that had been received and inventoried, in addition to those items which had been accomplished in the past. It became apparent that to progress the organization would have to project toward the future. Items that had to be analyzed in depth for the future were: (1) educational programs by subject areas; (2) faculty evaluation procedures; (3) total organization of faculty and their relationships with students and administration; (4) faculty, student, and administrators strengths, weaknesses, and potentials; (5) program and institutions evaluation procedures being utilized at the time and modifications needed to implement merit pay; (6) buildings and facilities; and (7) soft spots in management and leadership.

The Systems Approach to Administration as it was perceived in this plan is a device which prevents omissions as well as repetition in the curriculum and programs. It is believed that this plan influenced students, teachers, department and division chairpersons, district administrators, and the entire community. The systems approach also involved long-range planning, quality control, priorities, staffing, facilities, programs, financing, and innovations. To accomplish specific goals, the decision was made to define roles for personnel and staff. Objectives of the educational programs on the campus also had to be defined in detail. Therefore, the question was asked, What

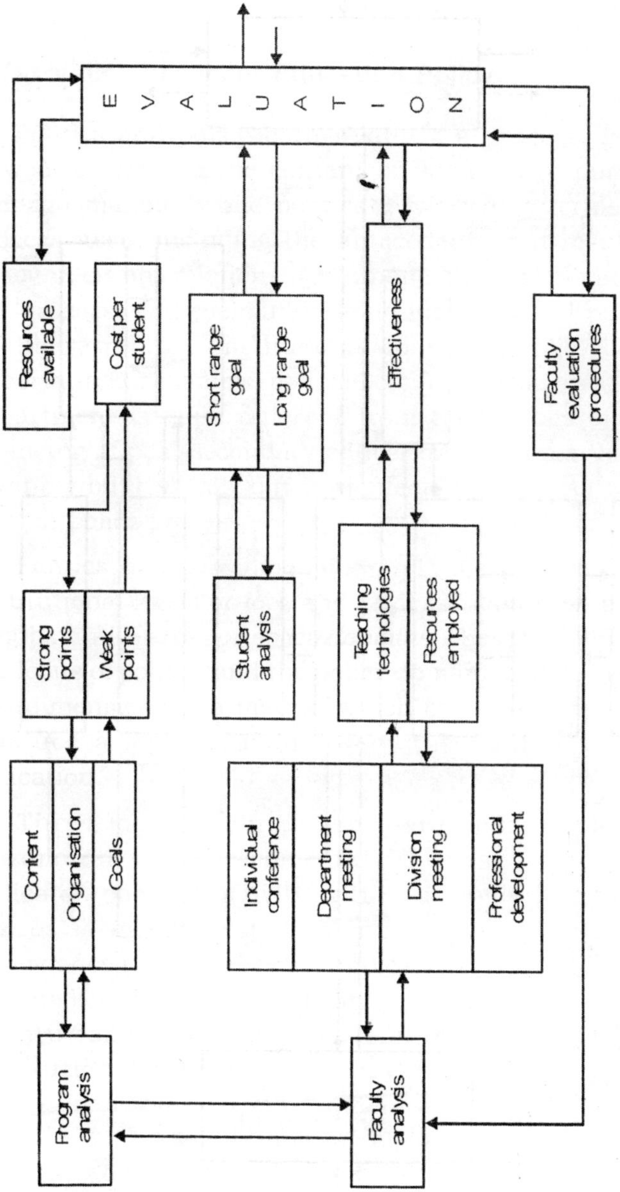

Figure 8.2. Systems Approach to Administration: Past

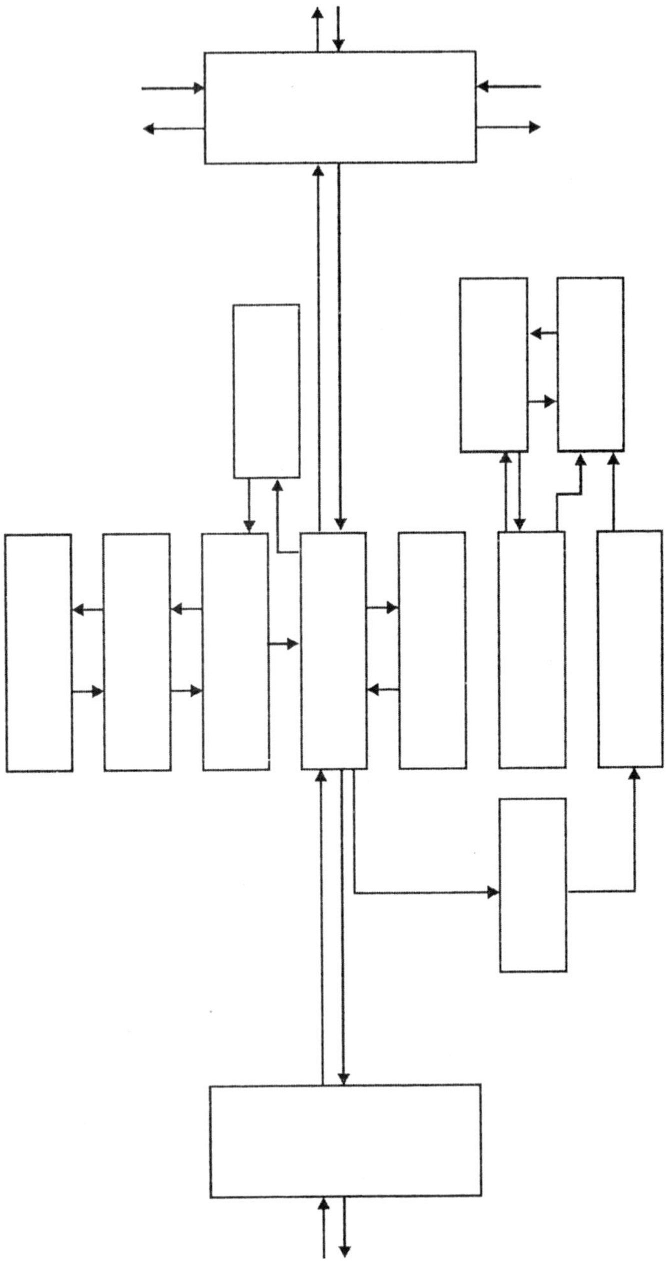

Figure 8.3. Systems Approach to Administration: Present

are the goals and objectives of the campus? Samples of the answers received are: an open-door policy; university parallel programs; technical occupational programs; continuing education or adult education; instructor and professional counseling of students; students do not become numbers on a computer; each instructor should know the students personally; the college should meet the needs of business, industry, education, cultural development, and recreational activities; and the student is number one in priority.

A sample of campus program goals and objectives involved such items as meeting the individual needs of students, correlating instructional and student services programs, utilizing campus and community resources, and having the instructor do his best to relate to each individual student no matter what the student's potential might be. The job of educators was to provide the most effective and efficient instruction possible. Next the academic dean had to define his role in relation to the president, division and department chairpersons, and instructional faculty. The whole process can be reduced to the basic areas described below.

Academic dean (role or job description): (1) supervises the total instructional program of the campus through leadership of division and department chairpersons and faculty members; (2) constantly evaluates the total instructional program; and (3) constantly feels the pulse of all facets involving faculty and programs. This is accomplished in three basic ways: delegate, trust, and hold these same individuals accountable for results.

The next area for task definition is that of the division chairpersons.

The academic dean cannot delegate away his responsibility on a legal basis. Even though many tasks are delegated, the dean still is legally responsible for these tasks.

Division chairpersons (role or job description): (1) supervise the total instructional programs of all departments within the division (includes planning, organization, supervision, administration, implementation, and evaluation) for department chairpersons, instructors, and students; and (2) provide leadership in production of effective and efficient syllabi.

Supervision and evaluation include visitation in classrooms; two-way, positive communication with instructors; student evaluation, and self evaluation. Additional included items were: evaluation by video and audiotapes; interaction analysis; staff development in evaluation procedures; professional development; continual evaluation of classroom instruction; curriculum revision; flexible scheduling; correlation of all subject materials and instruction; advanced placement with credit; the "teacher and staff" concept (which involves the master teacher, instructor, teacher assistant, teacher aids, and media technician); inter-divisional team teaching; team teaching (modified/non modified programs); and released time for instructors for innovative educational programs (reduced load).

Department chairpersons (roles or job description): (1) assist in preparation of the college catalog, curriculum brochures, faculty policies and procedures manual; (2) assist in planning professional development programs for the department faculty; (3) coordinate work with the bursar, registrar, bookstore, and student service personnel that applies to the department; (4) assist in the selection of department full and part-time staff; (5) recommend policy to the division chairperson; (6) conduct departmental long-range planning; and (7) constantly feel pulse of students and faculty within the department.

Sample faculty responsibilities also were defined on the campus.

Faculty (role or job description): (1) utilize community activities and facilities; (2) place less emphasis on textbook teaching than on supplementary and learn-by-doing techniques; (3) emphasize meaning and understanding of

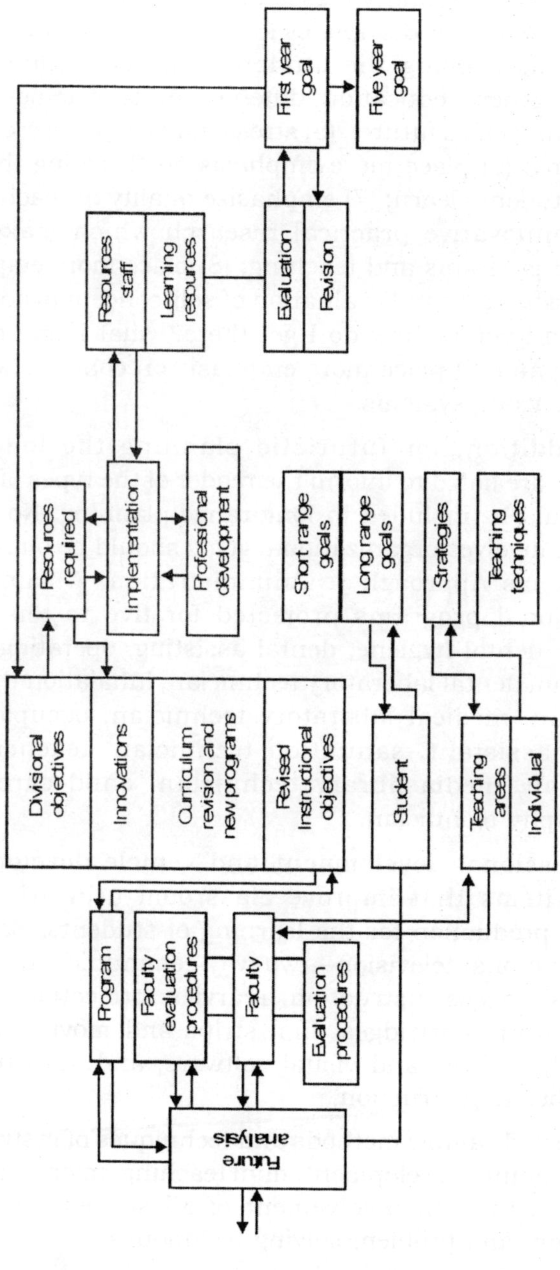

Figure 8.4. Systems Approach to Administration: Future roles differed from that of the Division Chairpersons and the Academic Dean.

concepts (involves and stresses understanding of structure and purposes of the disciplines for students); (4) curriculum design emphasizing the student, society, community-centered/general education, different levels of achievement (present as well as future); (5) stress importance of creativity in learning; (6) place more emphasis on "learning theory," or how students learn; (7) emphasize quality in teaching as well as innovative practical research which makes for improved programs and teaching; (8) place more emphasis on understanding and evaluation of self-concept (who am I? where am I going? how do I get there? what is my role in society?); and (9) place more emphasis on contributions to students' value systems.

In addition, for futuristic planning the following examples are listed to inform the reader of the types of items that should be included in long-range planning. No single area that involves organizational goals should be omitted in the Systems Approach to Administration. A sample of occupational programs projected for five to ten years includes: dental hygiene, dental assisting, operating room technician, dental laboratory technician, inhalation therapy technician, medical laboratory technician, occupational therapy assistant, sanitation technician, teacher aide technician, media library technician, child care, and photography technician.

Professional development and vehicle development include items that improve classroom utilization and software production for the learning of students. Samples are: educational television—two-way communication; video tape; dial access instruction; rearview projection; 8 mm single-concept cartridges; film strips and movies; slides, overhead, opaque, and visual software; and auto tutorial approaches to instruction.

Projected sample methods and techniques of instruction include: inquiry development, mini teaching, microteaching, dyadic interaction, involvement of all students in class discussion, and problem-solving techniques.

Sample buildings and facilities that have been developed on the drawing board include: academic classroom building, auditorium, pods for team teaching, remedial diagnostic center for learning disorders, multimedia center, addition to faculty office building, technical-vocational building, model child-care center, and learning styles mall.

Another part of the systematic approach developed for the campus is a curriculum flowchart or curriculum revision process. Curriculum and instruction revision begins in October on the campus. Students and faculty make suggestions or recommendations in written form for further consideration during the revision process. The recommendations then go to the department chairperson, who modifies changes, makes additions to, or approves the proposal. This process is continued at each administrative level in the curriculum development sequences. Forms developed by campus and district officials for curriculum approval contain questions such as: What is the cost for staffing, multimedia classrooms, and other items required of the budget? What is the rationale or justification for the course or particular program? What do community environmental needs require for the future? How many students will be enrolled each semester?

From the department chairperson, the proposals go to the division chairperson. In this system an "open hearing," the date for which is set by the academic dean, is scheduled once the division chairpersons have accumulated all proposals from the department chairpersons. All interested students or faculty members are invited to this hearing, and anyone in the community may attend. The deans and president are not present at this conference because they do not want to influence decisions related to curriculum at this time. During these hearings, no one complains about other divisions' curriculum changes. Participants may make points, ask questions, have general discussions; but if anyone opposes some curriculum change that affects his or her division or department, he or she submits a written protest to the academic dean. The academic dean invites this person to the hearing of the division chairperson who proposed the curriculum change. The division chairperson and the academic dean converse on a one-to-one basis and go over all the proposals for the division. Division chairpersons justify proposals with rationales. The educator making the written protest is invited to present his or her argument and rationale before the academic dean. A number of questions are asked, and a defense of the proposals is carried on. The academic dean invites the dean of student development and the dean of learning resources to these hearings so that they may be informed regarding any programs that affect their administrative areas.

After these curriculum proposals are approved or rejected by the academic dean, the two or more academic deans of the different district campuses meet with the campus presidents and make their recommendations to the presidents on a face-to-face basis. Once the proposals are given to the presidents, the presidents modify (with approval of the academic dean) and submit them to the chancellor. The chancellor then makes recommendations to the board of trustees and to the various state agencies involved in the approval process.

Strategies for Working within the System

In the process of selling the Systems Approach to Administration to subordinate division chairpersons, an unusual technique or strategy was utilized. It was stated earlier in this chapter that steps taken included: studying the quality control system and engineering of space vehicles at Cape Canaveral, Florida; hiring a consultant and building a past, present, and future model; and explaining the model and selling the concept to the campus president.

The past, present, and future model was then presented by the academic dean and the consultant to division chairpersons for their consideration. After the presentation, there was considerable pro and con discussion of the major concepts involved. Three of the division chairpersons were convinced this was an excellent plan. Two or three of the chairpersons were definitely against the Systems Approach to Administration model. Several other administrators attended these division meetings on a weekly basis. Those attending and participating in the meetings included the dean of student services, dean of learning resources, registrar, bursar, and director of the computer center. The purpose for their attendance was to integrate all aspects of the organization, especially for support services of the educational program.

Convincing the Chancellor

The president of the campus was contacted and his permission sought for the academic dean to inquire as to whether or not the chancellor would be interested in long-range planning. The president agreed that the dean should contact the chancellor and present the overall plan to him. The dean appeared before the chancellor and presented the plan in detail. The chancellor was positive toward the entire planning model. The dean then asked if the chancellor would be willing to spend seven to nine days on the campus to have the long-range plans presented orally and visually to him.

Models to be presented were those of the academic deans, the president, and six division chairpersons. The chancellor agreed to this, and to bring along the vice chancellor for financial affairs, the vice president for research and development, and any other staff members that he might deem appropriate.

Facing the Division Chairpersons

The academic dean returned to the campus and related the information to the president. The next week during the

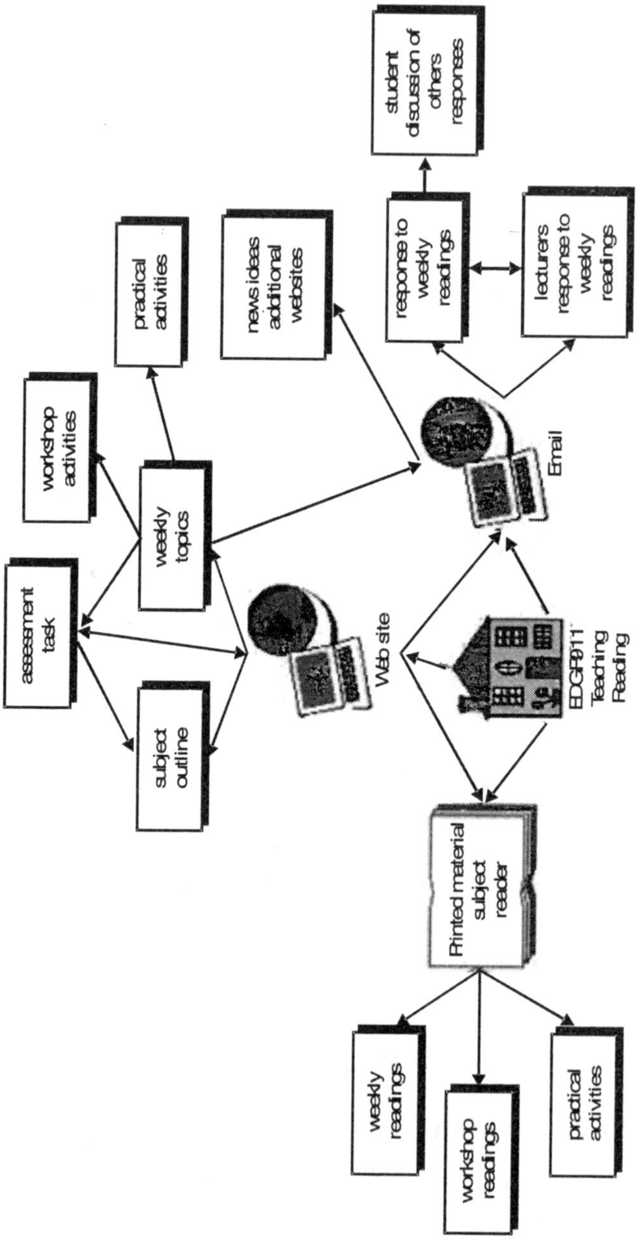

Figure 8.5. Sample of flowchart curriculum revision

division meeting, the chairpersons were given the following notice.

Six months from now the Chancellor, the Vice Chancellors and their staffs will come to the campus for seven to nine days to analyze your "Systems Approach to Administration," (long-range planning models) as well as the models of the President and the Academic Dean. The models will be presented by each administrator, both orally and visually. For the first time in each of our lives, we will have the opportunity to present total information on the past, present and future of education for students on this campus. The Chancellor will react to those things he sees as strength and weaknesses of our plans, and will make suggestions for future improvement. Samples of items which will be projected for the future are as follows:

1. Educational Programs
    A. University Parallel
    B. Occupational
    C. Adult and Continuing Education
    D. Community Services
2. Professional development and in service
3. Methods and techniques for instruction
4. Buildings and facilities to house education programs
5. Staffing for educational programs
6. Cost of financing educational programs
7. Curriculum flowcharts
8. How programs will be evaluated
9. Software and hardware for educational programs

Needless to say, when the division chairpersons found out that the chancellor and president were willing to participate and provide leadership for the plan, a new emergence of motivation took place.

After the division meeting, specific instructions and information were given to each division and the president in regard to time frame, support services for media, and printing. It was also pointed out that a model of each division's plan would be placed along with those of the president and academic deans, for display in the foyer of the administration building. Each division would write its plans and place the written plans in a pocket on its specific model.

Developing Individual Models

During the next six months, planning and production occurred everywhere from the president's office all the way down to each division office. Because departments and faculty were involved, the fever of planning became contagious. Even department and faculty members began to place long-range planning charts on bulletin boards and walls in their buildings. Everyone throughout the campus seemed to be in on the planning process. Eventually the time came for the appearance of the chancellor and his staff.

The System: A Look to the Future

Education should cause a student to know what he has not known before, to think about facts or ideas he hitherto has not contemplated, and to develop certain new attitudes, abilities, and modes of behavior. Unless education brings about some or all of these changes, it serves no real purpose. In the field of education, therefore, a system should serve the function of more effectively and more efficiently bringing about change in students.

Systems Approach to Instruction

A course or program must meet the needs of society and/or the individual. Needs are in a state of flux, therefore, the program must adapt to reflect this constant change. A developmental mode and delivery system must be utilized to assure that the product of the program is trained to perform in a changing societal situation.

The four basic elements of a systems approach, as shown in figure, are: *input*—the capacity and interest of the student, plus the needs of industry; *output* the student's terminal behavior; *resources*—institutional personnel, media, texts, etc.; and *operations*—the course or program. Attached to each of these elements and relating all four elements is *feedback*.

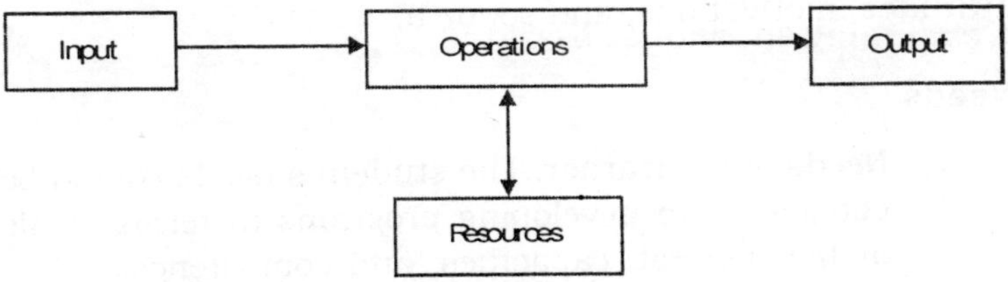

Figure 8.6. Basic elements of a systems approach

Components of the System

This section describes in detail the components of the system illustrated in figure 8.7.Society. Society establishes, controls through an elected board, and provides the funds for the educational institution.

Resources: Other institutions of society and industry are resources for the educational program. These resources provide facilities for work experience, consultant and advisory personnel, and an economics input.

Institutional management: Management is the professional staff selected by the controlling agent to administer the policies and goals of the educational institution. The institutional management contributes to the education model by: (1) establishing institutional goals and objectives based on its educational philosophy; (2) providing the educational facilities, auxiliary services, and financial support for programs; and (3) appointing qualified faculty and staff who reflect the goals and objectives of the institution.

Faculty: The faculty is the professional staff whose responsibility is to analyze and develop the various components of the model. They serve as the managers of learning.

Learner: The learner is the consumer of the model and is its expected product.

Learner capacities and competence: Characteristics of the learner consist of knowledge, skills, abilities, attitudes, motivations, and so forth.

Needs

1. Needs of the learner. The student's needs should be considered in developing programs in terms of his or her interest, capacities, and competence.
2. Societal needs. The need for a course or program can be assessed in terms of national, state, and community manpower demands. An additional need could be for fulfilling the general education or cultural interest of society. The educational institution must constantly assist society in assessing its own needs.
3. A positive answer to the following questions is necessary before a decision about curriculum development is made.

Can well-qualified faculty be obtained?

Will suitable space for classrooms, laboratories, and shops be available?

Can tools, instruments, and specialized equipment of high quality be provided in sufficient quantity?

Will the budget permit expenditures for replacement of worn-out and obsolescent equipment?

Can coordinating, placement, and guidance services be provided?

Are students with the necessary ability and interest available in sufficient numbers?

Will all these factors result in a program that will satisfy student and community needs at a reasonable unit cost?

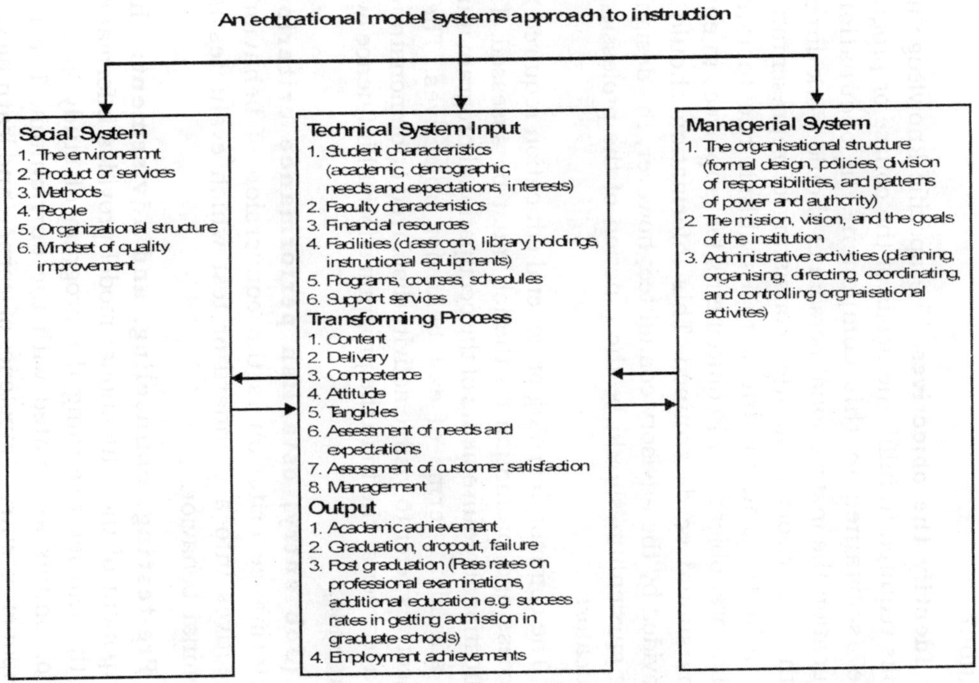

Figure 8.7. An educational model systems approach to instruction

Can the institution sustain the program for a five- or ten-year period?

Can the manpower demand not adequately be accomplished by other programs in the region, state, or nation?

Identify the objectives: The specific knowledge and skills required to fulfill the needs of the course or program are ascertained in this component. In occupational education the instructional personnel should work directly with an advisory committee consisting of representatives of industry and business to establish the terminal behavioral objectives. Requirements for employees in entry jobs should be determined. This information should be provided by the advisory committee; however, the design of the curriculum should be the function of the professional educators.

The common learning or general education required for success and promotion on the job must be assessed. The educational requirements of the occupational program must be stated in terms of exit behavior objectives. These objectives refer to visible activity displayed or demonstrated by a learner at the time the program's formal influence over him ends.

(Job entry) establish performance criterion: Performance criterion is the conversion of behavioral objectives into a standard or test which evaluates the terminal behavior.

Pre-testing, counseling, and advisement: This component of the educational model provides information for the learner regarding the program of study and the opportunities associated with the curriculum. The two components, entry competence of learner, and learning style of learner, are established from data produced in the pre-testing, counseling, and advisement component. This component also interacts with the basic studies and/or developmental activities component.

Basic studies and/or developmental activities: Data may indicate that a learner has a general educational weakness and should be counseled into the basic studies program as an attempt to strengthen his or her general competence and improve his or her learning style. If the learner demonstrates a weakness in a particular area (mathematics, English, reading, and so on), remedial or developmental activities should be provided for repairing that area.

Entry competence of learner: Pre-testing reveals the input, or entry, capabilities of the learner. These capabilities are then utilized in determining the learning task required by the program. The entry competence also provides information pertaining to the starting point for the learner in the program and may lead to advanced standing or course waiver in the curriculum.

Learning style of learner: Additional data indicated by pre-testing is the learning style of the learner. This information is useful in studying the learning task.

Analyze the required learning task: The performance criterion is what the learner is expected to exhibit in the output component (achievement of performance criterion). Analysis of learning tasks identifies the learning required to enable the learner to demonstrate the performance task.

Intellectual learning task: The behavior objectives in the cognitive domain are analyzed as the intellectual learning tasks. These tasks involve mental and intellectual processes (memory, understanding, problem solving generalization, concept, and so forth).

Emotional learning task: Emotional learning tasks stem from the affective domain of behavioral objectives. These learning tasks are associated with the feelings and attitudes of the learner.

Manipulative learning task: Manipulative learning tasks are those requiring motor skills that primarily utilize muscular coordination. These tasks stem from the behavioral objectives in the psychomotor domain.

Learning Theory—Strategies—Media: The concern in these components is the identification of everything that must be done by the components to attain the learning task. One must consider the various theories of learning; the strategies, methods, media, and other resource materials that can be utilized in accomplishing the learning tasks. In this phase our interest is in the organization and selection of program content along with the various alternatives to accomplishing the learning experiences.

Package the program: Packaging the program is the final organization of the program content into different courses along with the selection of instructional approaches and resource materials from the various alternatives. In this component catalog course descriptions are written, detailed course syllabi are constructed, and software materials are developed.

Conduct the learning activities: Scheduling the learning activities involves the decision of when (dates and time), where (location), and by whom (assignment of instructor) these activities will occur. Students must be enrolled and formal instruction be conducted.

Evaluation and feedback: Evaluations are made for the purpose of determining if the objectives of the model are being achieved and if any adjustments to the model are required to improve the achievement of those objectives. If a learner is able to demonstrate proficiency with performance criterion, then he moves into the achievement of performance criterion component and becomes a product of the model. Feedback, or quality control, in the model assists the designer in adjusting or reassessing: (1) needs of the learner and society; (2) inputs of societal resources, institutional management, and faculty; (3) objectives of the program and the job entry performance criterion; (4) entry competence and learning style of the learner resulting from the pre-testing and counselling; and (5) required learning task of the course or program along with the selection of the most effective and economical instructional approach in meeting these tasks.

Achievement of performance criterion: The learner reaches this component by being able to exhibit an output performance relative to the terminal behavior objectives of the course or program. The learner is thus a product of the educational model.

Follow-up studies: Follow-up studies provide feedback into the model after a product has graduated or completed the course or program. Studies should be conducted at specific intervals after the project's completion date.

Department of Basic Studies

Philosophy General

1. The Basic Studies program attempts to combine remedial skill education with college level cognitive and affective curricula.
2. The Basic Studies program may be viewed as a service department for the campus insofar as it prepares some of its students for success in A.A. and A.S. programs.
3. The Basic Studies program fosters the philosophy of the open door by providing a success niche for students who may find little success (initially at least) in other programs and courses.

Specific Basic Studies allows students to:

1. realistically assess themselves.
2. enrich their inter-personal experiences.
3. have a successful educational experience, especially where Basic Studies is the student's educational experience.
4. obtain a general educational foundation.

Five-Year Projection (Case Study)

Basic Studies is five content areas plus reading. It tries to take the relevant and make a general education for its students :

1. Greater emphasis on reading skills in the content areas; this emphasis will continue if it is found by evaluation in the succeeding years to be effective.
2. Greater cognizance of the affective content of our teaching; this emphasis will continue in the direction of humanizing education if it is found beneficial for our students and program.
3. Summer program to be evaluated for continuation or expansion.
4. Greater ecological emphasis in the content areas; this will continue until the environment is safe.
5. By the end of the second year portions of all the content areas will be packaged; further packaging will depend on evaluation of the packaging concept and of the individual packages themselves.
6. By the end of the second year, we will have prepared pre and post-tests for a majority of the content areas. The data gathered from this will be used as a partial basis of program evaluation which will become continuous as soon as we have the measuring instruments and time. These should be refined in the future.
7. Development of a public relations program to reach students, community, and college, to continue through the life of Basic Studies.
8. We will try to refine the criteria for selection of Basic Studies students; hopefully, by better identification techniques we should increase the enrollment to a number approaching 180-200. This would of course mean that we should need two Basic Studies teams by the second academic year. Like so many of the

items in this list, refinement of screening techniques is an ongoing process, as it has been in the past.

9. We would like to see the possibility of scheduling one large lecture period per week per class; this desire continues through the years until it is fulfilled, or perceived as no longer necessary.
10. A progress report should be written at the end of the first year; then, every two years.
11. By the third year, a two-year general education program should be instituted as part of the continuing search for the successful placement of our students here at the college.
12. After the first academic year, the emphasis in this document will be none save for the note that most, if not all, of items 1-11 are merely ways of defining what should be done in the Basic

Studies program: Items 1-11 are thus continuous in that evaluation, and feedback will take place with respect to them in the second through fifth years and beyond.

Department of Behavioral Occupations

Purpose

Improvement of instruction is basic to the rationale for the establishment of programs within the Department of Behavioral Occupations. Our role is to train para-professionals for an educational setting or for organizations that give full or part-time care of children. This may be in a public or private setting or in the educational program of business or industry.

The use of para-professionals in educational settings is in its infant stage, and indications are that we are witnessing the beginning of a booming era. Emphasis on individualized instruction, early childhood education, new state legislation, the U.S. president's call for adequate care for children of working mothers, new dimensions in education such as differentiated staffing, plus a growing shortage of money present a convincing picture for training people to meet these manpower needs.

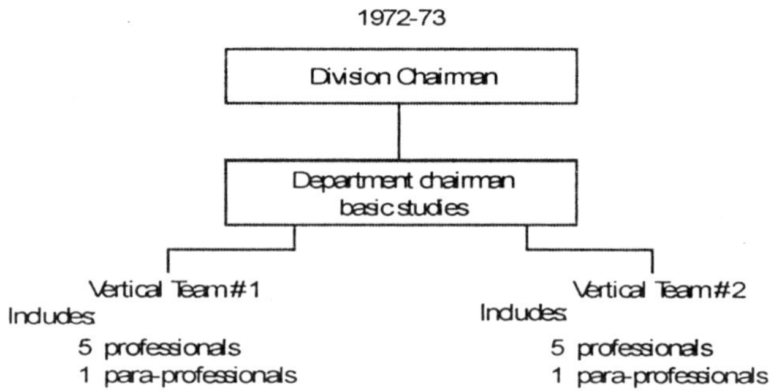

Figure 8.8. Department of behavioral occupations

If we are to properly train our students, we must have adequate space, equipment, supplies, and staff. Otherwise we will only continue the mediocrity that is all too prevalent in our current educational settings. This department shall strive to provide the maximum in learning and to develop within the student:

1. An understanding of the basic philosophy of modern education.
2. Knowledge and understanding of child growth and development including the physical and psychological needs of all children.
3. Knowledge and understanding of the importance of the family and parent-child relationships and interaction: the place of the young person in his family and culture.
4. Knowledge and understanding of a desirable working relationship as a member of a team.
5. A true understanding of the role of the para-professional.

Objectives

The following specific objectives have been adopted and will apply to the named program which operates within the Department of Behavioral Occupations.

Child Development Programs:

1. To provide the student with an understanding of his role and responsibilities as a primary caring person on the child development team in a day-care facility or a full-time care facility.
2. To familiarize the student with the basic qualities desired in an ideal child development person.
3. To teach the student proper methods of job management as related to the structure and service provided by the particular child development facility.

Teacher Assistant Program:

1. To enable student to be proficient in performing routine clerical tasks common to a classroom teaching situation.
2. To instruct the student in techniques and methods of assisting the teacher in classroom activities.
3. To instruct the student in the preparation and reproduction of instructional materials.
4. To familiarize the student with audio-visual equipment common to classroom instruction; to teach the student how to properly use the equipment.
5. To familiarize the student with routine library skills associated with the acquisition, organization, preparation, and preservation of library materials.
6. To provide instruction in the supervision of pupil activities outside the classroom.

Instructional Media Technician:

1. Exhibit appropriate utilization techniques and operating procedures for the various types of equipment.
2. Develop administrative skills in the various functions of an educational media program.
3. Prepare graphics, transparencies, still and motion pictures.

4. Exhibit appropriate utilization techniques associated with the acquisition, organization, preparation, distribution, and preservation of different types of media.

Department Goals

The first departmental goal is to develop curricula in the occupations that will be effective in the training of personnel to meet future certification requirements of state agencies :

1. Programs within this department have been established to train para-professionals either for an educational setting, residential homes, or for educational programs in business and industry.
2. As the curriculum continues to be developed, methods for effective teaching will have to be determined.
3. Liaison with state agencies, local agencies, and business and industry has been and must continue to be established. Personnel from these agencies must be utilized in planning curricula. Likewise, we should consider proper utilization of students we train and work with these agencies in effectively utilizing para-professionals.

To fully implement our behavioral occupations programs, plans must be formulated. Public schools, private day-care centers, residential homes, and business and industrial settings are and will continue to be utilized. However, the college will have to furnish adequate facilities for its part of the training:

1. Special day-care facilities will be needed in addition to classroom space.
2. Equipment for such a facility will be needed.
3. Additional laboratory space will be needed for the Instructional Media Technician Program.
4. Equipment—in addition to that utilized by the Learning Resource Center—will be needed.

5. A model day-care preschool program must be planned and implemented.
6. Additional teaching materials will need to be developed and/or commercially purchased.

To fully meet the needs of the community, it will be necessary to go into the inner city so that we may also train parents of the children that the para-professionals will be serving.

Five-Year Projection

A. Proposed Projects:

1. Further development of program for teacher assistants:
   a. Completing syllabi for courses in this program.
   b. Evaluating courses which have been taught.
   c. Exploring the possibility of redirecting one course in program and allowing it to be used as a practicum.
   d. Exploring possibilities of providing an opportunity for students to do further branching in program; allowing them to specialize in particular areas so that they might be better equipped to serve as assistants. Areas of specialization might include: Serving as assistants to counselors, special education, english, math, business, foreign language, and so forth.
   e. Planning and conducting a summer workshop for aides, assistants, teachers, and administrators from area schools. The purpose of such a workshop would be to promote the effective utilization of aids and assistants.
   f. Developing selective type criteria for admitting students to program.
   g. Contracting with students for work in particular courses.

2. Further development of program in child development (child care):
   a. Completing syllabi for courses in this program.
   b. Evaluating courses that have been taught.
      - Exploring avenues for recruitment of students.
      - Developing guidelines for a model day-care pre-school program which would be operated in the Child Development Center.
      - Contracting with students for work in particular courses.
3. Further development of Instructional Media Technician Program:
   a. Developing syllabi for courses taught in this program.
   b. Evaluating courses which have been taught.
   c. Exploring possibilities for recruitment of students; developing selective type criteria for admitting students to program.
   d. Adding additional equipment this year to update present laboratory.
   e. Packaging portions of some of the courses required in program.
   f. To attempt to have an open lab so that students may utilize equipment and facilities at their convenience.
   g. To contract with students for work in particular courses.

Additional Staff Requirements

First Year

1. 1 FTE (Full-Time Equivalent) coordinator of Instructional Media Technician Program.
2. 1 FTE para-professional—to be used to man open lab as well as to help in other areas.

A. Proposed Projects:

1. To provide training for people of the inner cities in the areas of child and family management. (Initially, we would go into the inner city to do this training.)
2. To begin concentrated effort of software development for all three programs within the department. This would be in the form of audio tapes, slides, transparencies, videotapes, films, printed materials, etc.
3. To explore possibilities of adding another program for training para-professionals. This program would be added for the purpose of training auxiliary personnel in social casework. This would necessitate a study conducted by the Office of Program Development to determine the feasibility of such a program.
4. To study the possibility of a core curriculum for the three programs now in operation in the Behavioral Science Department. Studies currently being conducted by the Texas Education Agency indicate there is some thought being given to including Early Childhood Education under education rather than home economics.

Additional Staff Requirements

Second Year

1. 1 FTE instructor who should qualify to teach in two of the three programs (Teacher Assistant and Child Development).
2. 1 FTE para-professional to be used in Teacher Assistant and Child Development programs.
3. 1 FTE secretary.

Third Year

A. Proposed Projects:

1. To design and equip a media laboratory in a facility that would provide adequate space for a class of

twenty-five students.

a. *Cost:* approximately $50,000.

b. *Size:* 2,200 square feet plus 200 square feet for office and storage: (1) 900 square feet classroom space, (2) 600 square feet equipment lab, (3) 1,200 square feet production lab, (4) 2,000 square feet TV studio, (5) 400 square feet individualized space for preview and recording (10' × 10' cubicles), and (6) 3 offices and conference room.

c. Cost of supplies would depend to a large degree on the number of students involved in programs.

Additional Staff Requirements

Third Year

1. 1 FTE instructor who would qualify to teach in Teacher Assistant and Media Technician programs.
2. 1 FTE para-professional.

Fourth Year

A. Proposed Projects:

1. To build and equip a child development laboratory that would provide adequate space for caring for thirty children.

   1,000 square feet indoors, 2,500 square feet outdoors.)

B. Additional Staff Requirements

1. 2 FTE instructors.
2. 3 FTE para-professionals

Fifth Year

A. Proposed Projects:

1. To conduct a pilot project on nutritional needs of children.
2. To fully implement child development laboratory.
3. To develop criteria for ongoing evaluation of child development laboratory.
4. To do additional packaging where studies have indicated a need.

B. Additional Staff Requirements

1. 1 FTE instructor.

Department of Developmental Studies

Purpose

1. To reinforce skills (such as reading comprehension, vocabulary development, study skills, basic writing skills, and written composition) that are needed in order for the student to succeed in every area of college work.

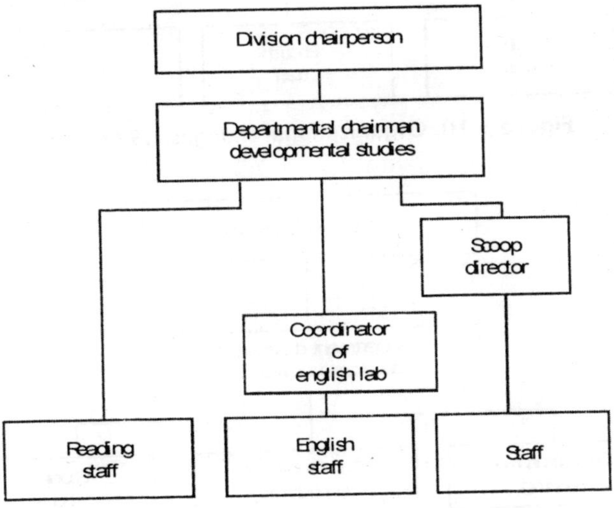

Figure 8.9. Organizational changes: 1971-1972

2. To give the physically handicapped student an equal opportunity to succeed in college on a par with the average student; for example, to act as liaison between the student and faculty members who have such students in their classes; to supply whatever is necessary in special equipment and tutoring; to make their learning effective; to make them an integral part of campus life rather than isolate them in a separate area.

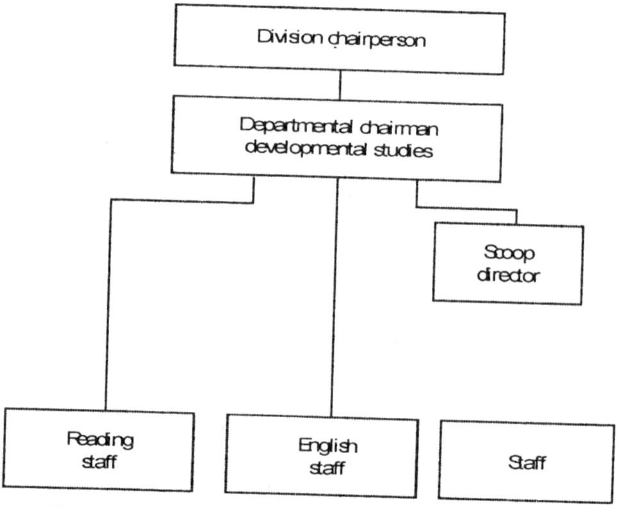

Figure 8.10. Organizational changes: 1972-1973

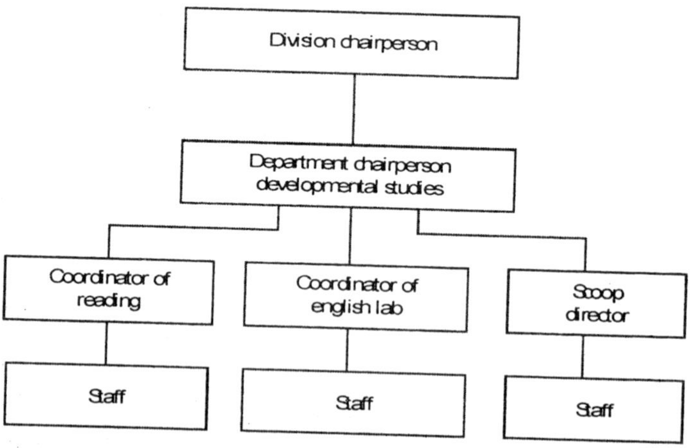

Figure 8.11. Organizational changes: 1973-1974

3. To help students who have been out of school for a number of years to regain confidence in their ability to succeed in college as they improve their reading and language skills.
4. To provide for students who are not working toward

a degree or certificate but who are interested in improving their reading and language skills.

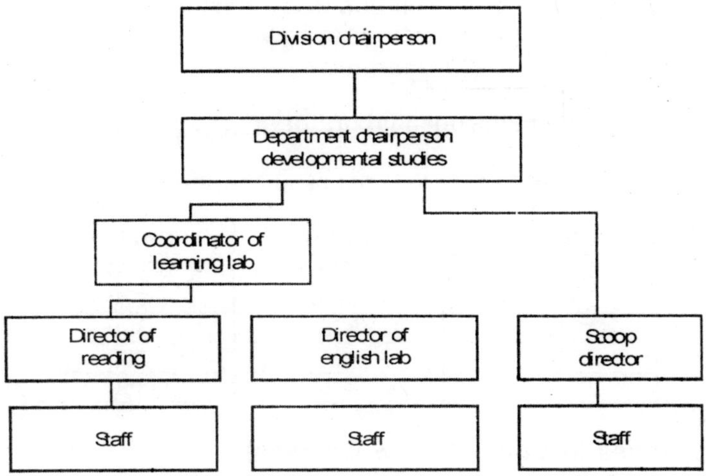

Figure 8.12. Organizational changes: 1974-1975

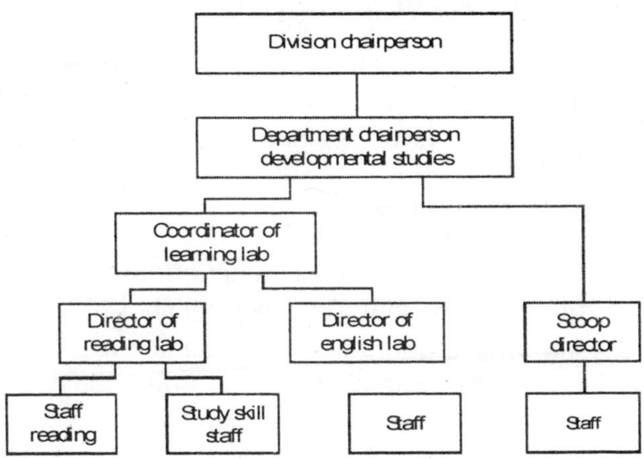

Figure 8.13. Organizational changes: 1975-1976

Programs and/or Projects

1. Learning center for physically handicapped.
2. On and/or off campus head-start classes.
3. English-language laboratory.
4. Saturday classes.
5. Study skills open laboratory.

Table 8.1. Projected number of students

Year	Reading	English
1971-72	275	180
1972-73	325	270
1973-74	375	300
1974-75	425	330
1975-76	475	360

Changes in Content (New Courses)

1. Report writing.
2. Mini speed-reading course—two hours for eight weeks—one semester-hour credit.

Changes in Types of Students

There will be a greater number of students who are not in the university parallel program but who are interested in the certificate and technical programs and in self-improvement.

Changes in Methodology

1. Increasing the use of instructional packages and programmed materials in English 1203.
2. Allowing students to contract for a grade and/or credit, thus enabling them to finish the course prior to semester's end or allowing them to continue the course beyond the semester's end if need be.
3. Permitting students to indicate their preference for the following methods of grading: credit or noncredit,

Table 8.2. Project Faculty needs

Subject	Year	Professional	Para-Professional
Reading	1971-72	2+ (Equivalent)	
English	1971-72	1+ (Equivalent)	
SCOOP	1971-72	3	7 (Equivalent)
Reading	1972-73	3 (Equivalent)	
English	1972-73	2 (Equivalent)	
SCOOP	1972-73	3	7 (Equivalent)
Reading	1973-74	3 (Equivalent)	1
English	1973-74	2 (Equivalent)	2
SCOOP	1973-74	4	8 (Equivalent)
Reading	1974-75	3 (Equivalent)	2
English	1974-75	2 (Equivalent)	3
SCOOP	1974-75	4	8 (Equivalent)
Reading	1975-76	3 (Equivalent)	3
English	1975-76	2 (Equivalent)	3
SCOOP	1975-76	4	8 (Equivalent)

Table 8.4. Staffing summary (full-time only)

	Basic Studies	Behavioral Occupations	Developmental Studies
Present Staff	5	2	2
1971 Additional Staff	0	1 Professional	
		1 Para-Professional	3 Professional
			5 Para-Professional
			2 Clerical
1972 Additional Staff	5 Professional	1 Professional	2 Professional
	1 Para-Professional	1 Para-Professional	
		1 Clerical	
1973 Additional Staff	0	1 Professional	1 Professional
		1 Para-Professional	1 Para-Professional
1974 Additional Staff	0	2 Professionals	0
		3 Para-Professionals	
1975 Additional Staff	0	1 Professional	0
Total Professional	10	7	8
Total Para-Professional	1	5	6
Total Clerical	0	1	2

pass or fail, letter grade.

4. Recommending students with unusually high performance records for advanced placement in English 1613.

India has been a centre of excellence in the field of higher education. Nalanda, Vikramashila and Takshashila were few of the oldest universities in the world and were the most renowned seats of higher education during their time. Students' from far off countries came to study in these universities. Today India has one of the largest higher education systems in the world and also some world-class institutions for higher education.

The present system of higher education dates back to Mountstuart Elphinstone's minutes of 1823, which stressed on the need for establishing schools for teaching English and the European sciences. Subsequently, the universities of Calcutta, Bombay and Madras were set up in 1857, followed by the university of Allahabad in 1887.

The first attempt to formulate a national system of education in India came in 1944, with the Report of the Central Advisory Board of Education on Post War Educational Development in India, which recommended the formation of a University Grants Committee, which was formed in 1945 to oversee the work of the three Central Universities of Aligarh, Banaras and Delhi. After independence, a full-fledged Ministry of Education was established on 29th August, 1947.

In 1952, the Union Government decided that all cases pertaining to the allocation of grants-in-aid from public funds to the Central Universities and other Universities and Institutions of higher learning might be referred to the University Grants Commission (UGC). The UGC was formally established in November, 1956 as a statutory body of the Government of India through an Act of Parliament for the coordination, determination and maintenance of standards of university education in India. In order to ensure effective region-wise coverage throughout the country, the UGC has decentralised its operations by setting up six regional centres at Pune, Hyderabad, Kolkata, Bhopal, Guwahati and Bangalore. The head office of the UGC is located in New Delhi.

❏❏❏

9

Capital Outlays of Instructional Technology

Introduction

There may also be pressing capital outlay requirements for long-deferred maintenance and repairs, and for renovation of buildings to suit changes in use, to meet increased environmental, health, and safety standards, and to provide for child care and the physically disabled.

The strategies to be discussed could reduce capital outlay for expanding facilities on existing campuses, developing satellite campuses, or building new campuses. Such savings would not necessarily fully offset the requirements for additional capital outlay mentioned above, but they would reduce the total capital outlay otherwise needed.

Coordinated Role for Facilities Planning

The planning of physical facilities should be considered in coordination with academic and fiscal planning. See, for instances, Haas; also the discussion of the use of a consultant for academic-fiscal planning.

Review Process for Proposed Campuses and Off-Campus Centers

Restraint in capital outlay commitments can be furthered by requiring that proposals for new campuses or off-campus centers undergo a careful review process. This is in addition to the measures discussed earlier for avoiding unnecessary duplication of programs through inter institutional arrangements. In the case of multi campus, public higher education systems, providing a campus at a geographic location not previously served by a conveniently located facility generally receives weight as an important consideration.

A source for updated guidelines for the review of proposed campuses and off-campus centers by a statewide coordinating body is available in a publication of the California Post-secondary Education Commission. Private and public colleges and universities within the state are requested to submit proposals prior to site acquisition that relate the proposed project to the state's educational policy goals. Effects on other institutions are to be identified and wide consultation should be arranged. A cost-benefit analysis of alternatives is to be included. Final proposals must include a completed environmental impact report.

Controlling Cost at Pre-Bid and Pre-construction Phases

Costs can be contained or reduced by attention to various matters at the pre-bid or pre-construction phases of providing educational facilities. Examples include attention to the following: behavioral needs to be served by the design of the facility; broad consultation prior to design so as to minimize the expense of change orders; coordinating obsolescence so that outlays are not made for facilities that are dependent on the continued use of facilities that have a shorter remaining service life; investing additional capital funds currently if long-run operating and maintenance costs would be significantly decreased; allowing time to receive bids that detail the quality of construction that would be provided; expediting the construction phase to minimize inflationary increases in cost; and so forth. A source drawn on in this connection is Engelhardt.

Adherence to Space Utilization Standards

We turn attention next to containing the capital outlay cost of serving larger enrollments through more intensive use of existing campuses. We start by mentioning, in this and the next several sections, measures that could be employed to expand the number served within the conventional nine-month academic year.

Space standards as to the number of assignable square feet of space per demand unit in a category of space are employed initially in planning the capacity of new buildings and subsequently in making an initial allocation of space by administrative unit and function. Improved efficiency in the utilization of classroom and teaching laboratory space is sought by monitoring the number of hours per week that a room is used and the percentage of student stations therein that are occupied.

Space standards should be applied as an average for a large block of space so that flexibility in the use of space is preserved. Thus, to provide the array of courses needed for a degree, a large enrollment lecture course may be used in combination with several upper-division or graduate courses with small enrollment. This would satisfy the desired intensity of use of space as an average, but not on a room-by room basis.

As space is released over time, it is absorbed, but not always in accordance with space-utilization standards. Periodic review of space usage may free up some usable capacity and lead to more intensive use.

A survey of space and utilization standards in all 50 states indicates that only 25 use formal space standards or guidelines in their budgeting process. Most states pattern their standards on work done in the 1950s and 1960s in California. See, for instance, the California Coordinating Council for Higher Education. California requires that classroom space be used more hours per week than do other states, and allows somewhat less space per student station, with the result that the assignable square feet allowed per student or student hour is less than in other states. The latest statement of California space standards is in CPEC.

Internal Pricing of Space

Certain types of space departmental administrative and faculty offices, conference rooms, and storage can be conserved, and the need for additional capital outlay can be reduced, by placing an internal rental price on such space and permitting its exchange for other resources needed by the department that are held by other departments or by the central administration.

Compensatory Redirection to Other Campuses

Redirection is feasible when the problem of capacity is not present throughout a system of campuses. However, attention needs to be given to the appropriateness of compensatory payments (mileage, differential living costs, foregone income of student and possibly that of the spouse) for students redirected to campuses that are significantly less accessible to the student.

When there is unused capacity at private institutions, an offer to applicants at a public campus to subsidize at least part of the difference in tuition and fees charged should reduce or eliminate the need for expansion. A possible complication is that students who initially plan to attend a private institution at their own expense may apply to the impacted public campus to qualify for such an inducement.

A less campus-specific approach would be an expansion of the provision for state student assistance that is applicable at institutions, whether public or private. A recent study showed that the proportion of students attending private higher education institutions is very responsive to a "relatively slight movement" in the percentage that a state student grant is of private institution tuition. The study also showed that the increased cost thereof to the state would be less than the total cost of providing for them within state-supported higher education.

Use of Campuses of other Institutions

Arrangements could be made for the joint use of a site or physical plant of another institution to the extent that the latter has capacity in excess of its current needs. This may involve the separate use of specified buildings combined with the shared use of other campus facilities. It may be either distinct from or another manifestation of efforts to reduce duplication of programs among institutions. Examples of what is referred to are to be found in Florida, Washington, Arizona, and California, and are described in Technical Report 6 by the CPEC. Such arrangements, in addition to conserving on capital outlay, make attendance more feasible for students who are at a considerable distance from the main campus, and they may encourage students to continue beyond the first two years when a community college is host to programs of a four-year institution.

Where new campuses are planned for different systems of higher education in proximity to each other (two-year and four-year systems, for instance), joint use of facilities on a single campus could serve the functions of the different systems until there is sufficient growth to justify separate installations (State of California, Governor's Survey on Efficiency and Cost Control, 1967, Recommendation 14).

Joint use of Educational Parks

Distinct from the foregoing is the proposal for an educational park, in which physical facilities are administered by a separate authority to which all users have a similar relationship. While this proposal has the potential for ultimately conserving capital outlay and operating cost, it would require considerable reorganization of the delivery system for higher education.

Extension of Hours of Instruction

Extension of hours depends for its appropriateness in part on the size of total enrollment relative to the breadth of the curriculum. For an institution having an enrollment that would not otherwise support multiple sections of courses, offering evening or Saturday sections in addition to those during the day would eliminate the need for more buildings for daytime use, but would result in smaller attendance per class and higher cost for faculty. If single-section course offerings are spread over more hours, difficulties would arise for students attempting to set aside a block of hours for outside employment that is stable from term to term.

Increased intensity of use of physical plant in the conventional academic year involves some increase in operating cost per FTE student. In addition, differential pay for faculty assuming a heavier percentage of night or Saturday teaching would be in the best interest of an institution if its options in attracting and retaining faculty of a given level of quality are not to be narrowed.

Expansion of Institution Size

More intensive use of the buildings and site of an existing campus, consequent on an increase in enrollment ceiling, may require that installations for basic utilities, and possibly the extent of access routes, be increased. Increases in campus population may elevate the importance of restructuring an institution with respect to curriculum, administration, and physical facilities into clusters of smaller units. The need for financial provision for this should be recognized. In the choice between expanding the physical capacity of an existing campus or establishing a new campus, the point to be noted is that there is an enrollment range below which level there are facilities that are utilized significantly below full capacity. The stricture is not against establishing new campuses but against establishing such campuses as would tie up capital resources without the prospect of rapidly reaching an enrollment that would put the facilities into full-capacity use. What would be important for a new campus would be early achievement of a threshold enrollment.

Earlier Culmination

Capital outlay cost could be reduced by offering the option of earlier culmination. A degree or other form of credit could be made available to students at least every two years, and the time required to obtain a baccalaureate degree could be reduced to three years. Looking ahead to about the year 2005, Fisher projects that the new instructional and learning technology will speed up learning in the primary and secondary schools so that part of higher education's job will already have been done. Earlier culmination of higher education will be facilitated, realizing a saving on capital outlay. However, earlier levels of schooling will require a large investment in the new technologies. Culmination of baccalaureate study in three years, with saving in capital outlay, can alternatively be accomplished by a change to the ten-month academic calendar, or through year-round operation.

Further Options

Additional options that would reduce space requirements include:

- Reducing marginally the contact hours for selected courses, with offsetting increases in the preparation expected of students outside class.

- Substituting courses that are already available through distance education in place of offering low-enrollment sections on campus that would underutilize classroom space.
- Permitting requirements for selected courses to be satisfied through credit by examination.
- Having the same facilities serve different groups of full-time students by students alternating fixed periods of college study with fixed periods of mutually agreed, off-campus experience. The latter could be foreign travel, independent study, public service, or professional employment (with students sharing a job alternately).

Academic Calendar Changes

An institution may change its academic calendar for reasons related to student achievement rather than saving on capital outlay. There is a trade-off between (1) calendar time, which permits the development of the material in discrete steps in class and the opportunity for reflection and consolidation outside of class, and (2) blocks of clock-time, which prevent one's energy and concentration being diffused over many subjects. The trade-off could differ by subject matter or discipline. It may also differ with the method of teaching. Appropriateness for learning should be the fundamental consideration. Examples of innovative changes in the academic calendar drawn from experience at six institutions are given in Adelman.

The extent to which a new calendar arrangement is satisfactory depends in large measure on the extent to which individual courses are thought through by faculty members in terms of the new calendar, and adjustments are made accordingly. Where strong feelings of opposition to change exist prior to a change in calendar, the needed adjustments may be slow in coming, thereby fulfilling the initial predisposition as to the unsatisfactoriness of the outcome to be expected.

Our focus will be on academic calendar change from the standpoint of containing capital outlay cost. The incremental cost of year-round operation depends on the academic calendar from which the conversion is made and the academic calendar selected. Either a trimester or four-quarter academic calendar would permit terms of equal duration, with the latter more likely to facilitate articulation for new freshmen or transfer students. Our discussion will be in terms of movement from a two-semester calendar to a three-quarter academic year, and from that to four-quarter year round operation.

A cost model for semester calendar operation has been developed for the conventional academic year which lends itself to formal marginal, incremental, and marginal incremental analysis of program changes. The incremental cost of a change to a three-quarter academic calendar includes the cost of the portions of the work that have to be repeated three times rather than twice and other costs to maintain the quality of educational opportunity made available. Included is incremental cost that is fixed relative to changes in enrollment as well as incremental cost that is variable, as determined by studies by the author in connection with budget recommendations for a large urban university. The cost of operating the conventional academic year under the quarter calendar was determined to be from 2.5 percent to 2.9 percent over the cost under a semester calendar, when the same level of service is maintained. A further consideration, which tends to be demoted in significance since it is non-quantifiable when proposals are considered at a series of levels, is that faculty experience some fatigue from relating to an additional set of classes within the conventional nine months.

Of the program elements in the cost model cited above instruction, research, community service, student service, and instruction-related institutional service the focus is on the first and last mentioned. Capital outlay for residential facilities is not discussed.

Instruction has the following program components: curricular program; faculty development; admission, registration, and records; academic advisement; library; instructional media; ancillary organizational units; and summer session. Instruction-related institutional service has the following program components: faculty government; executive; planning, analysis, and evaluation; campus development; business management; communications; publications; automatic data processing; plant operation and maintenance; and security. There is provision for cross-classification by type of expense, by level of instruction, subject field, and year.

A sub-model is used for building space requirements, and another is used for annualizing the cost of capital outlay expenditures for land, site work, outdoor facilities, building space, and equipment.

The analysis of the incremental cost of a program change to four quarter year-round operation builds on the foregoing.

Costing Capital Outlay

As noted in the section on inquiry into institutional cost in Chapter 4, the inclusion of the full amount of capital outlays in a particular year would cause expenditure per student to be affected by the rate at which institutions provide increments in physical plant facilities in response to encountered or anticipated changes in enrollment. That method was used by Bowen in developing the data underlying the computation of the rate of increase in the cost of providing higher education over the period from 1929-30 to 1977-78.

An alternative approach is to use current-year commercial rental rates per square foot for comparable space. This was discussed by H. Bowen and Douglass and was used in their joint study, as well as by Bowen in a different part of the 1980 study from that mentioned above. The latter study used estimates of space in existence in the current year, which means that for years in which additional space became available, the cost for that year would abruptly rise, even though a portion of the space was being added for future use. If rental cost were based instead on space utilization standards corresponding to the actual enrollment in a given year, a better indication of the unit cost of providing instruction in that year would be obtained.

Another approach is to compute the value of the capital stock used by a college or university, including newly added facilities, and then charge to each year an allowance for depreciation and for obsolescence, and an estimate of the interest foregone in that year by not having invested the value of the capital stock in its next best alternative. The value of the capital stock could be computed from the outlays in the years they occur or from current replacement costs in the year for which the estimate is made. Modifications of this are given by O'Neill.

Amortization offers a method of allocating a capital outlay over a period of years in a series of equal amounts composed of two components: (1) interest on such (declining) portion of the original outlay as has not been acknowledged to that point as being a cost; and (2) the remainder of the annual amount, which is the portion of the original outlay charged to that period. Were the series of annual amounts discounted to present value, the total interest would equal the sum of the amounts (1), and the total present value would equal the amount of the original outlay.

In the model for annualized cost developed by Simpson, provision is made for different rates of discount to be employed to approximate the opportunity cost of displacing spending in sectors other than higher education in different portions of the period over which the outlay expenditures are amortized. The method yields results that fall between those obtained by annualizing each outlay on the basis of the original book value and discount rate of the year in which an outlay occurred, and those obtained by annualizing, using the latest figures for resource prices and interest rates.

Amortization and the variation thereof mentioned above have an advantage over the commercial cost of rental space approach and the depreciation and obsolescence approach that they provide a method that can be applied uniformly for capital outlay for various purposes: purchase of land, site work, building space, outdoor facilities, and major equipment.

Fourth-Quarter Enrollment Demand

Full-time equivalent enrollment in a summer term, as expressed for the case of the quarter calendar, may be classified as follows:

- Program acceleration by students who attend four consecutive quarters.
- Spread of a three-quarter program over four quarters voluntarily, or because of lack of opportunity to obtain needed courses.
- Shift to the summer quarter by students who nevertheless limit attendance to some two or three out of four consecutive quarters.
- Full-time equivalent enrollment corresponding to enrichment units taken in the summer quarter by students who have been or will be attending also in the conventional academic year. These units are both beyond those required for graduation and beyond what would have been taken had attendance been limited to the conventional academic year.
- Enrollment in the summer quarter by students not attending in other terms.

In such cases as an existing summer session term is not comparable to the terms of the conventional academic year (the typical summer session, for instance, offers institutes, workshops, and "popular" courses, for varying periods from several days to several weeks duration), the distinction may be made between demand for educational services that is contingent on there being a summer term comparable to those of the conventional academic year, and demand that is non contingent.

In the case of public higher education, a conventional academic year in which tuition and fees are at a nominal and not fully supporting level is often combined with one or more summer sessions (such as described above) for which the incremental costs of operation are to be fully covered by tuition charged the students who enroll therein. What could be considered is the establishment of a summer term comparable to those of the conventional academic year as to accessibility of courses and course content and as to quality of the educational opportunity provided, with the fees not more than those of the state-supported conventional academic year (and possibly less, at least initially, as an inducement to attendance). The summer session could be retained alongside the summer quarter to serve the specialized need for workshops and so on of short duration, with its costs being fully covered by those electing to attend.

Effects on Peak Capacity

Under year-round operation, capital outlays at the same or at an added campus are postponed or reduced by incurring operating costs that permit part of the enrollment in the conventional nine-month academic year to be taken care of in the existing facilities, through the provision of a regular term of instruction during the summer months.

Acceleration and enrichment through attendance at a state-supported summer quarter increase the total annual full-time equivalent students to be supported by the state in the immediate period. The number of teaching positions to be filled is thus increased. In addition, the extent to which supporting staff and physical facilities have to be drawn on is greater than otherwise. In the case of contingent acceleration, but not in the case of non-contingent acceleration or of enrichment, there is the benefit over a longer period that graduation releases educational resources in the conventional academic year at an earlier date.

An increase in spread occasioned by the introduction of a summer quarter does release resources in the conventional academic year but does not contribute to an acceleration of student programs. Undertaken voluntarily, it reflects a gain in flexibility. Undertaken due to lack of course offerings within any particular nine-month academic year, spread reflects a cost imposed on students.

Shift is similar to spread insofar as the latter is described above, except that it leaves the student with some complete quarter other than summer available for other activities.

The extent of growth relative to shift and spread combined (and contingent acceleration as well, as its effects on the conventional academic year are phased in) is of importance in two respects: the net effect on total enrollment in the conventional nine-month academic year, and the effect on average class size.

If the extent of earlier graduation and of shift and spread of student programs occasioned by instituting a summer quarter were greater in absolute terms than the growth in the customary academic year fulltime equivalents (figured prior to that shift and spread), student positions in classrooms would be released within the conventional nine months to a greater extent than required by growth. Some savings in instruction cost within the academic year could be offset against the cost of the fourth quarter itself. However, a determination of the extent of such savings would require attention being paid to the likelihood of the released resources being sufficiently concentrated as to permit, without impairment of the educational program, the shift (but not the spread) of teaching positions into the summer quarter. Such capacity as is released but is not shiftable may become unutilized. This would be corrected by subsequent enrollment growth, except in such case as an institution has a ceiling on total enrollment for reasons other than shortage of capacity.

Guiding Attendance by Fees

The most immediate gain in capacity would be realized were acceleration, enrichment, and spread disallowed, through students being assigned to attend three out of four quarters on staggered attendance schedules that differ as to the quarter taken off. This requirement, however, would seem unduly restrictive.

Also too restrictive is the policy implicit in the conclusion offered in a technical background paper for the California Post-secondary Education Commission that for capital outlay savings to occur, summer quarter attendance would have to be mandatory.

Policies that encourage awareness and examination of options are to be preferred over those that make particular behavior mandatory. One approach would be to charge a student a nominal additional fee per unit of course work in each third quarter he or she attends that is other than a summer quarter (whether consecutive attendance or not, and at any campus within a system) except on the number of units equal to those for which the student enrolled and successfully completed in the preceding summer quarter. This retains for a student the option of taking either three quarters of workload per 12 months or four quarters per 12 months at the normal fee level if the summer quarter is included as one of those attended, but subjects the student to a fee (imposed to influence the choice of options rather than for recovery of full cost) for the number of units taken each third quarter during the peak period that could have been taken during the summer. However, there are administrative costs in implementing such a policy.

In any event, some increase in use of the summer quarter can be expected over time with increased awareness by students of the availability and advantages of attending the summer quarter and as students rearrange the pattern of their employment for the year. Moreover, balance can be more closely approached in a reasonable number of years by developing close relationships between the college or university and the schools that supply it with its students schools that may in fact be adopting some form of year-round operation themselves to meet increased demand for their facilities.

Applicability of Year-Round Operation

Institutions of higher education that are sufficiently new or small to still experience significant economies in per-student cost with increases in enrollment within the conventional nine-month period should take into consideration the extent to which such economies might be foregone or at least postponed were year-round operation introduced. At the other extreme, a mature institution in which enrollment is "topping out" at a ceiling determined not by shortage of physical plant but by the extent of potential enrollment from the area served would need to weigh the advantage to students of being able to accelerate against a possible increase in unit cost due to less than full use of existing capacity during the conventional nine months.

Effect on Building Program

For the institution entering upon year-round operation, three options for the building program may be noted :

- Reliance on existing buildings to serve future enrollment levels.
- Addition of more buildings (but fewer than without year-round operation) in preparation for an enrollment ceiling already set for a subsequent year.
- Continuance of the planned program of buildings but handling a higher ceiling than otherwise, construction being phased in more slowly.

All three options assist in serving additional enrollment while postponing the need for additional campuses, the second option more than the first, and the third more than the other two. However, the first option is not feasible, in the absence of excess capacity in the conventional academic year prior to year-round operation, to the extent that the space required due to enrollment growth exceeds the sum of (1) the space released for conventional academic year enrollment by shift and spread of enrollment into the summer quarter; and (2) such space as is released gradually as earlier terminations occur as a result of students who accelerate their attendance. Moreover, the second and third options have the advantage over the first in that they allow for the construction of buildings having specialized characteristics in accordance with the physical master planning of the campus.

For one or more reasons the provision of space pending the phasing in of earlier terminations, the need for a functionally balanced set of structures, or the adoption of a higher enrollment ceiling the discontinuance of new construction immediately on adoption of year-round operation in order to demonstrate "savings" may be unwarranted.

In the event that several institutions of higher education contemplating year-round operation predominantly draw their students from the same geographic area, consideration should be given to sequencing that conversion over a period of years. This will facilitate those campuses that introduce a summer quarter in achieving the level of enrollment needed for economical operation, and will avoid institutions having to recruit too heavily from the potential faculty appointees of a particular year.

Findings as to Cost

Total institutional cost under four-quarter operation is built up from total semester cost and incremental quarter calendar cost (obtainable from the models referred to earlier) by the addition of the incremental cost of year-round operation. The latter is based on maintaining access in the added quarter and the regular academic year to the quality of educational opportunity that is comparable to that in other quarters and not less than before the introduction of year-round operation, in spite of the increased complexity of planning and implementation. Comparable access to a variety of courses in the summer quarter, with at least initially less enrollment per class than in the conventional academic year, will require a number of faculty positions that at first is more than proportional to enrollment. Of the several staffing options extension of an appointment to a 12-month basis, addition of academic year appointees to replace those who, by rotation, fill the added academic quarter, one-quarter appointments of visiting personnel, or addition of 12-month appointees the second option is preferable in order to maintain student access to the same quality of faculty throughout the year and to avoid infringement on time needed by faculty for professional and personal development.

In pilot studies in California, the emphasis on offering a comparable quarter in the summer distinguished the approach followed by the primarily instruction-oriented campuses from those that are more research-oriented. The former designed a summer quarter curricular offering that was comparable to the other three quarters, as indicated above (which initially requires a planned-for more-than-proportional faculty staffing); the latter did not (although unplanned more-than proportional staffing occurred through student attendance that was less than expected). While other considerations were also operative, it may be noted that the first-mentioned approach was accompanied by a high initial enrollment in relation to the conventional academic year, which enrollment increased in subsequent years. In contrast, the summer quarter in which a comparable quarter was not stressed was less successful and was subsequently terminated. The other considerations operative at the research-oriented campuses included a slowing down of total student enrollment combined with high enrollment in their student-supported summer sessions.

Year-round operation adds (1) operating expenditures during the fourth quarter itself, and possibly the capital outlay cost of adding air conditioning for the summer; and (2) added costs incurred during the conventional nine months in order to conduct the instructional program on a four-quarter basis. Average operating cost per full-time equivalent student is initially higher than in the conventional academic year, but the extent of this will decrease in subsequent years (but not to the extent of being equal in view of (2) above) as the level of summer quarter enrollment approaches balance with enrollment in the conventional academic year. Offsetting this is the lesser annualized cost per student resulting from the containment of capital outlay. Whether total cost is increased or reduced, however, will depend on whether or not more students overall are retained by or attracted to higher education by its availability year-round. A different experience with year-round operation is reported and analyzed by Balderston and Weathersby and Hopkins.

Distance Education

Developing and expanding distance education programs that serve a "university without walls" can reduce capital outlay for space to the extent that participants in distance education are individuals who would otherwise have studied on campus. However, there may be some added enrollment and space needs due to individuals whose interest is aroused by the distance education program.

Components of the Open University (distance education) program include, in the case of Britain: a correspondence package; radio and television programs; access to group tutoring for each course and to a counselor for the student's work as a whole; one week of required summer school attendance; and possibly, on-loan experiment kits and access to a computer terminal.

There will be capital outlay for equipment, whether the radio or TV programs are prepared to be broadcast or distributed as cassettes. Moreover, there is a large outlay for the preparation of distance-learning teaching materials that is a function of the number of courses offered and the frequency of update but not a function of the number of students served.

The portion of cost that is fixed relative to change in enrollment is much larger than in conventional education. However, the portion of cost that does vary with the number of students is less in absolute amount per student for distance education than for conventional education. Beyond a certain number of students, distance education is the more economical technique. Further, there are considerable economies of scale corresponding to a larger enrollment.

The relative importance of fixed and variable cost, and their absolute levels as compared with those of conventional education, differ according to the media employed. The cost of distance education in Britain is compared with that of conventional education by Wagner, Carter and Rumble. A comparison of the cost effectiveness of the Open University with campus universities has been undertaken by Mace. Audio-teleconferencing as a low-cost technology for external networking is discussed in Robertson. Three successful Canadian operating models are discussed, as well as a University of Wisconsin model.

With distance education as with year-round operation, while average total cost per student can be reduced below that of conventional education when enrollment is sufficient, total cost is not likely to be reduced, since more students than otherwise will be served. Moreover, were the curriculum offered by distance education to include higher level courses of small enrollment, or other courses of small enrollment, the per-student comparison would become less favorable.

The Open University in Britain has had to restrict the number of courses it can offer, with the result that a graduate cannot take an honours degree unless it is in two subjects. In only Britain's distance education system among those of nine countries was the cost per graduate significantly below that of conventional institutions in the same country, reflecting drop-out and repetition rates as much as the intrinsic costs of each system.

❑❑❑

10

Student Assessment in Higher Education

Introduction

The assessment of prior learning in preparation for college-level course work or for remediation. To others, the term is the measurement of college-level learning after one, two, or three years of college. Junior examinations, as used in Florida is an example of this idea of post-secondary assessment. Finally, a third meaning, and probably the most widely used, is a measurement of college outcomes of what students learn when they graduate. The third interpretation of assessment places emphasis on the outputs or impacts of education, as opposed to the inputs into the education system.

Although the definition is simple, it encompasses a variety of assessment activities that occur at diverse cross-sections of colleges and universities in the United States. According to 1990 *Campus Trends* survey findings released by the American Council on Education (ACE), assessment initiatives at institutions of higher education occur in the following proportions:

Two-year colleges	:	88%
Baccalaureate colleges	:	76%
Comprehensive	:	83%
Doctoral universities	:	68%

The increased emphasis on student assessment establishes three challenges for assessment personnel in institutions of higher education as we approach the 21st century. The first challenge is to collect data that can help students enhance their learning potential and make meaningful choices about careers, programs, and courses. The second challenge is to aid in the evaluation and improvement of instruction, courses, programs, and the institution itself. The third challenge is to make the college or university accountable to its constituents: students, their families, government, and the public.

Student Assessment: A Historical Context

"Does the outcome [of a college education] bear the impress of a clear, consistent and valid purpose? Does the thing prove as education to have been worthwhile?".

These questions asked by Abraham Flexner in 1908 provide a historical context for student assessment and point the way for earlier methods of determining educational quality, such as comprehensive examinations taken at the end of the senior year. Flexner's determination to reform U.S. higher education became more intense as the Great Depression of the 1930s gripped the country economically. During this period, accountability questions posed by Flexner in 1908 resurfaced as government and institutions of higher education became frugal with their resources. In response, various institutions developed sound programs to assess student knowledge. These programs went beyond the snapshot approach, where individual instructors assigned grades to students based on their performance in specific courses. For example, as early as 1928 the University of Chicago used comprehensive examinations to measure student outcomes appropriate to the general education at their college. In 1932, the University of Minnesota followed Chicago's assessment efforts by establishing the General College. The General College's mission was described as "knowing what we are getting for what we were doing". In 1939, over 25 institutions representing a cross-section of the United States participated in the Cooperative Study in General Education under the sponsorship of the ACE.

As the country began to prosper financially during the late 1940s and into the 1970s, little attention was given to accountability measures such as determining the outcomes of the educational process. In fact, during this time period institutions of higher education (funded by federal and state governments) proliferated at a phenomenal rate to accommodate the growing student body. However, as the mid-1980s approached, another period of economic exigency affected higher education. Thus, attention again shifted to ensuring educational quality. During this formative period two issues dominated higher education: First, at issue for institutions of higher education was the philosophical need and justification for student assessment at institutions of higher education. Philosophical arguments relating to academic autonomy versus governmental intervention were voiced on college and university campuses. In addition many institutions, such as the College of William and Mary, felt that student assessment was not justified given the high quality of students admitted and its national standing. However, the impact of three reports: *A Nation at Risk: The Imperative for Educational Reform*; *To Reclaim a Legacy: A Report on the Humanities in Higher Education*; and *Involvement in Learning: Realizing the Potential of American Higher Education* established the need for improvements in secondary and undergraduate education.

A second issue for institutions of higher education that were resisting assessment was financial constraints. Many institutions found themselves faced with state mandates requiring student assessment but with no money to conduct the process. Thus, colleges and universities often took financial resources from other areas within their current operating budget. The 1986 *Campus Trends* survey found that 71 percent of participants felt there were no funds to develop procedures. This problem was virtually eliminated as the assessment movement gained momentum. State legislators appropriated the necessary funds during the budgeting process or offered incentive funding to institutions for their compliance.

With the easing of financial constraints, colleges and universities were now free to investigate important questions similar to those asked by Flexner in 1908. Hutchings and Marchese identified several questions that individual faculty, departments, programs, and entire institutions faced as they began to tackle the assessment issue:

- What is the college's contribution to student learning? How and what do we know of that contribution?
- Do our graduates know and can they do what our degrees imply? How do we ensure that?
- To what do the courses and instruction we provide add up for students? Are they learning what we're teaching?
- What knowledge and abilities do we intend that students acquire? Do they have opportunities to do so? Are they successful? At what level? Is that level good enough?
- How can the quantity and quality of student learning be improved? What combination of college and student effort would it take to achieve higher levels of performance?.

These and similar questions served as the foundation for the present assessment initiative.

Present Status

Arguments concerning the philosophical need and justification for student assessment and financial constraints at institutions of higher education are no longer the center of assessment controversy. Six years have passed since assessment of student learning re-entered the higher education arena, and now attention has shifted to other concerns such as technical problems associated with the how to of assessment, and political concerns about the uses of assessment results.

Technical Problems

In the 1989 *Campus Trends* survey, ACE found that 68 percent of campus administrators who responded felt that most faculty support the development of some kinds of assessment procedures. More importantly, ACE found that more than 33 percent of those who did respond felt that there were no good instruments available to assess their programs. Thus, attention has turned to locally developed assessment instruments to eliminate some of the technical problems associated with student assessment.

In 1990, 66 percent of colleges and universities that responded to the *Campus Trends* survey were developing their own instruments for student assessment. This figure is up significantly from the 1986 figure of 34 percent. Still, there is room for concern among assessment personnel as we approach the 21st century. Ewell suggests that one way to further lower this number is to link assessment personnel with the professional measurement community, which can aid in developing tests that accurately measure individual change in addition to tests that measure group change within a student body at institutions of higher education. Once the tests are constructed, they should be pre-tested on a random sample of the student population.

A second suggestion for reducing technical concerns is for similar institutions and disciplines to collaborate in designing their assessment programs and measurement instruments. This method appeared as early as 1939, when over 25 institutions participated in the Cooperative Study in General Education under the sponsorship of the ACE. Although the colleges that participated in the study had diverse missions, they felt they would benefit from a concerted effort to study many of the problems they faced. In addition, they believed that despite their differences certain basic problems were sufficiently similar to warrant a united effort. By sharing experiences, materials, and ideas, and by dividing the labor, certain complex problems could be attacked more easily. Such collaboration should be of particular importance and interest to two year colleges whose primary mission is preparing students to transfer to senior institutions. Since these institutions are not viewed as a final stage in the educational process, they must provide quality education for students seeking admission to senior-level institutions.

Political Concerns

Today's college and university campuses are essentially political entities that must respond to both external and internal calls for accountability. El-Khawas states that three-quarters of college administrators report their institutions are using assessment information in their internal decision-making process. Externally, each of the six regional accrediting agencies now require some type of student outcomes assessment in its review process. Also, at least 15 states use outcomes measures in their budgeting process, and another 13 have pending legislation, task forces, or commissions responsible for developing an outcomes assessment policy. Thus, it is important for assessment personnel to respond satisfactorily to all interested parties both external and internal.

External Accountability

In the 1990 *Campus Trends* survey, 73 percent of administrators expressed strong fears about the misuse of assessment results by external agencies. To further expand on the significance of this data, Banta points out that policy-makers as a group tend to ignore the individuality of institutions as well as the change process that institutions must go through to conduct successfully an assessment initiative on their campus. Not understanding the process, policy-makers have suggested that institutions simply adopt the assessment model proven effective at another college or university. In addition, policy-makers unfamiliar with assessment often suggest that institutions develop and use a single indicator of quality, when, actually, a complex multi-indicator method often is needed.

Lewis warns assessment personnel about providing simplified and trivialized information to such external parties as policy-makers. He states that the recipients of assessment information may use it to increase their role in making decisions that pertain to higher education, when in fact these decisions would best be made by individual institutions themselves. Although many student assessment programs are begun as a reaction to external calls for accountability, there should be a concerted effort by institutional faculty and administrators to internalize the program. This is the present challenge for assessment initiatives.

Internal Accountability

According to El-Khawas, to date assessment results are used most widely for internal planning purposes. The most popular uses include:

Program and curriculum evaluation	:	78%
Reports to deans and department chairs	:	76%
Reports to faculty	:	73%
Feedback to students	:	58%

Using student assessment for institutional accountability involves the active inclusion of assessment activities into the everyday functions on college and university campuses. This process, also known as institutionalization, occurs when assessment is incorporated into established institutional practices such as planning, budgeting, student development programming, and comprehensive academic program review. If a student assessment program is to be effective over a long term, it is necessary for both academic and administrative officials at an institution of higher education to resist the temptation to view assessment as a one-shot project. Assessment should not be a reactionary process, but should be viewed by those involved as a mechanism for stimulating change at the institution of higher education.

As student assessment programs approach the 21st century most will enter a stage of renewal or decline, depending upon the degree of institutionalization of assessment into college or university functions. As chief executive officers show increased concern with the costs of conducting these programs, many ask if the programs are as efficient as possible in providing maximum return of invested resources. What is being found presently is that assessment results often are placed on a shelf as opposed to being actively incorporated into the university's decision-making process. This should not be continued if indeed student assessment is to determine institutional effectiveness in achieving the goals and mission of the institution. If a college or university does not successfully incorporate assessment findings into its decision-making process, the program is probably headed for a rapid decline. If assessment results are useful and can be used successfully to justify decisions, then the program will be renewed. Hopefully, before entering the 21st century institutions already will have hurdled the technical and political concerns that presently plague assessment initiatives. Emphasis should then be shifted to the actual inclusion of assessment results into the decision-making process on college and university campuses.

At some institutions such as Alverno College and Northeast Missouri State University, including assessment results into the decision-making process is well under way, but for other institutions just beginning to develop assessment programs and tests, the bond between measures of student performance (within individual departments, programs, and schools) and overall indicators of institutional effectiveness will be at an infantile stage. However, once this bond is firmly established, decisions about goals and resource allocations should be made based on the interpretation of student assessment data. This will involve linking assessment performance with teaching, programming, and student career decisions.

Faculty involvement and support are critical to the long-term success of student assessment initiatives. Faculties at colleges and universities are composed of professionals who generally possess extensive knowledge that can be used to better assessment initiatives. In addition, if faculties are not included in the assessment process, they might respond with open hostility. This hostility might take the form of open or passive resistance to the process. For example, faculty members might claim there is no need for assessment within their disciplines or refuse to attend assessment meetings.

Future Concerns

The future of student assessment programs includes increased attention to their usefulness to colleges and universities as well as to external authorities that may have mandated assessment. As student assessment programs begin to generate both good and bad data that may or may not be a positive reflection on the school, it will be necessary to evaluate the effectiveness of the total assessment effort. Such a cost-benefit analysis has a goal of determining whether resources (financial, human, supplies, time, and so forth) have been used both efficiently and effectively at the institution, or whether these resources could have been better used elsewhere. Institutions will have to spend more time deciding how their student assessment program will be evaluated along with the very earliest planning and design of the program. This would insure that all the needed data is collected at the appropriate time before and during the implementation of the assessment initiative. However, with more and more states requiring some type of student assessment information, institutions of higher education are finding that assessment programs are being implemented in a crisis-oriented fashion, resulting in the omittance of critical program evaluations in their initial plans. Institutions of higher education must also realize that there is often a second inhibitor financial standing to the successful evaluation of student assessment programs. Institutions of higher education are finding they must tighten their financial belts at a time when more and more external audiences increasingly are questioning the quality of educational outputs and management techniques on college campuses. One effort to conserve resources has been cutting corners on student assessment programs. Since the evaluation component is not viewed by many as essential to program operation, it is often eliminated. However, evaluation is necessary before improvements can be made. Tracey states that improvement of any program can be affected by:

- objective and coordinated evaluation of every aspect of the operation;
- application of imagination and creative thinking by all personnel;
- deliberate collection of the observations, ideas, and thinking of all personnel;
- critical analysis and synthesis of findings, ideas, and alternatives; and

- systematic, time-phased development and try-out of policies and procedures as well as identification of resources (people, equipment, materials, time, space, and money) needed to carry out plans.

Student assessment programs should be evaluated by colleges and universities, but the process should not end there. As a final step, the evaluation should include a follow-up plan for the improvement of sub-programs within the overall program. The following suggestions may be helpful in preparing the follow-up plan:

Implement changes carefully. Once the evaluation has been conducted, action should be taken to implement some of the changes deemed necessary for the improvement of the student assessment effort. If no changes are made, the resources used in the evaluation were essentially wasted.

Do not try to improve every area at once, which will result in chaos and undue strain on available resources. A reasonable response would be to develop a time-phased plan for improving each sub-program of the student assessment program according to the findings of the evaluation.

Summary

The success of student assessment programs in the next decade depend upon the specific characteristics of each institution of higher education that implements them. These characteristics include mission, structure, control systems, goals, innovations, and ability to change. For most colleges and universities currently conducting student assessment, the programs generally are hampered by technical problems such as test development and implementation. However, as these programs mature approaching the 21st century, program changes must be tied to ongoing evaluation of the assessment data. At this point institutions of higher education may encounter the most resistance to their assessment efforts.

Despite the reasons for the development of assessment activities on college and university campuses, institutions of higher education must internalize the process. Internalization or institutionalization involves the active incorporation of assessment activities into the everyday functions of colleges and universities. A historical perspective can be used by colleges and universities in understanding assessment programs and for aiding administrators involved in the day-to-day decision-making process. Success in the 21st century will require that administrators respond to increased calls for assessment, outcome measurement, or accountability in a positive, proactive way if they are committed to improving their status in the higher education and surrounding communities.

❏❏❏

11

Developing a Campus Climate for 21st Century

Introduction

Some institutions have a narrow perspective on achieving diversity. For many, it is simply a matter of recruiting more under-represented minorities. There is a visible scramble among elite and prestigious colleges for well-prepared minority students, but they are reluctant to admit any at-risk minority students. At some publicly supported institutions, particularly in the western United States, legislative language may be in place calling for the increased representation of minorities and the economically and educationally disadvantaged on campus. Public colleges and universities that feel compelled, for whatever reason, to increase the number of under-represented students may adopt a target strategy, that is, they aggressively recruit minorities to maintain a desired enrollment level. However, if the campus climate is not hospitable to these students, many of them drop out after a year or more. We have learned that many underrepresented students leave for non-academic reasons. The aggressive recruitment and high drop out rate of these students is often referred to as the revolving door syndrome. How can an institution improve access and retention, and graduate an increased number of under-represented students?

Campus Climate

We cannot expect new types of students to adapt easily to a campus designed for another clientele. Such campuses are not well prepared to cope with these new students. Moreover, each campus has a unique culture that reflects to some degree the values and accepted practices of the local or regional society. While there are some constants within the academy, such as the role of the faculty and the educational and research mission of the institution, norms, and standards that affect attitudes and condition behavior, our prevalent college culture has deep roots directly traceable to Europe and England. Along the Atlantic Seaboard colleges and universities, especially the older, private ones, celebrate these English and European traditions. African Americans, Asian-Americans, Hispanics, and Native Americans were, for the most part, never involved in the development of these institutions and are, therefore, like "strangers from different shores". When minorities arrive on campus as new students, new staff persons, or as newly appointed faculty members, norms and traditions may be troublesome to them. Minorities learn to accommodate in order to survive. This does not mean, however, that we are pleased by the dominant cultural manifestations on a campus that relegate us to subculture roles and marginalize us. Even if we do adopt the outward manifestations of the dominant culture on campus, what price will we pay, and can we ever be certain of acceptance? The article by Reyes and Halcon provides an important insight on how racism continues to operate in academia and works against minorities.

Leaders in education must adopt a new commitment to make the transition from numerical diversity to interactive pluralism. It begins at the K-12 levels, where a new vision must be defined for schools as a place where all ethnic and racial groups can appreciate their differences in a process of mutual enrichment. At the college level new ways must be identified for minorities and those from the larger society to acknowledge and build mutual respect for similarities as well as differences. The following strategies should be considered.

Set Priorities

The president and top executives must publicly announce their goal for eliminating racial and ethnic disparities on campus and state their firm commitment to educational equity. Leaders within the faculty, staff, and student body must join with the president and senior executives to craft a program that will achieve educational equity. There are several models available. For the small liberal arts college, the work of the President's Task Force on Minority Presence at Saint Mary's College of California is exemplary. For a larger private university, the *Final Report of the University Committee on Minority Issues* at Stanford University is an important document. Finally, for a publicly supported university, the *Madison Plan* at the University of Wisconsin, Madison, offers much food for thought.

Crafting a plan for diversity, however, is not enough. The president must make the implementation of a diversity plan a key priority and back it up with needed resources and continuing commitment. Moreover, strategies must be devised to track and evaluate progress toward campus diversity regularly. A public self assessment is required to determine successes and identify areas that may require attention. Unless the president is completely committed to carrying out a plan for diversity, needed change will be more promise than practice. The implementation of a successful educational equity program at San Jose State University reflects continuing administrative support.

Provide Comprehensive and Integrated Support Services

The institution must develop support services that closely link academic and student activities. Programs that bridge the social and educational gaps minorities face are essential. Specialized minority enclaves that tend to marginalize these students must be phased out in favor of programs and activities that interface all students. This should include extended classes covering required materials, tutoring, learning laboratories, collaborative study groups, and active counseling that pulls students in the direction of a major. Majority and minority students should be encouraged to mentor each other, study together, learn from each other, depend upon each other, and socialize with each other. An important model is the Counselling and Academic Skills Development (CASD) Program at Pennsylvania State University, which provides individualized counselling and academic support services for minority undergraduates.

Establish a Non-threatening Social Environment

The campus climate and infrastructure must be examined carefully to determine how the dominant culture is manifested. Two critical areas for review are the academic structure and programs, and the out-of-class and social experiences encountered by students. Academic programs and staff services must be reviewed thoroughly to identify any attitudes and practices that are biased or culturally discriminatory. Staff in support services, like admissions and financial aid, must begin to understand how students from different cultural backgrounds perceive them. This review and change process must include everyone connected with the institution: faculty, staff, students, and especially trustees and alumni. Social machinery such as fraternities and sororities or social clubs must begin to incorporate different cultural attitudes and expectations and eliminate biases that rank one type of student over others.

The Madison Plan at the University of Wisconsin contains several initiatives to improve campus climate for minorities.

A key strategy to improve campus climate for minorities and other under-represented groups involves the development of a campus wide commission that includes representatives from senior faculty, staff and student leaders, alumni, a trustee or two, and two or more community leaders in the immediate area. Reporting directly to the president, this group should review all aspects of the campus for discriminatory conditions and assist with the development of strategies and activities to overcome racially biased attitudes and behavior. Such a commission should be long lived, and its leadership must meet regularly with the president and the presidents' chief advisors.

Stress Quality

The issue of high standards has traditionally cast minorities as at risk and deficient, particularly at some prestigious institutions. However, educational quality is often used as a double-edged sword. Selective institutions have in the past excluded minorities disproportionately: some because they do not meet high standards, others because they are perceived as over-achievers. Diversity and excellence are possible, but without diversity excellence is not possible.

Several programs have demonstrated how successful minorities can be at highly selective institutions. Brooklyn College provides a first-class education. One-third of its student body is African American and Hispanic, and it graduates students proportionately. The Mathematics Workshop Program affiliated with the Professional Development Program at the University of California at Berkeley is the brainchild of Uri Treisman. It is a highly successful program that should serve as a model for other institutions. It is critical for minority students to escape any stigma that casts them as second class or inferior students. If minorities are motivated to believe in themselves by faculty and staff, and if they are academically encouraged, they will excel.

Change the Curriculum

Colleges and universities that have been able to change their academic programs to include the experiences of minorities, women, and other excluded groups have done so by cultivating faculty and working in teams. The team approach involves students, staff, and faculty systematically reviewing target curricula to determine what new issues and supportive readings must be provided to students. The University of California at Los Angeles (UCLA) developed a fascinating approach to curriculum change. The campus secured financial resources so that the honors program could buy faculty release time during one quarter to add to their syllabi new readings dealing with the experience of women and minorities in the United States. Making any type of structural change in a curriculum is a thorny problem, as was evident by the debate at Stanford University to consider including non-Western themes. However, the UCLA model provides an incentive for faculty to transform their own courses. Another interesting approach to achieving curriculum change is the Odyssey II Program at Brown University. It is an effort that links faculty and students in developing reading lists and creating new courses.

A few words are necessary about ethnic studies graduation requirements. While a required course that will expose all students to the experience of ethnic and racial groups in the United States is a positive step, such a course must be comparative and "substantially consider at least three of the five main racial/cultural groups in American society: African American, American Indian, Asian American, Chicano/Latino, and European American". At many campuses, any discussion about imposing an ethnic studies graduation requirement will bring to light resistance by faculty and students alike. It took one defeat and over two years of discussion before the successful passage of the comparative ethnic studies graduation requirement at the University of California at Berkeley. As increasing numbers of minorities begin to attend U.S. colleges and universities, the curriculum must provide ways to sensitize all students to the experiences these different groups have had in the United States. A thoughtful and well-designed course, taught by an effective faculty, will do much to improve relations among different ethnic and racial groups on campus.

Diversify the Faculty

There will be many opportunities to add more minorities to our faculties. The demographic data on pending faculty retirements and new openings are known. It is not necessary to repeat that discussion. Instead, it is important to mention the development of a strategy that contains priorities and targets for faculty recruitment.

At most institutions, minority faculty recruitment is highly opportunistic. Some institutions set aside one or two positions in a particular school or college for minorities, and at others, the campus commits itself to hire a specific number of minorities over a five- or ten-year period. What is needed, however, is a systematic review of the institution to determine what colleges, schools, or departments have an immediate effect on the surrounding community. As for research universities, national priorities involving minority needs must be considered. Then, the president should make available new or replacement faculty positions to these units that should be filled by minorities. Prioritizing opportunities for minority faculty hiring is an important step in diversifying the professoriate.

Two other issues regarding faculty diversity are important. First, good teaching skills should be an important part of a minority faculty member's portfolio. The ability to reach a wide audience of students is an essential quality for a successful instructor. Second, ethnic and racial-related research and investigations should not be discounted in the tenure process. If we are ever genuinely to understand each other, we must be able to research and uncover our backgrounds and contributions to American life.

Preparing new minority faculty must be a priority for U.S. higher education. Most of the important steps that are needed to encourage minorities to consider careers as professors have been mentioned elsewhere. However, a few need to be underscored. Recruiting minorities for doctoral programs must begin in grade and especially middle schools. At the undergraduate level planning and preparing for graduate school must be stressed, and students working closely with faculty members who will guide and assist prospective doctoral students is very important. Selecting the right type of graduate program and securing a sufficient financial aid package will be essential to the student.

Several programs identify talented minority undergraduates and encourage them to pursue graduate degrees. The Early Identification Program at the University of Washington in Seattle is a well designed and operated model. Several programs are designed to increase the gender and racial and ethnic diversity of faculty in selected academic fields, and to link financial assistance with employment. Two important efforts are the New Jersey Minority Academic Career program (MAC) and the California State University Forgivable Loan/Doctoral Incentive Program. A highly successful state program is the Black Doctoral Fellowships provided by the Florida Endowment Fund. Some 25 fellowships provided by the Florida Endowment Fund are awarded each year for doctoral study at Florida public or private institutions. At the national level, the Minority Graduate Fellowships from the National Science Foundation, and the Patricia Roberts Harris Fellowship Program in the U.S. Department of Education, provide assistance for traditionally under-represented students who have demonstrated an ability and aptitude for graduate study in select fields. These efforts, and others, need to be expanded and new ones developed to ensure an expanding pool of women and minorities for faculty roles in U.S. institutions of higher learning.

Employ Minority Leaders as Change Agents

Academic colonialism can easily thwart an institution's attempts to diversify. Employing minorities in senior leadership positions sends a clear message about the value of cultural diversity among faculty and staff. Far too many institutions hire minorities for senior management roles in "soft" or marginal areas. Hiring them for such positions as dean of students, affirmative action officers, or special assistants to the president for diversity marginalize minorities into professional cul-de-sacs with little opportunity for advancement. At many campuses, this tends to trivialize their efforts. Michigan State University and the University of Texas at El Paso have successfully employed minority leaders as academic deans of different schools and colleges. A few institutions have identified and hired promising African-American academic leaders from historically black colleges and universities. These leaders are recruited as change agents. Creative change agents who understand the campus climate and can work effectively with staff, faculty, students, and senior administrators have been responsible for setting dramatic diversity trends. The president and her or his senior executives, however, must be prepared to support the efforts of these change agents and commit the institution to a program of continuing and long-term change.

Two areas that are critical for faculty recruitment are the sciences and engineering. The report of the Task Force on Women, Minorities, and the Handicapped in Science and Technology has some important recommendations for action. There is a coming crisis in the science and engineering work force of the 21st century. The projected shortfalls can be met by using our national talent, especially from those groups traditionally under-represented in engineering and science-women, minorities, and people with disabilities. Without world-class scientific and technical excellence, our international competitive prospects dim. The final report of the task force provides important steps that, if acted upon, will contribute to an improved educational climate and outcome for minorities.

Reach out to Off-Campus Groups

Colleges and universities need to carefully study demographic trends in their areas and determine what middle and high schools they will target for recruitment. In some places, particularly inner city areas, schools are becoming racially segregated. Outreach programs and services must be established with target schools to encourage minority students to consider going to college. Parents must be made aware of the preparation needed for their children to enter college. The liaison efforts with the schools require some important steps: role models need to be identified; the campus must be demystified; and the welcome mat for prospective minority students and their families must be genuine. Local agencies and community groups can be cultivated and work as partners to diversify the campus. Church groups and religious organizations are very helpful in stimulating interest and providing support for minorities to consider college as a realistic alternative. Business and corporate groups can provide motivation, human resources, and economic support.

The STEP Program: A Partnership for the Advancement of Learning at the University of California, Irvine, is a comprehensive effort to work with different groups to improve diversity on campus. It emphasizes inter institutional cooperation among school districts, community colleges, and four-year institutions to enhance the preparation of minority students for higher education. An important component of this model is the close liaison with parents, teachers and community groups.

Strengthen Ties with Feeder Institutions

It is a well-known fact that 70 percent of the minority students attending college are at two-year institutions. Yet, the rates of graduation and transfer to four-year institutions for these students is disappointingly low. Community colleges must play many important roles for under-represented minorities. They can serve as hospitable places within local communities to help students develop academic skills. They can provide transitional environments that prepare students for success at four-year colleges or universities. They can rekindle the motivation of minorities who have dropped out of four year institutions to continue their education. Finally, they can develop or enhance the skills of minorities to be productive members of our society.

An example of a very successful effort to improve the persistence and transfer rate of Hispanics to four-year institutions from two-year colleges is the Puente Project. Initiated in 1982 at Chabot Community College in Hayward, California, its purpose is to reduce the dropout rate among Hispanic community college students and increase the number who transfer from two- to four-year institutions. The program provides community college students with writing instruction; individual counseling in academic, personal, and career areas; and personal contact with mentors from the Hispanic professional community who offer each student a vision of career success and community commitment.

These are but a few alternatives available to assist colleges and universities to begin a process for cultural diversity. Numerous guides and handbooks are available that list and describe successful programs. Two need to be mentioned: the American Council on Education's book

Minorities on Campus: A Handbook for Enhancing Diversity and the publication prepared by John J. Halcon entitled *Exemplary Programs for College-Bound Minority Students.*

Three critical points need to be stressed that will significantly influence progress toward campus diversity in the future. First is the need for the president of the college or university to be genuinely committed to cultural diversity and change. The president and senior-level executives must have the will to take the necessary steps to diversify the institution. Without their commitment and enthusiasm, faculty, students, and staff will realize quickly that plans and programs for diversity will be praised but not implemented. A lack of commitment may cause such programs to be viewed by minorities as tokenism or lip service, prompting them to use confrontational or sensational tactics. In other places, minorities will vote with their feet and stay away from the campus. Second, if the faculty is not diversified and does not change the curriculum to include the experience of women and minorities in the United States, students will explore other options or may become militant. Third, staff, especially front-line personnel who deal directly with students, must become sensitive to minority differences and needs and learn to work successfully with this new clientele. The president and senior managers, the faculty, and the staff must view diversity as a challenge that offers new opportunities for growth and development. It should be an exciting and cooperative effort that makes people feel good about themselves. In time it will strengthen the active participants as well as the institution.

The inescapable fact confronting us is that the full participation of minorities in all parts of our society is vital to our survival as a free and prosperous nation. Changing demographics in the United States have made preparing and attracting our minority youth to U.S. colleges and universities a very high priority. Our fundamental goal should be to erase the inequities that characterize the lives of too many minority Americans. Access to our institutions of higher education must be improved for minorities, and programs must be implemented that will ensure their successful participation on the campus as students, faculty, staff, and administrators. The following quote should be carefully considered as we move into the 21st century:

> *Perhaps it truly can be said that no other nation on earth, at this point in history, has quite the opportunity that we do to create a fully functioning democracy where all citizens, regardless of race, ethnicity, creed, or sex, can participate completely in all aspects of national life. This dream need not be deferred any longer. Ours is the challenge; ours will be the prize.*

The 21st Century Campus Initiative Plan outlines seven priorities to increase the opportunities for students to attain the knowledge, skills and experiences that will prepare them for leadership roles throughout the state and beyond.

The initiative builds on student-centered traditions, calling for an enhanced focus on creating a diverse and inclusive learning environment; using innovative, effective teaching methods; and addressing important challenges of the 21st Century in the classroom and through institutional practices. The theme of sustainability is critical to global future and is central to the values, vision and economic interests of our students, state and region. Addressing this vital issue is a key priority of our plan and will become a signature focus for this campus.

To fulfill the vision campus must collaborate with a broad range of community partners in addressing workforce needs, as well as local and global challenges. Closer community ties will enable us to better understand the skills and programs students and employers need, while enriching the education of our students by providing real-world opportunities to learn from and give back to local communities.

The 21st Century Campus Initiative now serves as the exciting and ongoing process of further developing plans and moving forward in achieving the priorities.

❒❒❒

12

Role of Government in Higher Education Administration

Introduction

The number of people aged 35-47 will increase by 38 percent, those 48-53 will increase 67 percent, and those 65 and older will increase by 150 percent to become 20 percent of the population. Total population growth will be only 15 percent.

Minorities comprise an increasing proportion of the population. African-Americans, Hispanics and Native Americans, for example, represent one-fifth of the population today and will make up one-third within 20 years. More than half are being reared in poverty and are ill-served by our school systems.

Work Place Changes

Fifty percent of today's jobs will be replaced by new ones in the next generation.

New technologies will be the dominant vehicles for information storage, transfer, and personal communication.

Service occupations account for 71 percent of current employment and 68 percent of U.S. gross national product.

About 100,000 U.S. firms do business overseas, including 25,000 with foreign affiliates and 3,500 major multinational companies; one third of the profits of U.S. companies and one-sixth of the jobs are derived from international business.

Knowledge and Skills

Most persons can anticipate seven or eight lifetime jobs and three careers. Demand for high skills in science, engineering, and medicine will double.

Most available workers will come from minorities, disproportionate numbers of whom are dropping out of higher education.

An underclass is emerging in the United States. Nearly 15 percent of the population—27 million people—may be functionally illiterate, unable to read the simplest information needed for daily life. In our cities, 44 percent of blacks, 54 percent of Native Americans, and 56 percent of Hispanic adults cannot read or write English at the eighth grade level.

U.S. businesses spend $210 billion for on-the-job training and education, about the same amount expended for public elementary, secondary, and higher education institutions combined.

These facts signify major changes toward an aging, multi-ethnic population trying to adjust to an internationalized, information-based economy and society. Higher education will have to cope with these developments and help resolve the problems they entail.

Shifts in Federal and State Roles

These changes have been accompanied by shifts in federal and state roles in higher education. Russell Edgerton, president of the American Association for Higher Education, describes the federal role this way:

> There have been two major interventions by the federal government since World War II. The large dollar incentives for research caused a massive shift in emphasis which still persists. Most of these dollars have gone to major research universities. At the same time, as David Reisman tells us, backed by substantial research by Astin and others, it is really the private colleges which produce most of the good researchers; the research universities are not very good at producing their own. But this emphasis tends to drive the whole system, from institutional mission to faculty rewards. There are now about forty liberal arts colleges calling themselves "research colleges" in order to get under current federal funding guidelines.
>
> The other major intervention was the decision to fund students instead of institutions, taken in the late 60's. This decision created the market factor. But it also had major consequences for federal support of higher education. Congress would probably not provide 1/20th of what it now provides if the decision had been made to fund institutions. The problem is that parents and students, the "market," are not very good levers for improving teaching and learning or for changing the system.

During the 1980s, federal spending increased 110 percent for research and development ($29.8 to $62.5 billion) and 94 percent for basic research ($4.7 to $9.1 billion). Most of this has gone for military or defense-related projects, which increased from 50 percent to 70 percent of total spending. Federal support for non-defense research increased 59 percent, while support for defense-related research went up 191 percent. The proportion of federal research and development monies for university-based research fell from 14.3 percent in 1980 to 12.3 percent in 1988. In 1975 grants were 80 percent of student aid; by 1988 they were 49 percent. In recent years only 5 percent of state support is for need-based aid; 95 percent is a direct subsidy to all students.

While these changes were underway, the state role in regulation and budgetary control increased sharply. Statewide governing and coordinating boards became the major buffer among individual institutions, the legislature, and the governor, supplanting to a large degree the one-on-one lobbying that had dominated state dynamics before. Formula funding linked to institutional mission and grade level was adopted as the basic mechanism for allocating state dollars. New program approval became the major mechanism for controlling statewide redundancy and for monitoring institutional curricula. During the decade state initiatives, rhetoric, and limited dollars allocated to assessment, affirmative action, minority education, and centers of excellence have, at the margin, supplemented these basic roles.

As we enter the 1990s we are witnessing a withdrawal of government from its support of higher education. The privatization of higher education is proceeding apace, as the federal government devolves responsibility for a variety of governmental services to the states, and the states fail to accumulate the revenue needed to support these services. Faced with limited resources, state after state has taken actions that diminish the public's responsibility for higher education, imposing large cuts on the budgets of colleges and universities and passing on the burden of financial support to students and their parents.

These brief reminders about changes in society and higher education suggest some key characteristics for the 21st-century university. The Virginia Commission on the University of the 21st Century and an unpublished report on the impact of digital technology by Virginia Polytechnical Institute and State University suggest these basic ingredients:

- The university will be a network of resources, not a place.
- Offerings will give students a global, multicultural perspective.

- Widespread use of new technologies will improve the quality of instruction, increase contact between students and faculty, and reduce constraints on time, place, and space.
- Living and learning will be more closely integrated outside the classroom.
- Teaching will be more responsive to individual differences.
- Faculty roles, responsibilities, and rewards will expand and change.
- Colleges and universities will be increasingly interdependent with other educational providers and the private sector.

Some of these characteristics advocated for the future are being developed on an experimental basis by enterprising individuals or institutions, but these observations and recommendations deserve more systematic consideration because they have sweeping implications for the future of higher education and for government's role in this enterprise. To address the implications for higher education we have adopted two complementary strategies. We have selected one overarching issue the issue of boundaries that cuts across many observations and recommendations, and we have taken a matrix approach to illustrate how we try to think about this subject.

The fall of the Berlin Wall is an apt image for this era. Old boundaries are disappearing, dismantled by aggressive attacks, eroded with age, collapsed under the weight of change. Dichotomies that were the building blocks for an industrial age are being replaced by new categories intended to capture this new world, and new metaphors are arising to capture the imagination and serve as guideposts to action. What now appears as social disintegration and fragmentation may be prelude to a new order. Higher education, and the governments that support it, must understand these changes and their implications for the future. Colleges and universities must participate in this transformation and use these changes to the betterment of education and society.

The changes are organized as a set of dimensions of higher education, each of which is experiencing boundary shifts: teaching and learning, the generation and organization of knowledge, the relationship between schools and colleges, the dynamics among institutions of higher education, national and international developments, and the contributions higher education makes to its society.

Boundary Issues: Impact on Higher Education

Teaching and Learning

Impact on Learning Boundaries

Learner as "partner with technology" Break constraints of time and space—distance learning "Classroom" redistributed throughout campus and beyond Didactic pedagogy becomes interactive and facilitative pedagogy Customized learning replaces standardized packaging Nonlinear learning paths — "webs of knowledge" Break lock-step equations of credit-for-contact and semester as unit of knowledge Informal faculty-student relationships replace formal.

Impact on Research Boundaries

Expanded information professional exchange networks International networks of colleagues New "webs of knowledge" generate serendipitous connections Application and synthesis inform theory and method Expanded research on learning and technology New divisions of labor within professoriate—for example, non-instructional faculty "Reflective" practitioners replace professional "experts".

Impact on Service Boundaries

Integrated library-computing information centers Learning communities—networks of academic and non-academic interest groups Colearners replace professional experts and lay recipients of expertise "Service" becomes integral with teaching and research.

Impact on Organizational Boundaries

University distributed to urban villages and rural areas Units become increasingly decentralized and autonomous Departments and disciplines replaced by inter-disciplinary centers and institutes Joint learning ventures cross national boundaries.

Increasing integration of academic programs and shoot services 12-month calendar, 7-day week; 18-hour day.

Generation and Organization of Knowledge

Impact on Learning Boundaries

Overcoming "tyranny of the disciplines" Inter-disciplinary teaching and learning reflects knowledge frontiers Diversity of learning "packages" Faculty retraining Precarious position of non-sponsored faculty research Tension between professional and liberal education in curriculum Thematic and problem centered curricular foci Content plus competence New degree programs in emerging fields.

Impact on Research Boundaries

Frontier research creates new "disciplines" Science and technology focus of R&D Competitive knowledge development among university and non-university research centers Entrepreneurial uses of research Collaborative, multi-institutional projects Dispersed, global research networks.

Impact on Service Boundaries

National competitiveness focus Symbiosis of research and service in application of knowledge Program developments with local or regional rationales Community problem-solving teams Joint ventures—R&D and product development affiliates.

Impact on Organizational Boundaries

Privatization of research function Collaborative research—government, non-profit, private sector, and universities Multi-disciplinary centers and institutes Research projects cross-cutting governmental agencies Assessment of priorities for teaching and research Intellectual property/profits rights issues University/corporate degrees.

Education and Schooling

Impact on Learning Boundaries

Linked curricula Shared expectations for skill levels Dissemination of pedagogical innovations Overlapping transition zones Joint enrollments.

Impact on Research Boundaries

Student assessment Clinical settings research Study of student learning and developmental cycle.

Impact on Service Boundaries

Community-based programs—for example, early identification.

Teamwork to promote access —schools, foundation, and private support Collegial ties between faculty, teachers, and other educators.

Impact on Organizational Boundaries

"One system" — a "seamless web" Sectors — integration, articulation Alliances for joint projects Higher education as system—inter-institutional ventures Ties between higher education, "para-systems" and HRD in private sector Shared faculty/practitioner faculty.

Nation and the World

Impact on Learning Boundaries

Global perspective throughout curriculum Manpower needs for new occupations — program innovations Faculty development Reconceptualization of course content Satellite programs World regions programs Distance learning.

Impact on Research Boundaries

Collaborative international projects — global and multinational issues Applied research for national and international economic development Concern for national security and secrecy—intellectual property International data/researcher networks.

Impact on Service Boundaries

International consultation and sharing Scholar and student exchange programs International internships for professional programs Support for national competitiveness Monitoring and advising on international developments.

Impact on Organizational Boundaries

Internationalization of professional associations Foreign ownership of colleges and universities Partnership agreements with foreign institutions Facilities established at sites abroad Shared faculty appointments.

Contributions to Society

Impact on Learning Boundaries

Basic skill development Adapting the canon to multiculturalism Preparing for the information economy and society Values learning Generic cognitive/affective/ interpersonal competencies Lifelong learning.

Impact on Research Boundaries

National and international agendas for funding and support International competition and cooperation.

Emphasis on applied R&D Environment and health issues

Impact on Service Boundaries

Burgeoning demand for new services Leadership for community and nation Center for local and regional culture Joint programs for community development—partnerships with other sectors Retraining and contractual services Diversified services attuned to multicultural needs and providing access.

Impact on Organizational Boundaries

Interactive university Networks replace hierarchy Accountability demands Complex ties with other social institutions Creative financing of higher education enterprise Positioning supercedes planning

Boundary-breaking processes associated with each of these dimensions are altering the nature of higher education in teaching, research, and service and in the organization of colleges and universities. The complexity of these changes makes it difficult to elucidate each in the space available. We offer the figure as a concise way to capture this complexity. In the following text we do not aim to spell out all the information in the various matrix cells; instead, we aim to illustrate how we think about the interaction of these issues using this approach and to suggest the threads that weave through the details.

Teaching and Learning

Current standard instructional practices are artifacts of the industrial age. New technologies associated with the transformation to an information society offer opportunities for instructional innovation and new models for teaching and learning. Unlike earlier technological "fixes" for information transmission, these technologies are interactive and integrative. They enable networks of information and communication that overcome the boundaries of space and time. Hypertexts, for example, permit personal explorations of subjects that can take a student in uncharted directions, creating individualized "webs of knowledge" that can then be shared widely. Students can learn when and where they wish, transmitting questions and answers to teachers and others through electronic media, receiving instruction and feedback via the same mechanism. New forms of faculty-faculty, faculty-student and student-student interaction will result.

The boundaries for on-campus living and learning also can be blurred by distributing the academic enterprise to dormitories, student unions, and other sites traditionally peripheral to the learning experience. Beyond the campus, the same technologies permit distance learning, distributed throughout the emerging networks of "urban villages" to rural areas.

Faculty roles are also expanding to meet these needs. "Reflective practitioners" are confronting the conventions of instruction and exploring the impact of integrative technology on course design and the teaching and learning process including patterns of interaction between faculty and students and among students, feedback on student learning, and formats for assignments. Networks of faculty teaching the same subjects are forming, sharing course materials, making widely available the most up-to date scholarship, and transforming research on teaching into learning experiments and new instructional approaches.

The "new scholar" will not only be a teacher and scholar, but will engage in discovery, application, synthesis, and communication, reaching wider audiences than students and professional colleagues, venturing regularly into the world at large.

Generation and Organization of Knowledge

There is a subtle restructuring of knowledge in the late twentieth century. New divisions of intellectual labor, collaborative research, team teaching, hybrid fields, comparative studies, increased borrowing across disciplines, and a variety of "unified," "holistic" perspectives have created pressures upon traditional divisions of knowledge. There is talk of a growing "permeability of boundaries," even a profound epistemological crisis. To echo Clifford Geertz, there is indeed something happening "to the way we think about the way we think." These pressures have many origins and serve many purposes. However, they share one important commonality they have all been labeled inter-disciplinary".

Klein work *Inter-disciplinarity* describes experiments that undercut the distinctions between general and specialized education by combining disciplinary specialization with activities across disciplines. These experiments engage in problem-centered study that questions the sanctity of individual disciplines and professions and abandons traditional distinctions to study new subjects merging common features of related disciplines. The concepts of integration and collaboration permeate these innovations.

These experiments redefine boundaries of scholarship and learning, overcoming the "continuing rhetorical opposition of disciplinarity and inter-disciplinarity" by recognizing that both "are not only relative to each other but also time bound in character". In the process, these new forms threaten professional identities grounded in conventional academic life, forcing reforms in curriculum, in expectations of faculty, in competition for status within the academy, and in organizational alignments.

Much of the impetus for generating and organizing knowledge comes from the research enterprise. Recent developments blur the boundary between pure and applied research and challenge the primacy of academic research. The dominance of research and development, tied to corporate and national concerns with economic performance and potential, has stimulated a diversified research agenda and expanded the range of participants. The parameters of problem-focused, "field induced" issues, which cannot be subsumed within disciplinary or institutional categories, encourage new relationships among knowledge, action, and novel organizational arrangements to pursue these issues.

Education and Schooling

Indictments of U.S. schooling—the skill levels of its students, the preparation of its graduates for higher education, the profession of teaching, the participation and success rates of minorities have inspired a belated recognition that schools, colleges, and universities share a common bond, the education of youth. In response educators are pursuing a variety of partnerships that break down the wall between secondary and higher education. The appeal for one system, an integrated and articulated educational enterprise, captures the theme of these innovations. These linkages, involving faculty beyond schools of education, establish new roles for both teachers and professors.

Alternatives to traditional schooling and higher education also are emerging. Joint ventures in corporate education and training by U.S. business and industry in cooperation with two and four-year institutions are growing rapidly. Local school systems "have recently begun delegating financial and educational decisions to principals and teachers. Now the Dade County school system [for example] has extended this notion of site-based management to its logical conclusion: Let them design and run their own schools". Dade County invited not only teachers and administrators but also businesses and citizens to submit proposals for organizing its schools. Corporate foundations and corporations, seeking radically different approaches to education, have offered the financial incentives for these proposals.

Nation and the World

On the political front, events in Europe in 1990 made it abundantly clear that the world is undergoing a dramatic transformation. The dichotomies between East and West, between the Communist world and the free world, are obsolete. National boundaries are being challenged by sub-national emancipation movements. Those who view the world as comprised of a set of national economies are being overtaken by the emergence of a global, inter-dependent economic system. Once again, technology has played a major role in these developments. Information conveyed by telecommunications media crosses national boundaries with impunity, rendering useless governmental efforts to control what is available to citizens and opening a new era of instantaneous communication with others. The information society is quintessentially a global village. Higher education is responding to these revolutionary changes by redefining its involvement with the world beyond its borders. It is taking advantage of opportunities to develop new and expanded networks of relationships. It is being enlisted in support of national participation in the international arena. It is creating multinational research enterprises redefining its own perceptions of this new world within the curriculum.

Contributions to Society

For example, a recent publication, responding to concerns about the quality of education, calls for a revitalized system of higher education that will :

- restore a common sense of national purpose,
- affirm the dignity of work,
- recapture the belief in the future,
- rekindle a sense of values,
- cultivate our human resources,
- prepare and adapt U.S. workers to a changing world,
- nurture the talent of the people of the United States for creativity and inventiveness,
- cope with illiteracy, and
- incorporate minorities into society's mainstream.

Faced with an increasingly fragmented society, intensive international competition, and challenges to U.S. hegemony, society must turn to its colleges and universities for contributions at many levels.

Some institutions of higher education are responding by becoming self-consciously interactive, committed to work directly with business and political leaders of local, regional, and national communities. Programs are being developed that prepare students for life in the information society. Research is being conducted that applies to real-world problems. Partnerships are being established to sustain dialogue on community needs, offer joint services, and finance common enterprises that commingle educational and commercial activities. The classic ivory tower institution, walled off from town, is tumbling down.

The pace of change, which engenders perceptions of fragmentation and loss of purpose, makes decisions about how best to contribute to a complex society. Uncertainties abound, making conventional planning unsuitable. The recent emergence of chaos theory is a timely framework for an uncertain world, emphasizing as it does the non-linear nature of complex systems and the potential impact of seemingly small changes.

Interactive colleges and universities strive to position themselves to respond to unanticipated changes and developments, to take advantage of opportunities that arise. The institution's orientation toward and interaction with its environment is more like a surfer than a hiker. The hiker selects a predetermined destination, lays out the route, estimates resources needed with some provision for unanticipated circumstances, loads the pack, and sets out. The surfer reads the waves carefully, waits for the right one, and then, with a delicate sense of timing and balance, sets out to ride just ahead of the wave. Once started the object is to stay upright and ride for maximum speed and distance. Success involves being in an intimate relationship with the environment, attuned to fast changing conditions. The destination is not critically important; what counts is making the most of that wave. Having done that, it is time to move back out and be ready for the next.

Role of Government

The ability of U.S. higher education to assume a position of social leadership depends on political action at the federal and state levels, within executive, legislative, and bureaucratic offices. Each of the five boundary dimensions undergoing change is influenced by government's role. It gives a set of recommendations for governmental actions that can support rather than impede these changes.

The proposals are organized under three kinds of governmental roles: *rhetoric*, by which governments and their agencies influence "the climate, attitudes and intellectual agendas or conceptions of the role and purposes of higher education"; *initiatives*, "working through incentives or sanctions to encourage or discourage particular policies and practices"; and *regulation*, "exercised through the processes for approving [and monitoring] institutional activities, missions, budgets and programs".

Boundary Issues: Impact on Government's Role Teaching and Learning

Rhetoric

Call for pedagogical revolution. Articulate vision of learning society. Support distribution of learning throughout campus. Charge institutions to establish joint learning ventures in communities and abroad. Promote teaching mission. Endorse "principles of good practice" for learning.

Initiatives

Support instructional innovation. Fund telecommunications infrastructure. Sponsor research on learning styles and settings. Create distance learning networks Convene and support networks of teachers and scholars. Facilitate institutional cooperation to provide learning services. Fund faculty development for individualized education.

Regulation

Rethink "production line" guidelines. Revise faculty work-load measures. Reconceptualize categories of space needs and use. Enable organizational changes that support interdisciplinary, decentralized or autonomous learning units. Redefine concept of campus. Support integrated alternatives to branch campus. Change budget structure that separates instruction, academic support, and student services Revise staffing guidelines.

Generation and Organization of Knowledge

Rhetoric

Challenge discipline dominance. Preserve balance between professional and liberal education. Define higher education's role in economic development. Recognize knowledge as central resource for society. Promote creation of full range of new knowledge, pure to applied. Celebrate inventiveness and entrepreneurial spirit.

Initiatives

Support inter-disciplinary learning and frontier research Facilitate collaborative research. Fund faculty development to explore beyond disciplinary training. Make available to faculty up-to-date data bases. Provide financial incentives and rewards for research. Sponsor applications of knowledge for community service. Support curricular and research alternatives under Centers/Institutes. Encourage certificate/credential and noncredential alternatives to supplement current degrees.

Regulation

Enable creation and implementation of degree programs in new disciplines Establish intellectual property guidelines Avoid excessive control of research Re-examine antitrust laws for R&D. Monitor impact of entrepreneurial activity on educational mission. Facilitate coordinated support of research across agency lines. Develop sound policy for R&D activities. Approve new programs that serve emerging local and regional needs.

Education and Schooling

Rhetoric

Establish "one system" vision. Promote importance of education for 21st century world. Encourage cross-sector staffing and teaching. Encourage the primacy of human resources for an information age. Require articulation of skills needed for college level work Celebrate "model" programs.

Initiatives

Create cross-section programs. Establish alliances among agencies. Provide incentives for institutional cooperation. Sponsor colloquia that convene broad range of educators to address common learning issues. Convene school-college efforts to define appropriate skill levels by field. Share information on pedagogy with teachers and other educators. Fund research on student development cycle. Support community-based programs. Reinforce clinical professional education in school settings.

Regulation

Require information-sharing on student assessment across sectors. Develop systematic articulation agreements. Continue reform of teacher education. Ensure student assessment for program improvement as well as accountability. Establish new one-system governance and funding structures. Assure access to higher education for all who can benefit.

Nation and the World

Rhetoric

Articulate importance of global knowledge and perspective. Define higher education's role in balancing national and international interests. Establish national research teaching and curricular agendas and priorities.

Initiatives

Support internationalization of curriculum. Increase research funding aligned with national and international agenda. Promote international projects. Establish accessible international information networks Fund faculty and student exchange programs. Use faculty expertise on other cultures. Create international scholarly exchanges.

Regulation

Approve new programs to infuse international elements in curriculum. Establish flexible guidelines to support partnerships abroad. Facilitate establishment of sites abroad. Evaluate impact of foreign ownership in higher education and U.S. investments in foreign sites.

Contributions to Society

Rhetoric

Demand that higher education meet its responsibility for societal leadership. Articulate need for support of multicultural society. Define and disseminate information on skill and educational needs of knowledge-based society. Maintain awareness of need for access and educational success. Encourage recruitment and retention of stronger leaders.

Initiatives

Establish state and national agendas for higher education in global world. Fund research and development to address social needs. Promote joint community development programs across institutional sectors. Support cultural activities for communities. Encourage joint degree/certificate programs. Assemble faculty and administrative leaders as participants on community problem-solving teams.

Regulation

Approve programs developed in collaboration with community. Delineate new forms of accountability compatible with institutional autonomy. Re-examine institutional missions for the 21st century. Facilitate creative financing options developed in partnership with private sector. Provide incentives for expanded continuing education. Substitute initiatives for regulation to enable quick response to unanticipated change.

The proposals in the exhibit are based on some underlying propositions that derive from our understanding of the developments and processes outlined above. The following text summarizes those propositions for the five boundary dimensions.

Our recommendations for teaching and learning reflect our belief that governments and their agencies should recognize that the conventions of instruction and the categories of bureaucratic planning are barriers to more effective learning. Self-conscious, shared reflection and study about learning must be undertaken by those engaged in the teaching enterprise where teaching and learning take place in schools, colleges, and universities. These investigations must be related directly to each institution's own students and to the areas of knowledge, competence, and human development pertinent to that institution's mission.

Miami-Dade Community College has tackled this issue. Its Teaching/Learning Project, begun in 1986, has created a powerful mix of policy changes, concrete actions, and fresh resources. A steering committee, bolstered by sub-committees involving over 100 faculty members, have formulated recommendations for new, part-time and non classroom faculty, for classroom feedback and learning to learn, for faculty advancement and support, and for the role of administrators in supporting teaching excellence.

President Robert McCabe has convened college-wide small group meetings on faculty excellence and faculty advancement. The President's Council adopted recommendations to improve the teaching/learning environment. The college offers classroom feedback workshops and classroom research graduate courses, and 70 percent of participants are practicing new techniques to improve their teaching. Over two-thirds of the faculty voted to modify the institutional reward system to include improved teaching among the criteria for promotion and tenure. A publication to recruit new faculty includes a Statement of Faculty Excellence and a Statement of

Teaching/Learning Values. Teaching/Learning Resource Centers, staffed by at least two professionals assisted by outside experts as needed, are placed on each campus. One hundred endowed teaching chairs are being established by corporate and individual donors.

Other efforts like this are gathering momentum across the country. They need to be encouraged and facilitated by local, regional, and state governments so that all two and four-year colleges can give priority to teaching and learning.

Governmental rhetoric, initiatives, and regulations must proceed from the realization that a knowledge-based society requires the vitality of good teaching and the good practices of active learning. Governmental actions must enable institutions to test and take advantage of new technologies that can be effective in the service of learning, to experiment and innovate, to replace antiquated practices and forms, and to radically reshape campus life.

Proposals for the generation and organization of knowledge argue for actions recognizing that the goal of research is to achieve a knowledge-based society and economy. This goal requires diverse forms of support. New arrangements will be needed to pursue knowledge, both within the academy and outside departments, and between higher education and other knowledge-generating institutions. Problem-centered research will overlap governmental agency lines and levels, requiring increased collaboration and coordination.

Georgia Institute of Technology, for example, has borrowed the land-grant model and applied it to engineering. Georgia Tech Research Institute houses an Industrial Extension Division, a statewide network of regional offices linked to the Atlanta campus, its experiment station, and the engineering faculty of the university. Each office is staffed by engineers who serve a range of industrial clients and technical needs. They respond to requests for assistance on problems, usually with projects involving manufacturing processes, facility and materials planning, methods improvement, or cost control. When regional agents do not have the expertise to solve a particular problem, they draw upon the research services of the institute. The mission of this system is to help small, technologically unsophisticated firms achieve greater economic and competitive equity by offering free service for several days and contractually negotiated services for longer projects. The state provides limited funding, and staff seek additional resources through contract work.

Suggestions for improved education and schooling call for actions that implement the concept of education as a seamless web for lifelong learning. This implementation must radically alter relationships among secondary schools, two and four-year colleges and universities, and corporate human resources development. This requires greatly strengthened communication and coordination among educators and between educators and employers to avoid redundancy, increase efficiency and facilitate student transitions from one educational sector to the other.

The Institute for Educational Transformation (IET) in Northern Virginia that aims to find new answers to who teaches and who learns what, when, and where; to develop new structural relations among public, private, corporate, and professional institutions and individuals; and to strengthen the character of diverse educational partnerships. This collaborative effort includes the high-tech corporation IBM, a law firm, a venture capital business and a development corporation, a city council, city and county public schools, the local five-campus community college, and the regional university's school of education and its research and development center.

These partners establish the direction and evaluation of the institute; develop projects, proposals, and plans; implement agreed upon projects; and disseminate knowledge of the institute's work. The first IET project, a $1.7 million effort funded in part by a grant education, and corporate partnerships will be needed to address social fragmentation and the creation of a multicultural democratic society.

The Center for Conflict Analysis and Resolution and the Conflict Clinic, housed at George Mason University and comprised of scholars, practitioners, graduate students, and organizations in the field of peace-making and conflict resolution, are engaged in a partnership to address the conflicts associated with social fragmentation and multiculturalism. The mission of the center is to advance the understanding and resolution of persistent human conflicts among individuals, groups, communities, identity groups, and nations through research, instruction, and clinical and outreach activities.

Summary

Federal legislation and significant state support created the land-grant colleges that became the major vehicles for improving agricultural production and responding to the social changes provoked by the industrial revolution. There was widespread recognition that the prevailing model for higher education small, private, mostly church-related colleges though useful, was not sufficient to provide the skilled human resources, research, and technological assistance needed for that new age.

During the 1960s and early 1970s states and local communities, with some federal assistance, invested heavily in community colleges throughout each state across the country. Once again there was a powerful response to new social conditions. There was widespread recognition that the existing four-year institutions, and the sprinkling of junior colleges, though useful, were not sufficient to meet the needs for skilled workers and a more broadly educated citizenry. During the early and mid-20th century higher education had moved from an aristocratic orientation aimed at educating upper and upper-middle-class men, to a meritocratic orientation aimed at educating the best and the brightest. By the 1960s the United States recognized the need for an egalitarian orientation that would make higher education accessible to all who could profit from it. Four-year institutions became more open, often simply revolving doors. A new institution was needed that would take seriously the need to provide useful post-secondary education to all who desired it.

Now the nation faces a similar challenge. Although existing two year and four-year institutions, public and private, organized around traditional conventions concerning mission, content, campus, and calendar will continue to be useful, a new thrust in higher education is needed, similar in significance and scope to those that inspired the land-grant university and community college movements. Governments ought to play a major role in establishing and supporting this thrust, recognizing that a knowledge-based society requires the presence of viable, socially productive institutions of higher education. At present, it is unclear whether either the public or its political representatives understand the role that higher education must play in preparing us for the world of the 21st century. It also is unclear whether faculty and administrators at our institutions comprehend the systematic changes necessary to accomplish needed reforms and legitimize the new roles expected of them. The task is to create a viable vision of the 21st-century college and university; to mobilize educators, governments, and the public in support of that vision; and to create new coalitions across sectors to accomplish the vision. Failing that, higher education will be inadequate to serve the polity and unprepared for full participation in the global era.

❑❑❑

Bibliography

Apple, Michael W. *Official Knowledge: Democratic Education in a Conservative Age*. New York: Routledge, 1993.

Ashcroft, Kate and Lorraine Foreman-Peck. *Managing Teaching and Learning in Further and Higher Education*. London: Falmer Press, 1994.

Barnes, Louis B., C. Roland Christensen, and Abby J. Hansen. *Teaching and the Case Method : Text, Cases, and Readings*. 3rd Ed. Cambridge, MA: Harvard Business School, 1994.

Bensimon, Estela M. and others. *Making Sense of Administrative Leadership: The "L" Word in Higher Education*. Washington, DC: George Washington University Press, 1989.

Bloom, Benjamin. *Taxonomy of Educational Objectives*. New York: David McKay, 1956.

Campbell, William E. and Karl A. Smith, Eds. *New Paradigms for College Teaching*. Edina, MN: Interaction Book Co., 1997.

Catelli, Linda A. "Teaching the Teaching Process: Reflections and Strategies at an Urban College," *Teaching Education*. Vol. 1 No.1 (1990): 89-101.

Diamond, Robert M. and Bronwyn E. Adam. *Changing Priorities at Research Universities, 1991-1996*. Syracuse, NY: Syracuse University, 1998.

Diamond, Robert M. *Designing & Assessing Courses & Curricula: A Practical Guide*. Revised Ed. San Francisco, CA: Jossey-Bass, 1998.

Edgerton, Russell, Patricia Hutchings, and Kathleen Quinlan. *The Teaching Portfolio: Capturing the Scholarship in Teaching.* Washington, DC: American Association for Higher Education, 1991.

Egan, Kieran. *The Educated Mind: How Cognitive Tools Shape Our Understanding.* Chicago, IL: University of Chicago Press, 1997.

Escobar, Miguel and others. *Paulo Freire on Higher Education: A Dialogue at the National University of Mexico.* New York: State University of New York Press, 1994.

Farquharson, Andy. *Teaching in Practice: How Professionals Can Work Effectively with Clients, Patients, and Colleagues.* San Francisco, CA: Jossey-Bass, 1995.

Fiol-Matta, Liza and Mariam K. Chamberlain, Eds. *Women of Color and the Multicultural Curriculum: Transforming the College Classroom.* New York: Feminist Press, 1994.

Fleming, Neil and Colleen Mills. "Not Another Inventory, Rather a Catalyst for Reflection," *To Improve the Academy.* Vol. 11 (1992): 137-155.

Frost, Peter J. "Creating Scholarship and Journeying Through Academia: Reflections and Interpretations from the Field," *Journal of Applied Behavioral Science.* Vol. 25, No. 4 (1990): 399-418.

Frost, Peter J. and M. S. Taylor. *Rhythms of Academic Life.* Thousand Oaks, CA: Sage, 1996.

Gage, N. L. *The Scientific Basis of the Art of Teaching.* New York: Teachers College Press, 1978.

Gallupe. R. Brent and William H. Cooper. "Brainstorming Electronically," *Sloan Management Review.* (Fall): 27-36.

Gardiner, Lion F. *Redesigning Higher Education: Producing Dramatic Gains in Student Learning.* Washington, DC: George Washington University, 1994.

Gardner, Howard. *Frames of Mind: The Theory of Multiple Intelligences.* New York: Basic Books, 1993.

Hannigan, Jane Anne and Hilary Crew. "A Feminist Paradigm for Library and Information Science" *Wilson Library Bulletin.* Vol. 68, No. 2(October 1993): 28-32.

Hannigan, Jane Anne. "A Feminist Standpoint for Library and Information Science Education," *Journal of Education for Library and Information Science.* Vol.35, No. 4 (Fall 1994): 297-319.

Jalajas, David S. and Robert I. Sutton. "Feuds in Student Goups: Coping with Whiners, Martyrs, Saboteurs, Bullies, and Deadbeats," *The Organizational Behavior Teaching Review.* Vol. 9, No. 4 (1984-85): 94-107.

Katz, Joseph and Mildred Henry. *Turning Professors Into Teachers: A New Approach to Faculty Development and Student Learning.* Phoenix, AZ: Oryx, 1993.

Kecht, Maria-Regina, Ed. *Pedagogy Is Politics: Literary Theory and Critical Teaching.* Urbana, IL: University of Illinois Press, 1992.

McKeachie, Wilbert J. and others. *Teaching Tips: Strategies, Research, and Theory for College and University Teachers.* 9th Ed. Lexington, MA: D.C. Heath, 1994.

Meyer, Richard J. *Stories from the Heart: Teachers and Students Researching Their Literary Lives.* Mahwah, NJ: Lawrence Erlbaum Associates, 1996.

Nilson, Linda B. *Teaching At Its Best: A Research-Based Resource for College Instructors.* Bolton, MA: Anker, 1998.

O'Brien, George Dennis. *All the Essential Half-Truths About Higher Education.* Chicago, IL: University of Chicago Press, 1998.

Roberts, Helen and others. *Teaching From a MultiCultural Perspective.* Thousand Oaks, CA: Sage, 1994.

Schoefeld, A. Clay and Robert Magnan. *Mentor in a Manual: Climbing the Academic Ladder to Tenure.* Madison, WI: Magna Publications, 1992.

Schon, Donald. *The Reflective Practitioner.* New York: Basic Books, 1983.

Shulman, Judith H., Ed. *Case Methods in Teacher Education.* NY: Teachers College Press, 1992.

Sykes, C. J. *Profscam: Professors and the Demise of Higher Education.* Washington, DC: Regnery Gateway, 1988.

Tapscott, Don. *Growing Up Digital: The Rise of the Net Generation*. New York: Mc Graw-Hill, 1998.

Tompkins, Jane. *A Life in School: What the Teacher Learned*. Reading, MA: Addison-Wesley, 1996.

Vaill, P. *Managing As a Performing Art: New Ideas for a World of Chaotic Changes*. San Francisco, CA: Joseey-Bass, 1989.

Vandergrift, Kay E. *Children's Literature: Theory, Research, and Teaching*. Englewood, CO: Libraries Unlimited, 1990.

Vocate, Donna R. "Teaching Communication Theory in the Professional School, " *Journalism & Mass Communication Educator*. Vol. 52, No. 2 (Summer 1997): 4-14.

Whicker, Marcia Lynn, Jennie Jacobs Kronenfeld, and Ruth Ann Strickland. *Getting Tenure*. Newbury Park, CA: Sage, 1993.

Wolf-Devine, Celia. *Diversity and Community in the Academy: Affirmative Action in Faculty Appointments*. Lanham, MD: Rowman & Littlefield, 1997.

Woolfolk, Anita E., Ed. *Research Perspectives on the Graduate Preparation of Teachers*. Englewood Cliffs, NJ: Prentice Hall, 1989.

Wright, W. Alan and Eileen M. Herteis, Eds. *University Teaching and Learning*. 3rd Edition. Halifax, Nova Scotia: Dalhousie University, 1994.

Zamel, Vivian and Ruth Spack, Eds. *Negotiating Academic Literacies: Teaching and Learning Across Languages and Cultures*. Mahwah, NJ: Lawrence Erlebaum, 1998.

Zanna, Mark P. and John M. Darley, Eds. *The Complete Academic: A Practical Guide for the Beginning Social Scientist*. New York: Mc Graw-Hill, 1987.

Zuber-Skerritt, Ortrun. *Professional Development in Higher Education: A Theoretical Framework for Action Research*. London: Kogan Page, 1992.

❑❑❑

Index

□□□